Your Child's Divorce

Your Child's Divorce
What To Expect – What You Can Do

MARSHA TEMLOCK, M.A.

Impact Publishers®
ATASCADERO, CALIFORNIA

ATTENTION ORGANIZATIONS AND CORPORATIONS:
This book is available at quantity discounts on bulk purchases for educational, business, or sales promotional use. For further information, please contact Impact Publishers, P.O. Box 6016, Atascadero, California 93423-6016.
Phone: 805-466-5917, e-mail: info@impactpublishers.com

Library of Congress Cataloging-in-Publication Data

Temlock, Marsha.
   Your child's divorce : what to expect? what you can do / Marsha Temlock.
     p. cm. (RebuildingBooks)
   Includes bibliographical references and index.
   ISBN 1-886230-66-8 (alk. paper)
 1. Divorce—United States. 2. Parent and adult child—United States. I. Title
  HQ834.T46 2006
  306.8740973—dc22

                                             2006013856

Impact Publishers and colophon are registered trademarks of Impact Publishers, Inc.

Cover design by Gayle Downs, Gayle Force Design, Atascadero, California
Composition by UB Communications, Parsippany, New Jersey
Printed in the United States of America on acid-free, recycled paper
Published by **Impact Publishers®**
POST OFFICE BOX 6016
ATASCADERO, CALIFORNIA 93423-6016
www.impactpublishers.com

Dedication

Dedicated to my aunt and literary mentor:

Sydell Rosenberg
(1929–1996)

Adventures over
the cat sits in the fur ring
of his tail and dreams.

Publisher's Note

Contents

Acknowledgements

I would like to acknowledge:

...my husband and soul mate Stephen. You are the wind beneath my wings.

...my adventurous children, Larry, Sandor and Eve. You are my pride and continual source of inspiration.

...Sidney Kramer, my agent at Mews Books; Bob Alberti, editor and publisher of Impact; Jeanette Morris and Cynthia MacGregor, copy editors. It would be difficult to find a more supportive or professional team to have launched this book.

...Wendy Prince, Esq. attorney and mediator, Greenberg and Prince, LLC, for her help researching the legal material.

...Dale Evva Gelfand, there from the beginning with sound editorial advice and wry wit.

...fellow writers Sheryl Kayne and Ina Chadwick, for shedding light in my darkest hours.

Finally, I would like to thank the many parents who openly shared their family rebuilding stories to help others become a source of comfort and strength to their divorcing sons and daughters.

— Marsha A. Temlock

Introduction

"Mom, Dad ... I'm getting divorced."

You just got that unhappy news, and you're struggling with a ton of emotions and questions. You're confused, disbelieving, saddened, and determined to help — somehow.

Only you know how devastating an experience this is for you and your family. Like your divorcing child, you are grieving. You want to be helpful. But how? You may be afraid to interfere, afraid that anything you do or say will make things worse.

It may help a little to know that your reactions are perfectly normal and that you have a lot of company. As you may have heard, the latest statistics reported by the U.S. Bureau of the Census show that we have about a million divorces a year in this country. For every divorcing couple, there are four (give or take) parents grieving just as you are. (The exact number varies because of deaths, stepparents, etc.) That's a lot of sad folks.

Go to any bookstore or library, find the self-help aisle, and in the "Relationships" section, you will — not surprisingly — be confronted with a sea of books about divorce. Books on contemplating divorce, books on recovering from divorce, books to help children adjust to the trauma of their parents' separation, books on single parenting and stepparenting and blended families — the list is endless. But hundreds of books about marital breakup notwithstanding, an enormous segment of society has been neglected: the parents of divorcing children. You — and four million other parents like you, every year.

Your Child's Divorce: What to Expect — What You Can Do speaks to all of those parents who are standing helplessly on the sidelines while their family is wrenched apart. This book makes these compelling promises:

- Parents can help keep the family together even in the midst of pain, sadness, and acrimony.
- Parents can strengthen their relationship with their child during and after a divorce.
- Parents can be instruments of family renewal and regeneration.
- Parents can and must be role models for their children and grandchildren who, unfortunately, carry forward the divorce legacy.
- Parents can hasten their own recovery as they make this journey with their divorcing child.

•◀ *Why This Book Is Important* ▶•

Your Child's Divorce: What to Expect — What You Can Do is your opportunity to focus on your role in your son's or daughter's divorce. This book addresses such parental dilemmas as:

- Wanting to lend support but being uncertain about the role you can or should play in your child's life.
- Dealing with your emotions and working on your recovery.
- Constructing healthy boundaries to avoid becoming consumed by your child's problems.
- Helping your grandchildren deal effectively with their parents' divorce.
- Balancing other family relationships to avoid conflict and sibling rivalry.
- Disengaging when the rescue period is over without abandoning your child.
- Maintaining communication with ex-in-laws without being disloyal to your child.
- Adjusting to your role as stepgrandparent when your child remarries.
- Broadening your view of family and accepting the patterns of change.

•◀ *Where This Book Takes You* ▶•

Your Child's Divorce... takes you through the process of divorce from the viewpoint of a set of parents who, like you, are struggling to make sense of their roles through each stage. You will move from the announcement of the marital breakup to the re-establishment of the family unit. This continuum is not always linear, and each family member moves along at his or her own pace. You may be further along than your spouse or divorcing child in accepting the decisions and realities. On the other hand, you may be steps behind. Chances are you are open to reading this book because you recognize that there are many stumbling blocks, and you are eager to get past them so you can be available to your child and grandchildren who need your support. You can and will achieve this goal. There are plenty of pointers in this book to help you get from step A to step B and so on. The "Guideposts" at the end of each chapter as well as the Workbook Exercises are intended to help you succeed.

This book will *not* tell you how to repair your son's or daughter's marriage. It deals with the divorce journey. It is realistic about what you can hope to accomplish, and it deals with these accomplishments in two aspects.

First, it addresses the emotional toll the divorce may be taking on you as a parent. You may be experiencing disappointment, disillusionment, anger, loss, wounded pride, guilt — a whole range of difficulties and emotions. If your child is already divorced, you may be feeling relief and guarded optimism that he or she can begin a new relationship. You may be worried that your child is expecting too much by asking you to embrace a new family unit.

When I decided to write this book, I wanted to know if other parents felt the way I did when their child got divorced. What were their concerns at the different stages? How did they show support when they were feeling conflicted? What boundaries did they draw when their child asked for help? How and when did they disengage? I listened. I commiserated. I took personal inventory of my own feelings. Thus, the book took shape.

You will notice that I have included stories with varying points of view. This is because I believe we each have a unique way of handling problems, and not all situations fit a particular model. I believe you will find that you are in good company when you go through each chapter, and you will come away reassured that you are not alone.

And the second aspect? In addition to registering the emotional impact of your child's divorce, this book looks at the divorce terrain — the legal, financial and domestic issues — but from a parent's vantage point. Undoubtedly, you will be facing a number of decisions should your child come to you for a loan, a place to live, or help with the grandchildren. At the end of each chapter there are exercises that will help you assess your values and beliefs, and weigh your personal needs against your parental obligations. You want to be there for your child, but you also need to keep your life in balance.

•◄ *Format of This Book* ►•

Your Child's Divorce: What to Expect — What You Can Do includes a fictional narrative written from the personal point of view of someone just like you — a parent whose child is divorcing. Each chapter focuses on specific and heart-wrenching issues that surfaced for "Nora" and "Gary" in their struggle to cope with the changes their son's divorce wrought in their own lives.

Also included are stories extrapolated and compiled from interviews I conducted with parents who have suffered through a child's divorce. For some, the divorce was fresh; for others, it was "a thing of the past." I noticed that even parents who began the interview by saying, "Oh, that was so long ago," had a great deal of feeling behind those recollections. Many admitted the wounds had never healed. I would like to thank all those interviewees, and as promised, I have changed names and places to assure them complete confidentiality.

Your Child's Divorce: What to Expect — What You Can Do is divided into three parts:

Part I — *Accepting the Decision* begins with the shocking announcement that Nora's son is getting divorced. Chapters 1–4 focus on her knee-jerk response, her rescue mission, parental obligations relative to financial and homecoming support, and the conflicts that arise when family members take sides.

Part II — *Dealing with Change* is about transitions. Chapter 5 addresses conflicting loyalty issues. Nora has difficulty severing ties with her daughter-in-law and subsequently jeopardizes her relationship with her son. In chapter 6, when her son's divorce begins to take its toll physically and emotionally on Nora and subsequently on her husband, she starts focusing on their own road to recovery. In chapter 7, Nora and Gary decide that it is time to withdraw support and allow Ben to rebuild his life, with Mom and Dad functioning as a safety net in the background.

Part III — *Strengthening Family Bonds* speaks to the important role grandparents play in the lives of their grandchildren. In chapter 8, Nora realizes that her grandchildren are struggling with their parents' divorce long after the fact. Chapter 9 focuses on the stabilizing role that grandparents play in the re-structured family. Chapter 10 looks at the postmodern family. Ben remarries, so Nora and Gary have the new charge of strengthening their blended family unit.

Appendix A is a Parent's Overview of Legal and Financial Issues, prepared with the help of a practicing attorney. It includes a discussion of types of divorces, division of assets, custody issues, and recent court decisions relative to grandparenting rights.

Appendix B lists helpful resources of divorce-related support services: books for divorcing couples and all affected family members, Websites, and advocacy organizations.

Throughout this book, you will find notations in parentheses such as: (Alberti & Emmons, 2001) or simply (2001). These entries are a form of footnote, telling you the author(s) and/or publication year of a book or an article you will find listed topically in the Bibliography (Appendix B).

•◀ *Who Can Benefit from Reading This Book?* ▶•

- Parents, grandparents, stepparents, and other family members interested in supporting individuals going through separation or divorce.
- Adult children who would like to reach out to parents for support during their divorce but are concerned about parents becoming overly involved in their lives.

- Counselors, clergy, lawyers, mediators, social workers, and family relations professionals who work with divorcing couples.

It's time to meet Nora and discover, as she did, how, as parents of divorcing children, you can be useful in binding wounds, providing appropriate support, and rebuilding your family brick by brick.

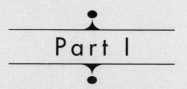

Part I

Accepting the Decision

Your Child's Divorce:
What to Expect — What You Can Do

Chapter One

It's Not Just A Rough Spot

Nora's Story

My son's phone call reverberated throughout the house — though at the outset it was strictly the ringing that resounded. It was eleven at night; my husband and I were accustomed to getting calls at odd hours from Seattle. The time difference and our schedules made it difficult for our son to call at times that were more convenient.

"It's Ben," my husband called down to me from our upstairs bedroom. "Pick up."

I was in the kitchen making a cup of tea, battling insomnia. I lifted the receiver, delighted to hear my eldest son's voice.

"Hi, honey. How are Jake and Janice?" Always my first question. My twin grandchildren had just turned eight. Regrettably, Gary and I had once again not been able to share the occasion. Too many missed birthdays, too many miles separating us.

The twins were great, Ben assured me.

"And Joan?"

"Joan is fine."

Did his voice sound a bit tentative? I confronted the feeling. "Is everything *okay?*"

"Everything's fine, Mom."

I proceeded to pester Ben with my usual inquiries about his job. Ben worked as an engineer and was always on the road overseeing some new project. I also wanted news about Mary and Todd, Joan's parents, who were our friends as well as my son's in-laws. I was continuously green with envy that Joan's parents lived less than an hour away from the kids and could see the twins whenever they liked. Gary and I tried to take two trips a year to see the kids in Seattle, but it always felt like a century between visits. Mary and I would chat on the telephone every few weeks, and the four of us usually got together whenever we visited or they happened to come to Pennsylvania. Gary asked about Todd, who had just had a coronary bypass, and was assured that our friend was doing well.

"Tell me everything the children are up to, and, of course, I want to hear all about the birthday party," I said.

The whole time Ben was talking, my "mother's radar" was picking up static. There's a saying that God created mothers to help Him keep on top of things. Maybe that's why, despite Ben's assertion that everything was just fine, something told me otherwise.

"Ben, are you sure everything is OK?" I asked again.

There was a pause at the other end — a long pause. Then I heard the dreaded words I don't think any parent is ever quite prepared for.

"Mom, Dad... Joan and I are getting a divorce. This is something we've been talking about for a while now. I know this comes as a shock, and I'm really sorry." His voice dropped into the shadows of Puget Sound. "We both think it's best if we move on."

So it began: with the announcement that shook the foundations of our family.

All that night Gary and I asked each other the same questions over and over: How was this possible? What did the future hold for Ben, Joan, and the twins? For us? How was this going to affect our family?

Gary and I walked around for days in a cloud of shock and confusion. Then shock gave way to feelings I was not prepared for: sadness, grief, anger. It took a while before I realized that I was in mourning for my son's failed marriage. Divorce is a kind of death, and, as with any death, there is a profound sense of loss. I had lost what I always thought was the impenetrable globe of family. Our seemingly rock-solid globe had developed a crack, shattering it like fragile glass.

It was hard to believe this was really happening. Divorce, we said, was something that happened to other families, not ours. Our children have good role models. Gary and I have been married for thirty-six years. We come from a long line of marital dinosaurs. Except for one cousin, everyone in our family is still with his or her original mate.

My husband has a theory about marriage that is probably as out-of-date as the RCA record player and his stash of 45s I still have in our garage. "When you sign on to get married," Gary used to tell the kids, "you sign on for life." We always laughed, anticipating the punch line. "And I've got a death certificate to prove it." It's a corny joke, but Gary made his point that our family was invested in marriage. There was nothing that love couldn't fix.

Ben must have known how devastated his dad and I were going to be when he dropped this bomb. How disappointed and hurt we'd be. How worried about him, Joan and the children we'd be. We, in turn, knew how painful it was for Ben to make that call and that he was going to need our support. This was going to be a stressful time for Ben and Joan. Naturally, Gary and I wanted to do what we could to help our children. But first, we had to get past our own emotionality and accept the decision. It would take time.

"Why didn't we see this coming?" we asked ourselves. True, thousands of miles separated us physically from our children, but we both felt so close to Ben and Joan. We shared everything. We were family, after all. Gary and I prided ourselves on being open and having good communication with all four of our children. We couldn't understand why we had been shut out, why Ben and Joan had come to this decision without talking to us first. It was impossible to imagine.

"It's not like Ben and Joan to just quit because they're going through tough times. They have two young children," Gary said angrily. "What's wrong with kids today that they can't stick it out?"

His words rang true. Ben and Joan were confirming what those divorce statistics we read in the magazines kept telling us, that couples today are finding it easier than ever before to walk away from their marriages. We had read about this being the age of "starter marriages" — marriages that last five years or less and end before children begin — and that about 50 percent of all first marriages fail.

Gary and I shook our heads in disbelief. "It's not like Ben to give up," we agreed.

The fault must lie with Joan, an inner voice told me. I felt guilty thinking ill of Joan. Joan was the ideal daughter-in-law, a loving mother, and a devoted wife. My friends envied my relationship with her. Yet blame reared its ugly head before I realized what was happening. I fully expected Joan to call me later that night, and I dreaded talking to her. What could I possibly say?

She didn't call until morning, and when she did, she was bitter. She flooded me with angry accusations about Ben while I bit my tongue and just listened.

"Ben was the one who wanted out," Joan insisted. "The whole thing was his idea, not mine. He waited until the children were asleep, and then he told me he was through with the marriage. He had his bag packed, ready to leave." No, he hadn't given her any reason for his behavior.

Of course, I wanted to know how the children were with all this going on.

Joan said Jake was upset and didn't want to go to school and that Ben told the children he would see them over the weekend.

"He must have told the twins he was going away on another one of those business trips." The way she said "business trips" made me cringe.

She asked me if I'd heard from Ben or knew where he was. I found myself hedging every word, afraid that anything I said would fly back in my face.

"Perhaps he was staying in a hotel or with friends," I suggested lamely. "Call me," I said close to tears before we hung up. "Call me anytime — morning or night — if you need to talk. I'm here for you." I wondered if my last words sounded as hollow to Joan as they did to me.

Gary and I clung to false hopes that Ben would reconsider his decision, and that he and Joan would get back together. We talked about the possibility of getting them into marriage counseling and even paying for it. I planned to suggest it to Ben the next time we spoke. Meanwhile, Gary and I argued back and forth, not knowing who was at fault. But, then, did it really matter? The fact remained: Our children had decided to seek a divorce, and suddenly Gary and I were thrown in with millions of other parents in the same situation.

Sitting helplessly on the sidelines, we struggled to understand where we fit. What was our role going to be? How could we help Ben and Joan through this crazy time without getting caught in the middle? Would we be able to maintain a relationship with our daughter-in-law after the divorce? And what about the twins? How would the divorce affect our relationship with our grandchildren? My heart ached thinking about the twins.

I've heard many painful stories from friends who have been cut out of their grandchildren's lives after the parents divorced. My friend Margaret complains all the time that she has to compete with her son on visiting day for her granddaughter's attention. She's been robbed of the unique grandparent-grandchild relationship she'd always dreamed about — instead, she's tossed a few meager crumbs every once in a while when her son brings them over to visit.

That wasn't going to be me, I vowed. I wanted my grandchildren to grow up knowing me. How I cherished my memories of my own grandparents! That thought triggered a long-dormant recollection: the delicious smell wafting in the halls as I ran expectantly up the stairs to Grandma Dory's apartment, and finding stuffed cabbage simmering in her enormous chipped blue-enamel pot. Those flavorful meat packages are to me as memorable as Proust's buttery madeleine cookies. And my grandfather, sitting in his chair doing the crossword puzzles, nibbling the end of his pencil while he ruminated about a clue.

Indeed, to this day my grown children have a unique bond with their grandmother — Gary's mother — who they regularly chat with online as well as on the phone. At eighty-six, my mother-in-law still pecks away her wise-owl advice to her grandchildren each week on her laptop in her own home. She is a role model for my children. They can spend hours on the telephone with their grandmother, just catching up. It is a rare and precious relationship that they will remember all their lives. She is their connection to the memories and lore of their heritage, an important part of their identity — who they are and what they will become. I desperately wanted to preserve our family, to keep our wonderful heritage intact, and I knew it would not be easy.

•◄ *Communicate Support* ►•

"Mom, Dad... I'm getting divorced." When these chilling words strike home, one of the first things you have to realize is that this is probably one of the most difficult decisions your children have ever had to make. After the initial shock (and not all parents are as shocked as were Nora and Gary; many anticipate the problem even before the child does), you have to face the fact that there are going to be major changes in your lives.

Divorce does not exist in a vacuum. Every member of the family is affected. There will be shifts in relationships, downswings and upswings, many shifts that are not within your control. The only control you can exercise is over the relationship you have with your son or daughter. Like Nora and Gary, you need to demonstrate your support from the very beginning.

There are no hard and fast rules as to when parents should undertake this mission to help their family heal. Nevertheless, there are some valuable lessons you can glean from Nora's experience. Let's consider her situation.

Her first reaction was to look for fault. Nora immediately sided with her son. Not all parents have this response when they learn the couple is splitting. They may have no choice but to fault their own child. And with good reason. There are unfortunate cases when a son or daughter has shown through past behavior that he or she is unworthy of parental support. In such cases, it is a good strategy to rally around the in-law in hopes of helping the spouse and grandchildren who have already suffered the abuses of that parent. But in most instances, when it is your child with whom you have developed trust and affection, you will want to be all you can be for that child. There are going to be tough times ahead.

Nora reacted with disbelief. "It's not like Ben to give up," she said. Obviously, parents will all react differently to the news of a child's marriage breaking apart. Some parents will be angry, some will become depressed, others confused, anxious, or fearful. Many parents are relieved that their child is escaping a bad situation. No matter how you react, it is important to remember that you are not the one taking center stage. Your child, son- or daughter-in-law, and grandchildren are the people who will be most buffeted by the winds of change. As a parent, you are expected to be there for the family to help steady the course while you hold your own emotionality in check.

Also bear in mind that when your child makes the announcement, he or she is already in pain and looking for family support. Your role is to communicate that support no matter how you feel about your in-law, whom you've learned to accept as your own child. Your child comes first. That doesn't mean you have make a vow to reject the son- or daughter-in-law or say terrible things about that person because you think that's what your child wants to hear. This is a time when your child is banking on your loyalty. What your child wants to hear is that you love and accept him — that you will be there to help her get through the tumultuous times ahead. Recriminations, if there have to be any, should come later, when you're less emotional. Understandably, absolute allegiance to your child may be difficult to carry out, especially if you know there is another side to the story — an unpleasant side, some behavior that you would rather turn your back on.

This is the key point: The way in which you react to your child's announcement will pave the way for your future relationship with your child, your grandchildren, and soon to be ex-in-law.

What if you've already acted with horror and said terrible things? You can't take back your words. The point is, you're only human, and you were thrown for a loop. Don't worry — this is only stage one. You'll have many opportunities to backtrack and make amends, as this is a long journey with many twists and turns. Chances are your child will be forgiving if you explain you were overwhelmed with the news and didn't have a chance to sort things out.

While there are no hard and fast rules, I think you will find the rest of the chapter has some good pieces of advice that will keep you on track as you journey through the first stage of your child's divorce, accepting the decision. The second is overcoming denial. This is what Nora experienced. Perhaps you can relate to her situation.

Nora Continues . . .

I was in a state of denial; I told myself: Joan and I would surely continue to talk on the phone — just not as often. Joan would still be invited to my niece's wedding, but she wouldn't sit at our table. The twins would stay with us for a week in August as usual. We'd instituted "Camp Gramps" a couple of years earlier, and it had become a family tradition. Previews of family get-togethers — holidays, birthdays, anniversaries — flashed across my memory screen. I fooled myself into believing that there would be full-length features, when the reality was that from then on there would be only film clips.

I decided not to publicize the news to our other children, but Ben let the cat out of the bag, and the whole family was abuzz. I'd asked Ben to wait before telling Gary's mother, to spare her the pain since she is so attached to Joan. I also delayed telling my friends. When I did confide in one or two whose children had divorced, they offered advice that I gracefully listened to but readily dismissed. My situation was different. My children would act civilly. No one involved would really get hurt. Least of all, me. I thought I was holding up well under the circumstances. I kept myself busy so I didn't have to think about Ben and Joan all the time. But then reality hit home. This is how it happened:

One day, my friend Anita and I went shopping, and I stopped to admire a cute sports watch in the display window. "Joan would just love that," I said without thinking. "Her birthday is in a few weeks. I think I'll send it to her." Then I caught my friend's pained expression reflected back at me in the glass, and I began to cry. Only moments before, I admitted that Joan and I hadn't communicated in weeks. When I telephoned, she was always rushing somewhere, and she never returned my calls. She ignored my e-mails — even the jokes and light-hearted messages I had so carefully crafted. When I called Mary, Joan's mother, she was cold as ice.

It was difficult to admit that I was losing a child. And Joan was our child. My husband and I had made a place for her in our family as soon as my son announced his great love. Life was never going to be the same. I knew deep within me that I had to move on and face facts. If I didn't, I wouldn't be able to be there for my son and my grandchildren. So easy to say, so hard to do, and I found myself grieving and looking for answers.

•◀ *Accepting Reality* ▶•

The next difficulty parents have is accepting the fact that their child's decision to divorce is a reality. Face it: their marriage is in big trouble. If the kids mean business (and they probably do, or they wouldn't have made the announcement in the first place), as a parent, you are going to have to get off the path of denial.

Like their divorcing children, parents have to grieve. Experts in marital and family relations compare the stages of divorce grief to the stages of death grief. And the level of stress is comparable (Holmes and Rahe, 1967), Following the initial shock and denial, there is a healthy period of mourning leading to acceptance and recovery. Nora thought that if she could just understand the reasons for Ben's decision, she would not feel so low. However, Ben was very shut down. He was not ready to talk about his marital problems. So Nora decided to take a stab at trying to figure out by herself what went wrong.

•◀ *Looking for Reasons* ▶•

Another mistake parents make is jumping to conclusions as to why their children's marriage failed. Nora and Gary spent many sleepless nights second-guessing how this could have happened to Ben and Joan, "the perfect couple." Nora came up with what she thought was a credible list of probabilities: Ben was a workaholic and spent too many hours at the office and not enough time at home. (Hadn't Joan referred to all those business trips?) Maybe the stress of work had gotten to him, and he was emotionally unavailable. Nora might have jumped to other conclusions, such as that Ben wasn't involved with the twins enough and that her daughter-in-law had the full brunt of responsibility, which wasn't fair. Her husband, in turn, might have argued that someone in Ben's position had to make sacrifices for the family's future financial security, and that Joan should be more sympathetic. Perhaps to keep the peace with Gary, Nora would have conceded that perhaps Gary was right, and then Gary would backtrack that Ben should have been more aware of the toll the children took on his wife. You can see how Nora and Gary might have waved back and forth like flags in the wind. The list of possibilities underlying their child's marital problems could have gone on and on. All unsubstantiated, of course.

Maybe in your case you know exactly why your children are seeking a divorce. A spouse has an addiction problem, is abusive, is a serial womanizer, or has taken a lover. However, for most parents, there are issues in the child's marriage that never surface. Perhaps over time, when your child's pain has diminished, you will discover the reasons. Or perhaps you never will. In the meantime, the best advice is not to look for answers while you are still in the dark, but simply to provide support.

Your son or daughter may recount chapter and verse of what went wrong in the marriage, yet be completely unaware of the underlying issues that really caused the downfall. As a parent and an outsider, you may think you see both sides. But is your child ready to hear your analysis? At this point, I would like to repeat the advice Myra offered when talking about her own experience comforting a stepdaughter who came to her when she separated from her husband:

> *Parents do not need to articulate to their child everything they think, feel, and observe. Some of this information hurts and cannot be retracted. And some of it is judgment, assessment, and not necessarily objective even though as parents we may feel we're better informed or more experienced or more objective than our children about these life situations*

The message bears repeating: Parents have an obligation to support their child without having all the answers about what went wrong in the marriage.

•◄ *A Barrel of Blame* ►•

Another mistake parents make when they get the news their child is getting divorced is to charge themselves with the failure. Like many parents, Gary and Nora fell into this trap by agonizing about what could have gone wrong. "Why didn't we see this coming?" Nora asked Gary.

According to author and grandparent Joan Schrager Cohen in her book *Helping Your Grandchildren Through Their Parents' Divorce*

(1994), parents do a tremendous amount of soul searching to try to figure out what went wrong. *Did we interfere too much? Were we not supportive enough? Shouldn't we have seen this disaster coming?* Because we want to protect our children, we come up with a hundred things we should have done: If only we had babysat more often, visited more often, given the couple more time to go off by themselves, contributed money toward a down payment when they bought their house. If only they lived closer. If... if... if....

Perhaps it's easier to blame yourself than to accept the fact that somehow your children have failed you by not living out your dreams. Many parents cannot accept the humiliation and embarrassment of their children's divorce, even though divorce is so much more socially acceptable today. A divorce lawyer I interviewed when I was researching this book told me her own mother did not tell the family she (the lawyer) was getting divorced.

> *Mom was too heart-broken, she said. She just couldn't believe an intelligent woman with two children would do this. When I got together with my aunts and uncles almost a year and a half later, they had no idea Jim and I had split up. My mother made the divorce harder for me, and I resented her attitude even though I understood where she was coming from.*

Parents who have more than one divorced child may dip into the barrel of blame each time: "How could this happen twice?" Rather than self-flagellate, acknowledge that there are many influences in our society today that make it easier for couples to untie the knot. Try this quick test: When you were growing up, how many couples among your parents' or, for that matter, your grandparents' peers would have split had society been more accepting of divorce?

Speaking of parents, what are you going to tell yours? Initially, you may feel the need to shield your elderly parents (like Gary's eighty-six-year-old mom, whom the kids adored), who are not in good health or are very attached to the about-to-be ex-in-law. Bank on the supposition that eventually, someone is going to let the cat out of the bag. If you aren't up to the task, choose someone you trust who can soften the blow. Prime that person. Tell your intermediary exactly what you want said and what you want omitted. It's not necessary to go into all the gory details. I laughed when one father I'll call Fred told me he kept the news under wraps rather than upset his ninety-year-old dad, who sniffed it out anyway when the grandson-in-law didn't show up for the granddad's birthday bash.

"So, Pip ran out on you," the old man said to his granddaughter. "Well, you're such a good-looking doll, you're gonna find someone three times better." Turned out the grandfather became a real morale booster to his grandchild, and a wonderful support to his son.

•◀ A Gallon of Guilt ▶•

Parents who got married in the '60s and '70s are only too familiar with the ravages of divorce in their own lives. This was the generation of self-fulfillment, when more couples divorced than ever before. Many parents are now burdened with the legacy of being a less-than-perfect role model for their children. They may very well ask, "Who am I to offer advice?" Unfortunately, statistics bear out this unfortunate legacy. According to U.S. Census Bureau Divorce studies (1995-6), children of divorce were 50 percent more likely to leave their marriages than were their counterparts from intact families. More than 43 percent of women whose parents were divorced got divorced within ten years of marriage as opposed to 29 percent of women whose parents stayed together in good or troubled marriages.[1]

Too many divorced parents bear the burden of guilt when they should be focusing on the strength and experience they can offer their children. I came across one such situation when I was talking to a young woman who initially blamed her divorced mother for her own marital failure. By the end of our interview, Barbara reversed herself and declared her mother had actually been a positive role model. This is Barbara's story:

My mother and father got divorced when I was sixteen. They thought that I was old enough to understand what was happening, and they never really considered my feelings. I was left pretty much on my own when they separated. My mother went back to college and worked part-time, so she was never around. I now understand that she was just doing what she had to do to take care of us kids; but at the time I resented what I considered her selfishness because she expected me to be so independent. A few years after the divorce, my father married Brenda, and I had a half-brother a year later. I used to think, "Is it any wonder my sister and I are so messed up?" Janet is almost forty and single. I was married for two and a half years before I realized what a big mistake I had made. I never thought I'd get divorced, but I've since learned that you have to rely on yourself, and you can be okay when things don't turn out the way you expected. My mother taught me that.

One other point I would like to make on the topic of the unfortunate legacy of divorce is that children of divorce should be able to count on the support of both parents. Understandably, a child's divorce can cause a certain amount of residual anger to surface in embittered parents who never resolved their own marital issues. It is much healthier if parents can work together instead of finding fault with one another and widening the breach. Your kids don't need more fallout.

•◀ *The Parental Knee-Jerk to Fix It* ▶•

Another mistake that parents make is the knee-jerk reaction to try to fix a child's marriage by insisting the couple go for marriage counseling.

Remember that Nora wanted her son and daughter-in-law to go for counseling, and she planned to talk to Ben about it. When she did, Ben told her that he knew what he was doing, and he refused to go. He felt his wife wanted out of the marriage as much as he did. He told Nora that before they broke up, Joan had been seeing a counselor. In fact, he'd gone to a few sessions but quit because he didn't like the therapist. Whereupon Nora suggested they see someone else. "It's the same thing as getting a second medical opinion before you opt for surgery," she instructed.

The rest of the story is that Nora admitted that she'd talked to Joan, even offered to pay if they'd see someone. Ben blew up. He accused his mother of being interfering, and he didn't speak to Nora for days. Was Nora wrong to suggest counseling? It seems a natural enough parental response. Her offer to pay was a caring gesture.

Psychologists I talked to about this issue said Nora's mistake was pushing on both sides and using counseling as a bandage, a way to save the marriage. One therapist explained that counseling is not a safety net. It is an opportunity for self-growth, a chance for individuals to understand each partner's personal agenda, to look at the power struggles, the defense mechanisms, and other negative behaviors that are causing strife in the relationship. It's a process, not a quick fix, to rebuild a marriage — which may or may not be possible (assuming rebuilding is still possible).

In general, parents should not force their child's hand and insist that they go for counseling. First, you may have no idea whether or not the marriage can or should be saved, and second, even if you know all the details, it is not your decision to make.

Let's say you are fairly sure what is causing the marital problems because it is so obvious. You know that Jack can't hold a job or that he and his wife blame each other for their child's antisocial behavior. Assuming the couple has not already filed for divorce, you might suggest and contribute toward professional help for some other reason than to get the couple back together. For example, you might suggest vocational counseling for your son-in-law or family counseling to help the parents deal with their child's misbehavior. Please notice I said suggest, not push.

•◀ Parents as Saviors ▶•

In the course of writing this book, I talked to parents who admitted they became overly invested in saving their children's marriage. One father spent thousands of dollars keeping his son's marriage afloat when his daughter-in-law subsequently discovered her husband was having an affair. The father paid for couple therapy, sent his son and daughter-in-law on a lavish vacation, and gave them money to buy a new house, thinking a change in domicile would solve their difficulties. When the matrimonial boat finally sank, the father refused to throw his son a life preserver when his son really needed his emotional support. By initially interfering, the father had assumed some responsibility for his son's behavior. Then when the marriage broke up, he took it personally and abandoned him.

Another mother, whom I'll call Glenda, sacrificed her privacy, ruined her health, and almost lost her job taking control of her daughter's marriage.

Glenda is a successful marketing executive from an upper-class, well-educated family. She is a single mother, who divorced Bobbi's father when the girl was three years old. When Bobbi turned eighteen, she dropped out of college to marry Vinnie, a garage mechanic. Glenda liked Vinnie, but she felt her daughter was too immature for the responsibilities of marriage, and she was concerned about the differences in the couple's backgrounds. Despite her reservations, Glenda paid for a lavish wedding. Not surprisingly, the marriage began to fall apart four months later. When Vinnie got laid off, the couple moved in with Glenda, and Bobbi became Mama's little girl again. Because his mother-in-law was taking care of them financially, Vinnie did not feel pressured to find another job. At night, he would go off with his friends and leave Bobbi sitting in front of the television. Ultimately, he got involved with an old girlfriend, who became pregnant. Vinnie swore he wasn't the father, and Bobbi believed him.

By now Glenda was developing all kinds of physical ailments and had trouble concentrating at work. Finally, she went for counseling and was told that she had to establish boundaries and set a deadline for the kids to move out. The marriage lasted six months longer, and when the two separated, Bobbi came back home to live. This time, however, Glenda insisted Bobbi go back to school or get a part-time job. Bobbi eventually remarried, and now she and her mother have a much healthier relationship and respect each other's boundaries.

It is helpful to stop and wonder what motivates parents to work so hard at saving their children's marriage. It is difficult to fault parents for wanting the best for their children, but in this area, they need to pull back and let their children take responsibility. One embittered man spoke up in a grandparent support group to say that to this day he has not forgiven his parents for their lack of support when he told them how miserable he was in his marriage. "My parents made me stick it out. I stayed married eight years longer than I should have, and it was hell. All that time wasted."

The following are examples of parental quick-fix compulsions. Note the end results:

- Margo convinced her son and daughter-in-law to give up their apartment in the city and buy a small house in the suburbs to be nearer to her - as if space or distance were the culprit in their breakup. The added cost of living only increased the strain on their marriage, and her daughter-in-law resented her mother-in-law's interference to boot.
- Gladys recommended her daughter give up her part-time job so she could devote more time to her husband, who resented her working outside the home. The daughter acquiesced but soon resented the loss of income and status that work gave her. The marriage continued to limp along, and when she finally left her husband, she blamed her mother for having to give up a good job she now needed to support herself.
- Jerry lectured his daughter-in-law about her spending habits. "If you cut back," she was told, "you won't make my son so angry, and he'll take you back." She tore up her charge cards, and the marriage went downhill anyway.

●◀ *Do as I Say, Not as I Do* ▶●

There are many other parental mistakes to note. One biggie is holding your own marriage or someone else's up to the light as a model. Marriages are as different as seashells. Moreover, while they may look perfect lying on the sand, when you examine them closely you see all the crannies.

The best advice is to refrain from holding one marriage up to the light as an example of how another couple rode out the storm. It's very tempting to say, "Look here. Aunt Betty and Uncle Barney had a really rough time a few years back, and they're still together."

Maybe that's the very reason your child wants out. He's afraid he'll wind up like Uncle Barney!

●◀ *Monday-Morning Quarterbacking* ▶●

Another point concerns the mistake parents make when they equate emotional support with in-law bashing. You may think you are consoling your daughter when you say, "You were right to get rid of the lazy bum" or you remind your son, "She was never top-drawer." No one wants to hear that she wasted all that time, money, and energy building a relationship that was doomed from the get-go. Instead, acknowledge how hard your child tried to make the marriage work. (Even if she didn't, she *thinks* she did.) You cannot win points by knocking the in-law. In fact, you are probably jeopardizing your future relationship with your child, who will resent your Monday-morning quarterbacking. Be mindful that the couple might get back together or stay connected after the divorce. (Hopefully they will for the sake of the grandkids, and where will that put you? Standing there with egg on your face.)

●◀ *Building Confidence* ▶●

Try this on for size. Which "parents" would you want in your corner and why?

Case A. Beverly was married for thirty-five years when her husband left her for a lap dancer. Beverly was devastated, and flew out to Florida to cry on her stepfather's shoulder. Her stepfather said, "You're going to be just fine. You're made of strong stuff, and you still have your whole life ahead of you."

Case B. Gayle was in her sixties when her husband told her he'd fallen in love with his secretary. Gayle got in the car and drove six hundred miles to seek refuge with her sister, who spent the entire week haranguing her brother-in-law, vowing she would never allow that so-and-so to darken her door again.

Case C. Terrence was inconsolable when his wife took the kids and went to live with his mother-in-law because she realized she'd outgrown him. He spent the entire weekend with his best friend and the friend's wife, bemoaning all he'd done to make Dolores happy —

the sacrifices to career and the financial hole he'd dug for himself building an expensive house and sending the kids to private school. Marty and Melissa just sat and listened. They let Terrence pour his heart out without defending him or attacking Dolores.

Case D. Monty spent the weekend with his father and his stepmother after his wife locked him out of the house. His father was irate that Monty was not being more aggressive. He told Monty to go back and demand to be let back in the house. "If she refuses, call the police," he said angrily. "It's your property. You pay the bills. She's the one who should be out on the streets."

Let's take a look at each scenario. I don't know about you, but if I were Gayle (Case B), I would run from all that gloom and doom. I'd much rather have my spirits lifted by talking to Beverly's stepdad (Case A) because he's so positive. No matter how old you are, it's comforting to be told that you are a survivor, that the future is bright. That becomes a wish-fulfilling prophecy. Of course, it can be difficult being this positive when your child comes to you and you are just as fearful. There is much value in just being a good listener. You need not say anything other than offer comfort (Case C). What your child wants is a shoulder to cry on.

Now let's turn to Monty's situation in Case D. This father wants to be his son's ally. He is trying to help his son, but he is escalating the problem by being so emotional. What's worse, he is giving his son bad advice. This situation calls for a third party (a lawyer or close friend) to act as mediator and resolve the house occupancy issue.

Even if you are able to see both sides of the picture and you have some ready advice, hold off awhile. Your child is not able to hear you when he or she is in so much pain. Problem-solving comes later. You may also find that your advice may change as you gain distance.

In summary, be someone your child can turn to. Be a trusted listener. Be a comforter. In addition, if possible, be an optimist. As one older divorced woman said, "If you can exorcise the demons of your past relationship, you are on the way to divorce recovery."

●◀ *Staying Together for the Sake of the Children* ▶●

No discussion about the difficulties in accepting your child's decision is complete without discussing the natural fears grandparents have about losing their grandchildren when the parents separate. In previous generations, people stuck it out for the sake of the children. That is just not the case today. More and more children of divorce grow up in single parent homes. (See chapter 10 — Sidebar "What Is Family?") The verdict is still out as to whether or not a good divorce is better than a bad marriage in terms of the children's emotional well-being. Researchers Judith Wallerstein, Julia Lewis, and Sandra Blakeslee (*The Unexpected Legacy of Divorce*, 2001) would argue that children of divorce carry the scars well into adulthood. On the other hand, Professor E. Mavis Hetherington and co-author John Kelley who conducted a longitudinal study, *For Better or For Worse: Divorce Reconsidered*, involving 1,400 families and more than 2,500 children from divorced, intact and remarried families, claim that while there is a deleterious effect as the result of a family's splitting up, other researchers — like Wallerstein — have exaggerated the negative impact. Instead of focusing on the minority who don't do well, Hetherington and Kelley point to the number of children of divorce who grew up, finished school, got jobs, formed families, and achieved impressive professional success. Twenty years later, when they revisited the two groups, they found there was more similarity in terms of overall adjustment than difference and concluded that children from divorced families are "uncommonly" resilient, mature, responsible, and focused.

I think it's fair to say that most grandparents are not interested in the research data when they learn that their grandchildren are caught in the crossfire. They are much more interested in the future, that is, the role they will play post-divorce. A grandparent's greatest fear is being denied access if the in-law gets custody and moves away. Close behind is the uncertainty of the grandparenting role in the changing pattern of family life when and if the divorced adults remarry (a very high probability, since approximately 73 percent of them do within an average of ten years).

Obviously, once the die is cast, you need to face reality. Your grandchildren are going to be affected one way or another, and you have no choice but to help them get through it as best you can. (See chapter 8 — "Grandchildren in Crisis.") Like their parents, grandchildren need your support. Rather than cry over spilt milk, go out and buy another carton.

Parental Guideposts: Chapter One

It's Not Just a Rough Spot

- Come to a reasonable acceptance of your child's marital difficulties.
- Avoid jumping to conclusions as to why the marriage failed.
- Guard against self-recrimination.
- Say goodbye to guilt.
- Resist the impulse to fix "perceived" problems.
- Acknowledge that your child's path may be different from your own.
- Avoid Monday-morning quarterbacking.
- Demonstrate ongoing support.

•◀ The Divorce Journey ▶•

Marriage has always held an honored place in our society. Understandably, people are cautious today, and there is more social acceptance for single status and cohabitation that ever before. Nevertheless, the wedding business is booming. In times of national crisis (9/11, for example), one of the biggest-selling items was expensive engagement rings! Americans are eternally optimistic. According to surveys such as the oft-quoted U.S. Census Bureau Household Economic Studies (2001), an amazing 90 percent of Americans express a desire to marry despite the 1997 oft-quoted statistic that one out of two marriages is expected to end in divorce. Recent findings are closer to 43 percent, still an impressive figure. Even more amazing is that 75 percent of divorced men and women will try their luck again within three to four years, especially those who do not have children. Furthermore, an astonishing 60 percent of those second marriages will break up within eight years. These statistics are elusive, as some states do not report their figures. The reality remains that a large number of parents can expect to travel the divorce journey twice with their children — a journey that is not any easier and has even more blind curves as families expand, blend, contract, and relationships become more complex.

When your child got married, you assumed your parenting role was over. You looked forward to reaping the rewards — grandchildren, family gatherings at your holiday table, an album full of photos tracing your family history. You anticipated new beginnings. It's understandable if, now that your child is getting divorced, you feel short-changed, angry, disappointed. You are entitled to grieve. However, the best antidote to grief is acceptance, adaptability, and having a sense of purpose. That purpose is getting the family back on track. It began with your "Accepting the Decision." Having done that, now you are charged with helping your child rearrange the disassembled puzzle pieces of his or her family.

END NOTES

[1] Researchers are now saying that the previous 50 percent divorce rate is based on inconclusive and incomplete data. The 50 percent figure as reported by the National Center for Health Statistics (NCHS) is based on a simple — and flawed — calculation: the annual marriage rate per 1,000 people compared with the annual divorce rate. "People who are divorcing in the given year are not the same as those who are marrying, and that statistic is virtually useless in understanding divorce rates. In fact, studies find that the divorce rate in the United States has never reached one in every two marriages, and new research suggests that, with rates now declining, it never will. The method preferred by social scientists in determining the divorce rate is to calculate the number of people who have ever married and subsequently divorced. Counted that way, the rate has never exceeded about 41 percent, researchers say." There are also questions about the trend because no detailed annual figures have been available since 1996, when the NCHS stopped collecting detailed data from states on demographic information about people who divorced. (*The New York Times*, April 19, 2005, Dan Hurley, Science Section, F1)

✎ *Chapter One: Workbook Exercises*

1. Describe your first reaction when your heard the words "Mom, Dad... I'm getting a divorce."

2. Review the eight guideposts. Arrange them in importance as they apply to you.

3. What are your obstacles in making peace with your child's decision to divorce?

4. How do you plan to overcome these obstacles?

5. Give reasons why you are not to blame for your child's mistakes.

6. What do you anticipate will be some of the biggest challenges you will face in helping your child (in-law, grandchildren) in the weeks and months ahead?

Chapter Two

To the Rescue — Putting the Pieces Together

Nora's Story

Once I was able to accept Ben and Joan's decision to get divorced, I thought I would be able to help the family move smoothly through the ordeal. It was *never* smooth.

Right after the announcement, Gary and I kept in close contact with Ben. We often spoke two or three times a day. Because he lived so far away, we magnified every sigh and looked for signs of distress. More than once, we were awakened in the middle of the night when Ben had a special need to talk. Even though he had the support of some close friends, he turned to family when things looked bleak. When he called, Gary or I would walk him through his sadness or anger. However, there was only so much we as parents could do. We listened, but we could not take away Ben's pain. We felt powerless.

Ben and Joan's divorce was moving along a predictable course. They had consulted lawyers and worked out a visitation schedule. On Tuesdays, Ben took the twins out to dinner; they spent the day with him every other Saturday. Because he'd rented a furnished studio, there wasn't enough room for the children to sleep over. So visitations were restricted to daytime excursions; they went to the park or the movies, depending on the weather. I felt sure the arrangement was hard on the children, who were confused and upset that their daddy was no longer living at home.

Ben told us that after he drove them home, Janice would sulk and cling to him when he dropped her off on the doorstep. Jake was much better at hiding his feelings when he was with his father, but he was acting out at school. His teacher reported him bullying some classmates, and he'd gotten into a fistfight on the schoolbus.

Gary and I wanted to fly out to Seattle, but Ben kept us at bay with excuses: he was traveling for business; all his spare time was taken up with the children. Naturally, we said we understood, but in reality, we were hurt. We wanted so much to *do* something. I can honestly say, never a day went by that Gary and I didn't talk about Ben and Joan. Their divorce consumed us. We were particularly worried about the twins.

Then, one day, Gary took the bull by the horns and announced that he was getting on a plane and going to Seattle. "No ifs or buts. Grandparents have rights too," he said tartly. Ben relented, and Gary went for a brief visit, hoping to work some magic that would stop this tragedy in its tracks. When he came back, Gary was gloomier than ever. "The marriage is definitely over," he told me when I picked him up at the airport. "They're both stubborn as mules," Gary reported. "I spent hours talking to Ben and Joan individually and got nowhere."

"What did Joan tell you?" All contact between Joan and me had long since ceased. I deduced she had installed Caller-ID and was blocking all my calls. I was eager for any information about her and her attitude toward Ben

"She's very bitter. She says Ben is never there for her. That while he's been moving ahead, she's been stuck in a rut and . . . . "

"You know Ben offered to pay for law school when she expressed interest in going," I interrupted.

"Well, that's her side of the story. When I told this to Ben, he said that Joan doesn't know what she wants, that she blows hot and cold. One day she wants to be a lawyer, the next day she wants to open a bookstore. He claims she's angry, confused, and taking her frustration out on him, blaming him that the world is passing her by." Gary sighed. "The long and the short is — they both want to end the marriage because things have not been good between them for a long time."

I found it astonishing that both Ben and Joan had put up such a good front. I guess I never saw any real cause for alarm, or maybe just saw only what I wanted to see. I always assumed they would iron out their own wrinkles, just as Gary and I had.

Gary returned from Seattle with a clearer picture of the situation and Ben and Joan's relationship issues. Ben was equally clear: he appreciated our interest, but he didn't want us there. He said he was getting by. Months later, it was a completely different story. This is what happened:

I was freelancing for an advertising agency and working at home. I was in my office when Ben called. Immediately, I knew there was trouble from the sound of his voice.

"I'm on my way to pick up the kids," Ben said. I checked my desk calendar. It was Thursday, not his usual visiting day.

"What's up?" I asked quickly.

"It's Joan. She had a mammogram Tuesday, and the doctor discovered some suspicious calcifications in her right breast. She's going to need some exploratory surgery — a lumpectomy."

I gasped. Five years ago, Mary, Joan's mother, had had a mastectomy, and Mary's sister died of breast cancer in her early forties.

"Joan's fallen to pieces," Ben said. "She's going to stay with her parents, and she wants me to come back and live in the house and take over the kids for the time being." He stopped, gulping some air. "I'm not sure how I'm going to work this all out."

I felt my pulse quicken. "Ben, do you want me to come out and give you a hand?" Given the situation Ben had just described, I didn't think Mary was in any position to watch the children. She clearly had her hands full with Joan. I could hear honking in the background and realized Ben was calling me from the car. Never had I felt so far away from my family.

"Would you?" Ben cried. "Mom, that would be great. How soon do you think you can get here?"

I looked at my desk piled high with stuff I needed to get out to a client. I had a tight deadline, but it would have to wait. I would do what I could from Seattle or farm the work out if I had to. "I'm going to call the airlines and check the flight schedules. I'll call you right back," I said.

Like Ben, I was operating on auto-pilot. The separation was bad enough. Now we had Joan's potential illness to deal with. Panic coiled around my throat. I knew I couldn't give in to my fears because Ben was going to need all my strength.

Nora and Gary's First Response

Nora and Gary discovered by trial and error that parents play different roles at different times, depending where they are on the slippery slope of their child's divorce journey. The most difficult stage is what parents perceive as "the rescue period." Some parents are called to arms right after the announcement that their child and his spouse are separating. Often the call comes months later, or it may not come at all. The lesson here is that in order to do the most good, parents have to respect their child's timeline.

In this part of Nora's story, Gary went to his son's rescue hoping to fix the marriage. His behavior was dictated by his own need, not Ben's. Let's talk about that instinctive urge to deliver first aid when you learn your children are splitting up.

The Parents' Call to Arms

It's hard to fault parents who want to help. Gary and Nora felt that their place was by their child's side, especially since Ben kept telephoning them, even waking them up in the middle of the night. Nora said it all when she said she felt powerless. She wished she could take away Ben's pain, but knew she couldn't. Gary was even more desperate. He announced, "Grandparents have rights, too," and took a plane to Seattle. He returned frustrated and saddened, realizing he couldn't fix the marriage.

What can you glean from Nora and Gary's experience? First, since you are dealing with an adult child, you need to acknowledge that your son or daughter may not want to be rescued. In addition, if your child does need rescuing, Mom and Dad may not be the ones she or he wants — at least, not initially. Second, keep in mind that a physical "rescue operation" may not be what your child has in mind when he or she calls — even in the middle of the night. Third, it is important to resist the urge to rush in to either save the situation or provide first aid. The key is to have patience and wait before responding. Do you remember what your own parents taught you when you were learning to cross a busy intersection? They told you to Stop, look, and listen. It's the same now when your child separates from a spouse. Stop before running to fix the problem. Look and survey the situation. Listen to what your child is asking from you.

Now, it may be that your son or daughter calls and immediately asks for help. Her needs are crystal clear — a place to escape an unsafe situation, a warm bed for a couple of nights, some money to appease creditors, a temporary babysitter, a cup of hot tea, a shoulder to cry on. Often, however, a child is so distraught or in so much denial that the marriage is over, he or she may not know what is needed. Here is one mother's perspective:

I think the only thing you can do for your child is to be there. I held my son in my arms as he tried not to cry. I did not blame anyone. I let him do that. 'It's your life,' I told him. 'And if you want her back, I will support you. It's your happiness that is important to me, with or without her.'

While doing the research for this book, I asked a number of sons and daughters what kind of help they wanted from their parents following their announcement. These were some of the responses:

"Everything"
"Nothing"
"Understanding"
"Feather pillows"
"Not to have to answer their questions"
"Space"
"The last thing I wanted was to involve my parents!"

I discovered that what adult children want most of all, without having to ask, is a hug. They want the knowledge that their parents are in their corner. What they *don't* want is to have to deal with their parents' emotionality or recriminations. They know on some level that their parents are disappointed. Nevertheless, the child has his own pain to deal with, and the last thing he wants is to be burdened with anyone else's.

Keep in mind that your grandchildren will be your child's number-one priority. Your son or daughter's first order of business is to explain the situation to the kids and to allay their fears. You, your spouse, your child's sisters, brothers, aunts, uncles, etc. must take a back seat.

•◀ *Avoid Jumping the Gun* ▶•

Listen to Faye and see if what she has to say has a familiar ring:

> *Sheila just separated from her husband. Now, I know she told me not to come, but I'm sure she needs help with the kids. She's all alone in Chicago, so I think I'll just pack a bag anyway.*

This mother has the best intentions, but she's probably making a mistake by not listening to her daughter. Faye should stay in touch with her daughter, wait for the door to open a crack, and continue to renew her offer. She should not act on her own.

There are a number of reasons not to jump the gun when you get the news about the separation. First, you may be getting a lot of mixed messages:

> *I want your advice; I don't need your advice.*
> *You are a big help; you are interfering.*
> *I want you here; you are just in the way.*

Second, your child is in turmoil and may not be ready to face you, especially if you've had problems getting along with him in the past. Third, your child may have other support systems in place. Before we get to the other reasons, let's look at the three different support systems:

The inner circle of family tends to "circle" around one another like old pioneers when there is trouble, according to Joan Schrager Cohen, who offers wise advice in her grandparenting book, *Helping Your Grandchildren Through Their Parents Divorce* (1994). The negative side of this is that some relatives can overstep boundaries and be overly critical.

The outer circle is composed of friends, colleagues, and acquaintances. There is a good chance your child has friends who know the divorce ropes and will save your child a lot of time and energy recommending legal counsel, etc. The negative to this is when a community of friends ostracizes the divorcee. One embittered former wife of a Wall Street mogul wrote this: "Once I was divorced, I became a social embarrassment to my old circle of friends and was left high and dry when I couldn't keep up with them anymore."

The virtual circle. Another source of support that has gained popularity is the Internet, where individuals share experiences and get advice online. It's one way to unload angry feelings. And while I am not discouraging this outlet, I caution anyone using this about giving out identifiable information.

A fourth reason you should not immediately board a plane is the reality that your son or daughter may not be quite as desperate as he or she may sound. There are going to be good and bad days with many emotional highs and lows. Your child more than likely called you on one of those bad days.

And the fifth reason — the one that may be hardest to accept — is that, quite honestly, as a parent you might just be in the way. In Sheila's case, having her mother with her at this moment in time when she is trying to manage three kids (Faye is a nervous wreck when it comes to three adolescent boys) might simply put poor Sheila over the edge.

When *do* you break the rule and rush to your child's side? When you think your grandchildren are at risk and their parents are too embroiled in their problems to take care of them. In that case, act on your instincts. In addition, when you know for a fact that your son or daughter has been victimized, is hurting, and is not able to take care of the situation, pack your bag.

•◀ *Survey the Landscape* ▶•

By now I think I've established my point that there are sufficient reasons why you should not rush in to save your child, notwithstanding a) the existence of an emergency situation or b) the fact that your child is absolutely clear he or she wants you there. Understand that your son or daughter may be more "divorce ready" than you realize, because while this breakup is news to you, your child has been plotting this event, or at least preparing himself for its possibility, for a long time.

Suggestion: If you can, find out whether or not your child has attended a divorce support group, sought legal or financial advice, and/or researched the state's divorce laws. You will feel better knowing your child has begun some preparation work, especially if the divorce settlement is going to be difficult. One mother told me,

By the time June went public with the news, she'd interviewed half a dozen attorneys and selected one. There were some custody issues at stake. I went to court with her for moral support, but she was pretty strong and definitely ready to do battle.

•◀ My Child Acts as If I'm the Problem! ▶•

Your child is trying to get his or her life back together. People going through divorce are juggling a lot of balls and making many decisions to keep their lives on course. Your son is looking for a place to live so his spouse and kids can stay put. The couple is deciding whether to hire a lawyer or seek mediation. Your daughter is struggling to work out financial arrangements to keep her and the kids afloat until the final settlement. He's unhappy about the visitation schedule; she's anxious about finding a job because she's been out of the workforce awhile. And those are only for starters - there are the day-to-day struggles such as childcare arrangements, dealing with angry or depressed kids, and handling the in-laws that make this time very stressful. If your child is bitter, angry, frustrated, and overwrought, you become a safe target for all that emotionality. Think back to that period of his adolescence when nothing you ever did was right and how much smarter and nicer you became when your child didn't need you so much.

Charlene and her daughter Jennifer found themselves constantly sparring when Jennifer moved back home with her two young children after her marriage broke up. Things got so tense that Charlene prevailed upon her live-in boyfriend, who owned a house, to rent it to her daughter. Charlene loved her daughter but desperately needed her life back. To make up for some of the lost revenue, Jennifer went to work part-time and gave a portion of her salary to her mother's boyfriend. The situation was much improved when Jennifer re-established her independence.

●◀ *When You Can't Go to the Rescue* ▶●

A final point before we return to Nora's story: You don't have to be physically present to give your child what he or she needs. Today more and more families live many miles apart, and for various reasons, many parents cannot rush to their child's side even if they feel they should be there. Obviously, feelings of guilt will linger for parents who cannot be there face-to-face to answer the call for help.

> *"I'm so far away," one parent wailed when she got her daughter's call that she was leaving her husband after months of quiet deliberation. "We're on opposite coasts, and I'm not well enough to make the trip. How can I be of any use?"*

The reality is you don't have to be there in person to give your child a hug. You can give her a hug by phone, e-mail, snail mail, instant message, text message, or fax. You get my drift. No matter what method you use, you want to convey the message, "I'm here for you. I support you." And you want to send this message often. It is likely your son or daughter will be too distressed to really hear it the first time it's offered, even if the breakup comes as no surprise to anyone. It is a message that bears repeating.

Nora's Rescue Operation

Ben met me at the terminal gate. The twins were with him. I hadn't seen my son in months. He looked thin and drawn. His eyes were darkly circled. Usually the twins break away as soon as they see me and embrace me in a long, tight hug. Now they pressed into their father's side. For some reason, the first thing I noticed was that Jake was wearing two different shoes and that Janice's hair needed washing.

On the drive home, Ben and I made an effort to keep the conversation light. We chatted about Honey, the twins' rough-hewn mutt, who was always getting into trouble. Last week she'd slammed into the sliding glass doors in the family room, trying to chase a squirrel she'd spotted in the backyard.

"Honey has ten stitches in her leg," Janice said. "And she keeps tearing off her bandage. Mommy had to take her back to the vet two times to get it fixed."

"Was Honey brave when they sewed her up?" I gulped when Janice said *Mommy*. I didn't know how much Ben had told them about Joan's going to stay with Grandma Mary and Grandpa Todd.

"Oh, very," Jake said soberly.

Ben carried my bag and led me through the house. It was the first time he'd been inside since he left. We both could hardly contain our surprise. Newspapers, books, and articles of clothing were scattered everywhere. There was a dark stain on the hall carpet, and the plants were dry as dust.

The children were hungry. I opened the refrigerator to see what I could find and winced at the odor of sour milk. When I peeked into the laundry room, I saw my work cut out for me. Joan's lackadaisical domestic attitude, she had admitted, was rooted in teenage rebellion. Joan's mother was a scrupulously neat housekeeper and a stay-at-home mom, a bit too compulsive for my liking. However, the condition of the house told me that something more was going on. I had never known Joan to be this lax.

While the children ate peanut butter and jelly sandwiches, I unwrapped the present I'd brought — a 500-piece puzzle of a Tracy Arms print I'd picked up on our cruise to Alaska. Purple-tipped icebergs poked through the water like uncut amethysts.

"We'll work on the puzzle while I'm here," I said cheerfully. "Let's keep it spread out on the dining room table. That way, anyone can just go over and fit a piece in. Shall we make a wager who puts in the last piece?" Of course, I had to explain what a *wager* is.

While the children sorted the pieces in matching colors, Ben and I sat at the kitchen table.

"Ben, will you finally talk about what's been going on?"

He shrugged and lowered his voice so the children, who were playing in the next room, wouldn't overhear him. "I know Joan blames me for her unhappiness, but believe me, Mom, I did the best I could to make the marriage work." He paused and looked down at his hands. "I know she's telling everyone I'm the one who walked out, but she's getting exactly what she wanted."

I looked at the disorder in the kitchen that became a kind of metaphor for the disorder in our lives, and then turned my head in the direction of the squabbling coming from the other room so Ben couldn't see the tears welling in my eyes. So many hopes and dreams for my children — gone forever.

"We'll all get through this," I said smartly. "Ben, you are going to be fine. Let's get started by dealing with this mess." I got up and went to the sink full of dirty dishes.

"Mom, I'm really glad that you're here," Ben said, standing next to me, helping me load the dishwasher. He reached over and touched my arm, and I put my hand over his and squeezed it.

I scoured the sink and scrubbed the inside of the refrigerator with a baking soda solution, glad to feel useful. Next, I took inventory of the pantry while I also took inventory of the situation. My first priority, I told myself, was the grandchildren, who needed security and continuity. Ben was feeling defeated and had to prepare for what might be a long haul as a single father. Until Joan got well, she was going to need our support to get through this medical crisis.

Somewhat hesitantly, I picked up the phone and called Mary to let her know I was at the house; to my relief she didn't resent my being there. We agreed that we should work out a schedule so the twins could stay over and spend time with Joan. She offered to help with carpooling so I could get some of my own work done, since it looked like I was going to be in Seattle longer than I had anticipated.

Fortunately, Joan's cancer was stage one DCIS, which I later learned, was *ductal carcinoma in situ*. The cells lining the milk ducts (the channels in the breast that carry milk to the nipple) were cancerous, but the cancer was contained within the ducts and not growing through into the surrounding breast tissue. Sometimes DCIS may be described as pre-cancerous, pre-invasive, non-invasive, or intraductal cancer. Her lymph nodes were clean. The prognosis was excellent, although there was obvious concern because of her familial history.

Joan opted for a series of radiation treatments. She elected to live with her parents while she was being treated. The radiation made her tired, but what was most alarming was the post-op despondency that set in. The children's visits cheered her up, but these visits were hard on the twins, who, after each visit, kept asking when Mommy was coming home. I had no answer and tried to keep up a good front. Finally, they stopped asking and accepted Ben in her place.

Ben grew increasingly anxious. He, too, kept waiting for some sign that Joan would be returning. When the eight-week series was over, Joan told him she still wasn't up to the responsibility of taking care of the children, so Ben's lawyer drew up a temporary physical custody order, and Ben moved his clothes back to the house. We boxed the things Joan wanted and took them to Mary and Todd's.

I emptied the medicine cabinet of her perfume bottles, nail polish, and scented soaps. Then I wept. Ben grew even more bitter about the divorce, now that Joan was over the crisis stage of her breast cancer. I knew that he was struggling to keep his own life in balance while marking time, uncertain, like Joan, about the future.

While Ben was at work, I continued to clean, shop, cook, and keep the house in order. I refused any new freelance assignments, hoping the ad agency would understand my predicament and use my services when I returned. Naturally, Gary was sympathetic, but my absence was hard on him.

Ben was accustomed to working late. A couple of times he called at the last minute to say he was meeting a client and wouldn't be home for dinner. One night he stayed out until 11:00 p.m., and I found myself pacing the floor the way I had when he was a teenager. When he came in, I was waiting at the door.

"I'm here to help you, not to be your babysitter so you can stay out all night," I lashed out.

"I need *some* time for myself," Ben yelled after me as I stormed upstairs to the guestroom, where I'd been staying for the past two-and-a-half months.

For the next few days, my son and I danced around each other, barely speaking. Nevertheless, after that explosion, Ben kept more regular business hours and brought work home so he could spend more time with the children. I finally had some respite from exhausting days taking care of two active eight-year-olds who missed their mother and resented Grandma always telling them what to do.

The weeks dragged; I began to see an unhealthy pattern of life emerging. I was taking on more and more parenting responsibility for the children, and it became clear that Ben was growing increasingly dependent. He asked my advice about everything: *Did the children need new sneakers? Should he take the children to visit their mother more or less often? Did I think he should change lawyers?* Clearly, these were decisions Ben could make himself. Sometimes my advice was direct: *Yes, the kids need new sneakers.* Other times I tried to bounce the ball back in his court: *Discuss the children with Joan and find out what she wants to do.*

Then one evening while we were watching television, I looked at Ben and the children and realized how far they'd come since I arrived. They were watching some silly sit-com and laughing their heads off. I realized Ben and the twins had regenerated into a new family unit, and it was time for me to leave.

Ben found a housekeeper, a part-time college student who was willing to live in. The children took to Brenda like a duck takes to water. Happily, I retreated to just being Grandma, while Brenda took over the household chores.

The night before it was time to go home, I stayed awake staring at the ceiling, thinking about Ben and his life's journey. He'd been thrown into the maelstrom of divorce, and like so many others who think they will never get past the crazy times, he was surviving.

When it was time to leave for the airport, Ben carried my suitcases to the car. I bent down and kissed my grandchildren, who were staying behind with Brenda.

"I'll call you every week," I promised.

"Grandma, what about the puzzle?" Jake said. "It's not finished."

"I have to go home now," I said. "You and Daddy will have to work on it without me. I wager you'll have it finished by Thanksgiving when Grandpa and I come back to visit."

"What's a wager again?" Jake asked.

"It's a bet," Janice said brightly. "The puzzle is nearly finished, you know."

"That's because Grandma did all the edges," Jake reminded her.

"Yes, she did." Ben said, smiling from the doorway. "And later we are going to work on the sky together."

●◀ *Nora's Response to the Crisis* ▶●

Take a close look at Nora's rescue operation in order to learn from her mistakes and her right actions. Her first response was to take control of the household and establish some normalcy for the grandchildren, who were at loose ends. Nora's efforts were rewarded when things fell into place. She knew that Ben appreciated her help. Obviously, he was relieved to have "Mom" there, so he could fade into the background and resume his hectic work schedule. The operation took a turn for the worse when Ben became dependent on his mom, who had not only taken control of the situation but also taken over. At one point, Nora realized she had overplayed her hand and was doing too much. She became physically and emotionally exhausted. However, what bothered her most was that Ben seemed to be taking advantage, resulting in parent and child sparring in the way they had when Ben was a teenager.

Nora could not stay forever. She and her son knew Mom had her own life. What was Nora's goal when she left for Seattle? It was to stabilize the family and to leave Ben stronger, more confident, so he could assume responsibility for the children and adapt to his new role as a single father, even if that role was a temporary one.

Nora knew that Ben was living with ambiguity, and she was sympathetic. She too was uncertain about the future. Nevertheless, when she went home, she felt that Ben was back on track and that they had established an adult parent-adult child relationship. And perhaps, that relationship was better than ever before.

●◀ *The Tendency Toward Parent-Child Regression* ▶●

During the rescue period, an adult child may become very dependent on the parent for advice, physical support, and/or emotional support. It's perfectly natural for a person in "overload" to want to be taken care of. You may find yourself taking center stage — taking over the chores, parenting your grandchildren, becoming the babysitter while your son or daughter goes out with friends to help get over the hurt.

In Nora's case, Ben became the self-centered adolescent and Nora reverted to the indignant mother. Fortunately, they were able to establish a more mature, adult-adult relationship. I think in times of crisis, the parent-child bond can actually strengthen. The rescue period should not perpetuate your child's dependency. It should re-enforce his or her self-confidence. The parent should encourage decision-making and help bolster confidence for good problem-solving behavior.

•◀ *In-Law Boundaries* ▶•

Oftentimes the son- or daughter-in-law, rather than the biological child, needs the support. It's not uncommon for parents-in-law to rush to the side of the abandoned spouse and do all they can to stabilize the situation. It is particularly heartbreaking when your own child is the cause of the marital discord.

Patty was distraught when her son left his wife and children for another woman, emptied out the bank accounts, cancelled the car insurance, and defaulted on their house loan. Patty's daughter-in-law had no place to turn for help except to Patty, who came through with flying colors and sought legal action against her own son.

Nora's situation was particularly difficult because she not only had the task of supporting Ben and his children, she had the additional concern about her daughter-in-law's health. Once she knew Joan was getting the best possible care, she focused on Ben and the twins. She had to shore up Ben's confidence and minimize the grandchildren's fears about their future. Nora learned quickly that she had to establish boundaries with Joan, who had actually already drawn the lines by not taking her calls or responding to her e-mails.

•◀ *Managing Stress During the Rescue Period* ▶•

The rescue stage is a difficult time for your family. Your child and grandchildren are grieving the loss of their family unit, the absence of a parent, and the adjustment in lifestyle. Oftentimes there are accompanying losses of friends and in-laws. The stress wrought by divorce can be overwhelming. Your child, your grandchildren, your spouse, or you may be in need of professional help if you notice any of these signs:

> Prolonged bouts of insomnia
> Loss of appetite
> Extreme lethargy
> Inability to make decisions
> Excessive crying or explosive rage
> Suicidal thoughts or behaviors
> Use of drugs or excessive amount of alcohol

As hard as you try, you may not be able to convince your child to go for help. You *can* do the legwork and make inquiries about the kind of mental health support services that are available in your child's community by checking the Yellow Pages. Crisis telephone services — Info-line, Hotline, etc. — can direct you to university clinics, local family service centers, community counseling centers, professional societies of psychologists and family therapists, women's centers, and various outreach programs. If you can afford to pay for counseling, this may be the time to make that offer. Problem-centered therapy, such as working though the issues related to the divorce, is usually a short-term process. There are excellent anger management workshops for individuals who are embroiled in adversarial divorces, especially those involving custody issues.

You might also contact your religious community to find out about divorce support groups. Ask if there is a fee to join a group (often there is not), and if there is, whether there is a sliding-scale payment schedule for new members. Also suggest that your child join a gym. Participating in a sport or simply fitness exercises can help work out some of that stress. Go to a public library or bookstore and thumb through self-help books that might be appropriate for your child's situation, but be wary of those that offer quick-fix solutions. Rebuilding takes time — two years or more, according to some researchers (Fisher and Alberti, 2000). I list a number of excellent resources for adults in Appendix B. Once again, remember that your child is an adult and should take responsibility for his or her own health.

By the same token, don't neglect your own health needs during this emotionally and physically draining time. Watch for signs of stress and head for the treadmill when things get overwhelming.

•◀ *Call up the Rear Guard — That Includes the In-Laws* ▶•

Now that you've responded to the call, where is it written that you have to shoulder the whole burden, especially if the rescue operation is a drawn out affair? It may take months before your child can comfortably manage on his or her own. Ask your other children or family members to pitch in.

Cody knew she was wearing herself out taking care of her four grandchildren (the youngest was a year old) from six in the morning until eight o'clock at night. Her blood pressure shot up, and her doctor warned her she had to take it easy. "My oldest daughter was a godsend," Cody told me. "She cooked for the two families, and her husband, Jim, took the two oldest boys on the weekends." Being able to count on family was not only a source of relief for Cody, it was important for the grandchildren, who needed a break from their frazzled grandmother. It was also comforting to have the orbit of aunts, uncles, and cousins around them.

The rescue operation can be an opportunity for parents-in-law to build bridges. Sadly, however, it's more often the case that families retreat to their enemy camps when the couple splits up, and do not band together even in times of crisis. Mary and Nora knew they had to get past their children's differences and be there for the twins. Like most parents-in-law who have been on friendly (even close) terms prior to their children's separation, undoubtedly Nora and Mary had become guarded. In a situation where there is illness or some crisis, like Joan's, parents often agree to come together for the sake of the family. It shouldn't have to take extenuating circumstances to rebuild relationships, and it is best if parents-in-law cooperate with one another during the separation and divorce. They can help with carpooling, take the grandchildren on special outings, and arrange sleepovers so the divorcing couple gets a break and the kids can forget about their parents' problems for a while.

A word of advice: If you are in a position to reach out to your former (or about-to-be-former) in-laws, this would be a good time to try. Strive to establish some kind of cooperative relationship, one that could carry over into the future. It will greatly benefit your mutual grandchildren, who can use all the support they can get from a loving family when their world splits apart at the seams.

◦◀ Call Up the Rear, Rear Guard ▶◦

Your own parents or elderly relatives can be additional pegs for the tent. Don't neglect to call them for assistance. The intergenerational divide has narrowed. Generally, the total population of today's seniors is younger and healthier than ever before. You may discover, like Gerard, that it's not age but capability that's important when you need an extra pair of hands with the grandchildren.

> *Gerard's daughter was at her wit's end when her husband left her. Gerard felt they both needed a change of scenery, so he called his great-aunt Peg because Aunt Peg had raised him and three foster kids by herself. Gerard said proudly. "She may be eighty, but she's sharp as a tack and is no stranger to trouble."*

◦◀ Modeling Behavior ▶◦

When your child was little, you taught him by example. You drilled into his head how to behave in church, in school, in a restaurant, and what was expected when company came to the house. By adolescence, you assumed your daughter knew the rules, could tell right from wrong, and would make good decisions when you weren't there. Your job is not over. Now that your child is divorcing, your role modeling is even more important because your positive attitude, your willingness to accept change, your ability to problem-solve, and the manner in which you deal with adversity are exemplars for the many, many challenges your child will have to face down the road. If you can keep a cool head, chances are so will your child.

The rescue stage is a transition period, the one time you as parents should come into the foreground, assuming you are asked. It's a time to be useful; it's a time for bonding with your child. It's the beginning of family healing. The sooner you can pass the baton back to your

---

Parental Guideposts: Chapter Two

To The Rescue — Putting the Pieces Together

- Carefully evaluate your child's desire to be rescued.
- Determine if your child is "divorce ready."
- Reserve judgment and criticism while you are binding wounds.
- Know the difference between help and support. Help is concrete. Support is intangible. Help says, "What can I do for you?" Support says, "I have faith you can do it yourself."
- Give advice in small doses. Try not to overwhelm your child with a list of things you think he or she should do right away. Help your child prioritize.
- Steer clear of burdening your child or grandchildren with your own emotions.
- Expect some regression. Your child may begin to exhibit adolescent behavior or become overly dependent.
- Create boundaries. Are you being useful or being used?
- Retool your parenting skills. Remember your "child" is an adult. The old rules simply won't apply.
- Build self-esteem by focusing on your child's strengths.

---

adult children, the better. Your goal is to help your offspring do whatever it takes to get a fresh start.

However, it is also vital that you carefully weigh your parental obligations and determine what you can and cannot do. During the rescue stage, your child may also want you to provide financial support or temporary housing. The next two chapters deal with these two important issues.

✎ *Chapter Two: Workbook Exercises*

1. What other support systems does your child have in place other than you and your spouse or partner? (Friends, therapist, marriage counselor, lawyer, support group, minister, rabbi, siblings, and colleagues)

2. How would you rate your child's "divorce readiness"?

   Very prepared   Somewhat Prepared   Unprepared

3. List any other obligations that might interfere with your ability to be there for your child.

4. How much time can you realistically offer your child right now to help him or her out?

5. Make a list of resources in your child's community that are available for help in an emergency or crisis. Call this list to your child's attention and suggest he or she keep it handy. (Keep your own spare copy, as it is likely to get lost under the deluge of divorce paperwork your child will be plowing through.)

Chapter Three

To the Rescue — Mom, Dad...
I Need Money

Most parents struggle with the ongoing issue of how much financial support to give their children. The problem becomes that much more pressing when their son or daughter seeks help during his or her separation and/or divorce. Whether it's a jump-start loan or a long-term subsidy, there will be issues you will have to deal with that will affect family relationships. Let's look at how Nora handled this one.

Nora's Story

Initially, Gary and I held off offering Ben money when he separated from Joan. He had a good job, and we were not aware of any unusually high credit card debt he and Joan had incurred during their marriage. I didn't anticipate any money problems after their separation, although I knew Ben was stretched trying to maintain two households. He also had the additional costs of his lawyer, doctor bills not fully covered by his medical plan, counseling for the children, and the expense of a full-time babysitter.

Gary suggested that Ben reduce his overhead by selling the house and finding a less expensive place to live in the same school district while the children were living with him — assuming, of course, Joan approved, since the property was tied up in the divorce settlement. Much to our surprise, we learned that there was a lien on the house. I then remembered some problems Ben had with the plumbing contractor when the house was under construction. While they were hooking the house to city water, a city mainline had been damaged. Ben was responsible for the repair and blamed the plumber, who refused to deduct the cost from his bill. When Ben withheld payment, the plumber put a lien against his house.

Joan was doing much better physically, but the ordeal had taken an enormous emotional toll. She was not ready to move back in with the children. Her therapist, who had initially advised her to live with her parents, now suggested that she find a place of her own. Joan's temporary solution was to share an apartment with a newly divorced friend and her three-year-old daughter. When Ben told me about the arrangement, I must admit I found it rather ironic that Joan could tolerate Georgina's toddler, who had to be a lot more demanding than the twins were. To her credit, however, Joan got a part-time job clerking in the Seattle University law library, although her salary barely covered the cost of her lunches. Ben was still responsible for her living expenses.

Now that Ben had all these financial pressures, he had decided to negotiate with the plumber. They agreed to split the difference. The problem was that Ben had to come up with $15,000 — $15,000 he did not have.

Gary and I discussed floating Ben an interest-free loan. When we made the offer, Ben jumped at the opportunity since Joan had agreed to put the house on the market. The next problem was that, as much as we would have liked to, Gary and I simply could not afford to give our son the money. As it was, we were dipping into savings we'd set aside for our last child's college tuition.

I asked myself, "What if the divorce drags on and on? Would Ben put the loan on the back burner? I wouldn't feel right if I had to pressure him to repay us when he has all these other worries. And what if our other children came to us for help and we had to turn them down?" Certainly, I did not want to be accused of playing favorites. Gary and I didn't know whether we should tell our other children that we were lending Ben money. We knew this would be setting a precedent and were not sure what or how much to disclose.

•◀ *Nora's Dilemma* ▶•

Gary's advice to Ben, who was struggling under the financial weight of his impending divorce, was to reduce his overhead. Cutting back on overhead depends on an individual's circumstances: For some, it might involve finding a less expensive apartment, or selling their home and renting a house or a condo. For others it means bunking temporarily (or long-term) with Mom and Dad, a sibling, relative, or friend. Perhaps leasing a less expensive car, carpooling to get to work, or using public transportation instead of spending money on gasoline would help; cutting back on entertainment or going to the parents' house once a week for dinner could be a solution; working out a mutual babysitting arrangement with a friend often saves hundreds of dollars a month. One young mother told me that after her divorce she decided to share her home temporarily with another divorced woman who had two children. The two split the household costs right down the middle and helped each other out with babysitting. They both knew it was just a temporary measure until they could get back on their feet. In a way, it turned out to be the best thing either woman could have done; they found support from one another, and their children had ready-made friends.

•◀ *Too Little Too Late?* ▶•

Gary intervened in a way he believed would best serve his son's needs and yet preserve Ben's dignity. Other parents, like Andrew and his wife, assume that their child is financially solvent or astute, and hang back rather than appear too interfering. It's another slippery slope that requires judgment, as you will see in this case:

> *My daughter Betsy was financially secure during her marriage and has always prized her independence. She made it very clear she did not want her mother or me involved in her divorce, and she kept us at arm's length. I just assumed Betsy knew what she was doing. I know that Betsy was hurt and humiliated that John had left her. That's probably why she never came to us. We decided to give her lots of space. Unfortunately, her lawyer*

didn't know enough about finances and misguided her. He advised her to make a cash settlement, and she missed out on some important assets. Now she blames me for not being there for her.

Andrew was not wrong to step aside and let Betsy handle her divorce settlement on her own. However, he went overboard in distancing himself, and inadvertently sent the message, "I'm not interested in your affairs." Betsy let her pride get in the way of getting help from her family. Had she been less self-protective, she would have been less fearful of someone taking control. Andrew said that had he been given the chance to do it over again, he would have volunteered to review the agreement. It would have been better to have his hand slapped than not to have extended it at all.

•◀ *How Much and for How Long?* ▶•

Nora wanted to get more involved with Ben's dilemma by loaning him the money he needed to settle the dispute with the plumber. She was in a quandary, however, as to how to do this without creating more problems in the future with her other children. Some parents feel they are not doing enough to help out a newly separated or divorced child financially. Sadly, there are many pitfalls for parents who are too eager to assume fiscal responsibility for a divorcing child. An offer of a loan or outright gift is usually a gesture of love and support. The issue of determining how to help without creating a long-term, unhealthy financial dependency, or, as in Nora's situation, resentment, is the task at hand. Circumstances vary in each case, but keep in mind that when you offer to help your divorcing child financially, you are establishing a precedent for the future - not only for that child, but also for any other child who might one day come to you with a similar request.

•◀ *Gift or Loan?* ▶•

They are not the same, are they? It's important for you to decide in advance of the gesture which form your financial offering will take.

It's important for you and your spouse to agree! And, you should consider the following in either case.

•◀ *If Your Help Is a Gift: No Strings, Please!* ▶•

Make your offer freely and avoid attaching any strings.

> *When Jess gave his daughter $500, he told her he was willing to pay for a lawn service, but not for those fancy art lessons she was taking, even though his daughter had previously explained that painting was a good way to get her mind off her problems.*

Let's face it. There are going to be times when you don't approve of how your son or daughter uses money, yours or theirs. It's important to remember that you are dealing with an adult who probably has been independent up until now and is in the uncomfortable position of having to ask for financial assistance. Once you give a gift — unless you specifically target it to pay for something such as your granddaughter's out-of-state soccer trip — I would say the worst thing you can do for your relationship is to attach strings. You not only run the risk of demeaning your child and taking away any pleasure you had in giving the gift (assuming you gave it out of the goodness of your heart), you create an unhealthy parent-child tug-of-war. You won't err if you *suggest* how the money should be spent if you see a crying need, and then let go, as in this situation:

> *Martha gave her ex-daughter-in-law, Jane, a check to buy a new clothes dryer when the old one broke down. Jane said she didn't mind hanging the clothes on the line. Martha then told her to use the money as she saw fit. Jane appreciated Martha's thoughtfulness and bought herself a winter coat she'd been eyeing and could not afford otherwise.*

Once the money leaves your hands, consider it a *fait accompli*. If you are truly unhappy with the plans for the money, once again, you have the right not to renew the gift. If your divorcing son or daughter has been financially irresponsible in the past - thrown away money, run up high credit card debt, taken money for granted — you may have to set limits right from the start.

◆ *When They Throw Caution to the Wind* ◆

When talking to parents, I've heard complaints about children who, in the middle of a divorce, threw caution to the wind and unwisely spent money for something they could ill afford in order to satisfy some adolescent impulse. Victor said, "I loaned my son five thousand dollars after he separated from his wife, figuring he'd use it to resettle himself in a nice apartment. Instead, he went out and purchased a BMW motorcycle and continued sleeping on the couch in his friend's place!" Victor was outraged with his son's behavior, knowing he was also three months behind in his child support.

This mother talked about her daughter spending money "she didn't have" to get back at her ex:

> *My ex-son-in-law took his girlfriend to Italy after he and my daughter separated. The next thing I knew, my daughter was making plans to go to London over spring break and taking my two teenage granddaughters with her. It was a 'we'll show him' act of defiance. My daughter and I wound up having an argument about all of this and not speaking to one another for weeks.*

It can be difficult to justify your child's irrational behavior because you as an outsider see it one way, and your wounded child sees it another. After divorce, many individuals develop a feeling of entitlement: "Because I was so hurt, I'll just do this to make myself feel better. I deserve to feel better. I'll show him/her!"

Try to accept the fact that your adult son or daughter is in emotional turmoil and using money to salve wounds. Obviously, it's a bandage solution. Healing will come in time and, hopefully, your child will develop more mature coping skills.

◆ *Hope for the Best* ◆

Here's another flashing yellow light! Avoid withholding money as an object lesson. Your child is already suffering the slings and arrows of misfortune and doesn't need more daggers pointed in his direction. When your children are so off-balance because of the dramatic change in their lives, it is more important to express some confidence in their ability to change than it is to make your point. Explain clearly and directly how you would like the money spent rather than charge your son or daughter with being more responsible than he or she has been in the past. The key here is to make positive assumptions. Disappointed once again? Don't renew the offer.

•◀ *Am I Being Selfish?* ▶•

Know in advance how much you are willing and can afford to give your child. It's not easy to draw the line when it comes to helping your own. If you have to refuse a request or withdraw support, it's hard not to feel guilty. Nevertheless, it is not wrong to consider your needs and your spouse's. Perhaps you are nearing retirement and trying to scale back on your expenses at just the time your child announces his or her divorce. If you are already living on a fixed income, you may already be stretching every dollar, cutting out coupons, and shopping for bargains. Today people live a lot longer, are much healthier, and can expect to have many years to enjoy the fruits of their labor. Resentment would be a normal response to having to forsake your plans to go on that world cruise, buy that vacation house you longed for, or pay off the mortgage.

Before you decide to take on the long-range responsibility of supplementing or supporting your divorced child, ask yourself how you feel about working past the age you had set for retirement or dipping into your savings to support two families. Ask yourself what other ways you can help your child gain financial independence. Perhaps encouraging him or her to go back to school, look for a better job, scale back on expenses, or just be more resourceful would be more realistic and less of a hardship on you.

•◀ *Money, Guilt, Resentment* ▶•

Be wary if a loan or gift to your child is going to compromise your lifestyle or cause you to put some plans on hold. Even if the plans are "frivolous," you have a right to use your money as you see fit without feeling guilty. Blanche and her partner talked about redecorating their apartment:

> My mother left me some money, and we'd just moved into our new space and wanted a whole new look. Then I thought about Samantha, who was struggling after her divorce, so I cancelled the furniture order. When my daughter, Samantha, found out, she was outraged that I was so small-minded to think she'd be resentful.

You don't have to rub salt in the wounds and flaunt your plans when you know your child is hurting financially, but you need to be honest about your commitment to your child, and whether or not your guilt is just being self-serving.

◆◀ Give Only What You Can Afford Not to Get Back ▶◆

Even if it's to be a loan . . . "Only give what you can afford not to get back." This was wise advice given to me by my father when I was in college and complaining about my dormmate, who was always short at the end of the month. Foolishly, I kept loaning Diane ten bucks here and there, and Diane conveniently forgot to repay me when her father sent her next month's allowance check. Meanwhile, I was drowning in her excuses. Ultimately, money problems drove us apart, and in the end, we split up. I switched roommates and learned my lesson. I was also out a few hundred bucks!

The same holds true for parents who loan their child money and realize too late that the child does not intend to repay it. Unfortunately, this is too often the case if the adult child is bitter and unwilling to take responsibility for the failure of the marriage, and is under the impression something is owed him or her. (Remember, you can become an easy target for all that anger.)

What do you do if your child comes back with yet another loan request? I would handle the situation diplomatically by suggesting other means for obtaining the money. Without doing a lot of muckraking, simply explain that you understand your child's difficulties, but you have expenses and cannot afford to fill the request. Underscore your sensitivity and you won't ruffle as many feathers.

Establish realistic timeframes within which you expect your child to pay you back. If you are specific about the way you would like the money spent and/or set a repayment timeframe, you can avoid creating a permanent dependency. Some parents take over paying the rent for a year or agree to supplement their child's temporary alimony until the divorce is settled. Others agree to help out with expenses until their daughter finishes school or goes back to work and is secure enough to take back the responsibility. One attorney suggested considering a promissory note to accompany a loan to your child. This then becomes a marital debt and is added to the financial affidavit, and has a better chance of being repaid once the divorce is settled and the assets divided. In giving a loan, be careful it doesn't violate court orders. A loan in this instance should be used for household expenses. By setting goals and being specific about how you think the money should be spent, you stand less chance of wounding your son or daughter's pride and taking on more than you bargained for. However, if you think a blanket loan is a better way to approach your child, just be clear on the amount, and once again, establish some limits — unless you are willing and able to assume financial responsibility indefinitely.

Be prepared to flex those timeframes. Circumstances change, but if possible, try to stick to the arrangement. If necessary, create a second, more realistic schedule and acknowledge any progress your child has made trying to pay you back. For example, you might say, "I know you tried to get more hours at work, but things are slow right now. I'm sure in six months things will improve or you will have found a better-paying job. So let's wait until then to talk about the money I loaned you." Obviously, if you see there is a crying need, if your child is struggling to make ends meet, you will want to come to the rescue without putting unnecessary pressure on her.

•◀ *Either Way, Know Your Child* ▶•

It may sound harsh, but consider your divorcing child's past behavior as well as his or her current financial situation before opening your wallet While many children expect their parents to come forward, others would rather struggle on their own than admit that they are having trouble making ends meet. If the latter is your situation, you can make your offer, but be wary. Money talks. It can say, "I see you are in trouble, and I want to help you" or "I see you are in trouble and you need me to bail you out." The first is a loving gesture. The second is subject to misinterpretation and can easily trigger resentment.

There are no clear-cut guidelines as to when you should come forward with a loan or a gift of money. A lot has to do with your child's circumstances. It also depends on how comfortable you are getting involved in your son's or daughter's financial affairs. There are ways to give money without diminishing your child's self-esteem. Keep in mind also that your child might be too proud to come to you for help, in which case it is up to you to take the initiative. You might say something like, "Since I shop at that grocery warehouse, let's consider splitting the major items since it will be a lot cheaper for both of us, and I can use my car so you won't have to use yours."

Suggestion: Frame your gift positively by acknowledging everything your child is trying to do to rebuild his or her life and supporting his or her efforts to be independent. You might say, "I know you took on more hours at your job, but I also see that babysitting costs are eating into your salary. Let me cover the childcare costs of those ten extra hours you are working, just until you get a raise (or find a cheaper babysitting situation, make more in commissions, etc.)"

●◀ *Special Cases: If Your Child Needs Ongoing Support* ▶●

In many instances, a temporary loan or outright gift will not be enough to stabilize your child's changed economic situation. Perhaps you have a child who has never worked outside the home, has emotional or physical health problems, is recovering from addiction, or is taking care of your grandchild, who needs special services and continual parental care. In such cases, you may be your child's only lifeline. It's not an easy position to be in. Only you can decide what financial sacrifices you are willing to make and what your role in your child's life will be. Sit down and problem-solve alternatives with your child and a family counselor so you can get some relief.

Janet and Jerry's daughter got divorced right after their grandchild was diagnosed with a rare eye disease. The parents own a two-family house. Their daughter lives in one half, and pays minimal rent. Their ex-son-in-law does all the maintenance work. Janet babysits her grandson during the week and takes him to the eye clinic for therapy so her daughter can go to work. Once the child's condition improves, Janet plans to enroll him in a daycare program that has services for physically challenged children. Janet is the first one to admit that life revolves around her divorced daughter and grandson, but she tries to make time for herself and her husband and accept her responsibilities with equanimity.

•◀ Money Is a Family Affair ▶•

Martha was outraged when she learned her husband had withdrawn money out of their retirement savings account without consulting her to help their divorced daughter. She loved her daughter and felt sorry for her reduced financial situation, but she had misgivings about how the money would be spent based on past experience. Her husband was more softhearted. When his daughter approached him, he decided to act on his own, knowing how Martha felt. He rationalized that his wife would become overly anxious if the loan was not repaid and so decided not to tell her.

Who's right in this situation? I'm afraid I'd have to side with Martha. Rule of thumb: Include your spouse or partner in your decision to make a gift or loan to your child to avoid conflict.

Couples should deal openly and honestly with each other and discuss the kind of financial help they want to give their separated or divorced child. Acting alone is a flint to surefire disaster. Nowadays, when both partners work outside the home and pool their resources, husband and wife expect to have equal say in how their money is spent. Even if one spouse or partner does not work outside the home, that partner makes an important contribution to the marriage, and his or her opinion should not be taken for granted. Partners may not always agree, especially if the loan or gift is going to a non-biological child or an ex-son or daughter-in-law, with whom one partner may not have as much sympathy. This is the time to puff on the peace pipe and negotiate before the smoke signals set the teepee afire.

Whether or Not to Tell the Other Children

As you may recall from reading Nora's story at the beginning of the chapter, she struggled with her conscience about whether or not to tell the other children that she had loaned Ben money. Surely you can appreciate Nora not wanting to violate Ben's confidence if he had asked her to keep this under wraps. But he didn't, so she was free to do as she wished as long as she discussed her intentions with Ben. I tend to believe that rescuing one child financially sends a message to your other children. I also believe in being open. Here's how Nora and Gary solved their dilemma.

In the end, Gary and I called the family together. Gary explained to our other children that we wanted to help Ben with his financial dilemma, but we were not in a position just to hand over money, especially since we were at that time in our lives when we needed to think about our own financial security. So she told them we had loaned him the money he needed to get the lien off his house, with the understanding that he would repay it as soon as the house sold. I think the children were embarrassed by our candor, but they appreciated our honesty, and I felt much better that we'd cleared the air.

It's not always easy putting your cards on the table and discussing your financial affairs with your children, who expect you to make sacrifices on their behalf. Some parents are more cautious about telling their children what's in their pocketbook, and I'm sure they have their reasons. I think the loving thing to do is to treat your children like adults and let them know what you can and cannot do. You might conclude any discussion you have with your kids by saying something like, "I'm telling you this because I want you to know that your mom and I are here to do the same for you, with similar terms, should any of you come to us with a special need."

The Financial High Wire

A number of parents have told me that their children didn't know where to begin when it came time to manage their financial affairs by themselves. Division of marital assets is a nasty business. Some partners go for the jugular; others are so demoralized, they are willing to throw the baby out with the bathwater. Julia's son Hank was set to give away his house:

> I reminded him that his wife had drawn out all the money in their savings and checking accounts and was leaving him to go live with her boyfriend. Hank was going to need a roof over his head. In addition, I reminded him that his dad and I had countersigned the mortgage, so we had an investment in his keeping it. Now Hank lives happily in his house with our grandson, who came back to live with his father because he hated living with his stepfather. The other day he told me, 'This is my real home.'

When your child is tottering on the financial high wire, you can help by providing some balance — as long as you maintain some objectivity and distance. Remember, this is not your battle. One of your goals is to create an aura of calm.

You might suggest setting priorities if you think your child is making some bad financial decisions. "Let's take a look at your basic expenses before we figure out when you'll have to replace your car." (See pages 226–233 for helpful ideas.) Perhaps you could diplomatically defuse a time bomb if your child is bent on getting back at the ex by going after some material item. "Is it really the end of the world if she takes the toaster and leaves you the coffee maker?" Without getting in the middle or taking control, find some opportunity to reiterate that Sesame Street lesson of "give and take."

Often the Best Kind of Support Doesn't Cost a Dime

There are many ways parents communicate love and support without opening their purse strings. You can open your home, fix dinner, offer to babysit or carpool, attend your grandchildren's sports events, be a stand-in room mom or fill-in scoutmaster on a camping trip, help with the grocery shopping, research lawyers and divorce tax consultants, type your children's resumes, help with budgeting, rent a movie, take them out to eat, return books to the library, pick up the laundry, mow the lawn, bring their car in for servicing, send them cheerful e-mails — and the list goes on. Taking the burden off your child by providing respite and being a shoulder to cry on is the best way to help your child. Listen to the ranting, join in the laughter, as one parent put it. Consider taking your child and grandchildren on a family vacation where you focus on fun and not money problems. Generous acts of good will do not take away from your son's or daughter's independence and go a long way in demonstrating your support.

●◄ *Let's Do It Together* ►●

Money issues are the number-one cause for hostility and depression pre- and post-divorce. The corporate wife who used to entertain lavishly resents spending more quiet evenings at home after her separation. A divorced father burdened with alimony and child support payments resents not being able to take his second family on vacation. A divorced single mom worried about the rent that's due is less sympathetic when her son complains about the bullies in the school lunchroom. The courts are filled with re-opened divorce cases, and lawyers continue to collect fees to renegotiate endless financial disputes. During the rescue period, in addition to all the other stresses, your divorcing child may be readjusting to a new, uncomfortable standard of living. The main thing you want to do is send the message, "I'm here for you. I love and support you. I am helping you out temporarily because you have a lot on your plate right now. Let's work together to ease your burden and get you back on your feet."

Your role is not to provide long-term financial support. Your goal is to point your child toward financial independence. Doing too much is as bad as doing too little.

Parental Guideposts: Chapter Three

Mom, Dad... I Need Money

- Encourage fiscal independence with transitional loans when possible.
- Respond to financial needs when children are at risk.
- Don't withdraw financial support to punish your child.
- Don't make assumptions about your child's economic plight.
- Avoid attaching strings to your gift or loan.
- Negotiate flexible repayment schedules — allow your child to suggest timeframes.
- Earmark your contribution if your child has mismanaged money in the past.
- Only give what you can afford not to get back.
- Money is a family affair - include your spouse in decision-making.
- Provide in-kind support such as babysitting, running errands, etc.
- Familiarize yourself with some of the financial issues underpinning divorce. (See Appendix A.)
- Be a resource to your child. Don't take control.

✎ *Chapter Three: Workbook Exercises*

Decision-Making Time — You may already feel boxed in, embroiled in your child's financial problems, and see no way out. Maybe your relationship with your spouse or partner is suffering. It's not too late to shift your course of action.

1. Answer these questions as honestly as you can and then decide what changes you are willing to make:
   • Does your child really need financial assistance?
   • If yes, do you want to offer help now or wait to be asked?
   • What can you afford to give outright?
   • How much money can you afford to loan your child?
   • Is a gift or a loan the best way to respond to your child's financial need?
   • Do you want to specify how the money should be used? If you do, list these specifics. In addition, list items you are not willing to pay for.
   • What terms do you think are fair for repayment?
   • If your child or ex-in-law is living with you, what can you realistically expect him or her to contribute each month? List the items.
   • What, if any, effect will giving money to your child have on: Retirement? Travel? Discretionary income? Your other children?

2. In the space below, list any questions you should discuss with a financial consultant.

3. In the space below, list any questions you should discuss with a lawyer.

Chapter Four

To the Rescue — Mom, Dad...
Can I Come Home?

Nothing throws life more off kilter than when your offspring, in the throes of divorce, returns to the nest that has become your private refuge. Is it any wonder that all the while you're putting out the welcome mat, you are also considering the alternatives?

Most parents are happy to do whatever they can to help their child get back on his or her feet. They're just reluctant to be Mom and Dad all over again.

Nora's Story

Ben and Joan's divorce was moving at a snail's pace because of the custody issues and the uncertainty surrounding Joan's breast cancer treatment and recovery. For the time being, the couple had decided that Ben would be the primary residential parent. Joan was thinking about going to law school and not sure where she would wind up. There was a lot of bouncing back and forth on her part. I was relieved that she agreed to have the children live with Ben while there was all this indecision, although it made me anxious for Ben and the children's sake. I felt we were all in limbo waiting for Joan to make up her mind; but Ben, to his credit was willing to wait it out.

The court had worked out a Parenting Plan in which both Ben and Joan were expected to share in decision-making to assure the best interests of the children. Both of them were to have access to all information concerning Jake and Janice. Ben continually reassured me things were fine.

Then Ben called one day to tell us that he had been offered a consulting assignment managing an engineering project with a pharmaceutical company based in New Jersey. The company was only a stone's throw from our town. Gary agreed with Ben that this was a good career move. So Ben applied to the court, and they granted permission to relocate the children out-of-state temporarily. At first, I was surprised to learn that Ben had volunteered for this assignment, especially during this unsettled time. Later, I surmised that he needed the support of family and had decided to come back to the nest because he was still at loose ends.

Naturally, I was delighted to have Ben and the twins nearby, although I didn't like the fact that the kids would be uprooted again. For the most part, they had settled into a routine living with their father and Brenda, the nanny. I was also worried about the twins not seeing much of their mother. All the research says children of divorce do best when they have access to both parents. Ben said Joan was okay with his decision to relocate and that she was planning to come out east to look at law schools. Since there were no obvious objections on either side, I prepared for Ben's arrival, anticipating what life was going to be like as a full-time grandmother. I hadn't forgotten how exhausting it was taking care of the children when I was in Seattle. Gary was far more optimistic.

"Isn't this just great?" he kept saying, watching me clear out drawers and empty shelves to make room for our guests.

"Sure," I said, not quite as enthusiastic. A visit was one thing. A long-term stay was quite another. Brenda had to stay behind to finish her college course work, so all week I'd been reorganizing my space and my commitments to make room for my grandchildren. For many years, I'd been working at home doing freelance for an ad agency. I was used to going into my office and shutting out the rest of the world. How would that ever work with youngsters around? I decided to finish my then-current project and not take on any more work for the duration of Ben's stay. I also arranged a leave of absence from a Town Council committee I headed and started looking for a substitute to take my place in my weekly bridge game.

Gary had a dental practice that included working every other Saturday, so the burden of childcare, even on weekends, would fall on my shoulders. Recently he'd cut back a bit so we could spend more time together. That would have to wait as well. I wondered if my son realized how much the pattern of his parents' life had changed since he'd left home more than fifteen years ago, and was about to change again! There is certain wisdom to Thomas Wolfe's famous saying, "You can't go home again." That wisdom was about to be tested.

During the first month after their arrival, Ben put in long hours at the plant, including Saturdays, when the project lagged behind schedule. Gary pitched in when he could on the weekends. Instead of spending time on the golf course working on his backswing, he shopped for groceries — we were now buying at one of the discount warehouses — and chauffeured the twins to their swim classes and soccer practices. Most Saturday evenings we were content to rent a video and order in; once Gary and I would have driven an hour to be with friends and enjoy a leisurely dinner in a restaurant. We'd gone from doing the foxtrot to the salsa, and we were having trouble keeping up with the rhythm — and becoming exhausted trying.

"Where has all our energy gone? Were our own kids this demanding?" Gary asked me one evening as we waited for Ben to come home. It was nine o'clock, and Gary was sacked out on the couch. He'd had a full day with patients, then bathed the children, read two bedtime stories, tucked them in for the night, and made his final trip upstairs to settle another argument. I was still picking up toys, assembling bag lunches, and rounding up stuff to put in their backpacks for the next day. Twice that week the twins had missed the bus and I'd had to drive them to school. It wasn't that Gary and I weren't happy having our family under the same roof; it was just that being thrown back in time, and having to deal with parenting again when we were that much older was getting to us.

●◄ *It's a Major Readjustment* ►●

While researching this chapter, I spoke to a number of parents who had opened their homes to divorcing children who needed a place to stay. Parents agreed that while it's important to support a returning child, it requires a major readjustment for the entire family. It can be particularly hard on other children who are still living at home and have to share both parents and space with returning siblings who are probably at a low point in their lives. The arrangement, even if it's temporary, puts a strain on the entire family if members are not prepared to make significant adjustments.

Betina described her family problems when her returning daughter and one-year-old baby came to stay.

"I was heartsick when Shana and the baby were turned out of their home after her separation, and I tried to make it up to her in any way I could while she was living with us. In the beginning, my sixteen-year-old daughter, Maddy, was very understanding. She followed my instructions and went out of her way to be helpful. But after a while, she began to resent all the attention I was giving Shana and the baby. To be honest, I didn't realize how hard all this was on her. One day, she blew up when I said she couldn't have her friend sleep over because the baby was teething and I was exhausted from being up the night before — the last thing I needed was more people under foot. Maddy said that it wasn't her fault her sister screwed up. Then she charged out of the house to stay at her friend's overnight. I felt awful because it was true. I'd been treating my younger daughter like a second-class citizen in her own home. I talked it over with my husband, and we agreed that we needed to encourage Shana to get back on her own two feet, the sooner the better for all of us."

An adult child's homecoming creates an imbalance in the family routine. When parents, siblings, the adult child, and his or her children are thrown together, accommodations and concessions are required all around. Even in the most loving and supportive families, there is bound to be some resentment when individuals must share space and sacrifice privacy. Happily, a balance can be restored if parents anticipate some of the challenges beforehand and establish some boundaries from the very beginning. Most family members are willing to put themselves out temporarily for the sake of the wounded parties. There is great satisfaction in knowing you have helped a relative when there is a crisis.

Problems occur when parents go overboard by doing too much, shouldering too much of their child's burden, and expecting other family members to feel the same commitment. It's particularly difficult for younger sibs who are self-involved and deserve their special time with parents while living at home. How do some families head some of these problems off at the pass? One way, according to family counselors, is to make sure everyone is in on the plan when the adult child comes back home.

•◄ *The Homecoming Contract* ►•

It's much easier for parents and adult children to live under the same roof when there is a strategy for re-entry and eventual exit. A good first step is to establish boundaries and treat homecoming as a transition to independence by drawing up a contract that addresses such issues as these:

"Flexible" timeframes for the homecoming and departure date. Suppose you know up front that your daughter and grandkids are planning to live with you for six months. Assume these end dates are flexible. Circumstances are bound to change. It's not easy to stick to deadlines during separation and not fair to insist on them when your returning family is scrambling for stability. However, it helps if you and other family members know that there is light at the end of the tunnel. Everyone's behavior and attitudes will be different if there is some idea when the "guests" will be leaving. In some situations, returning children are there for the long haul. Nevertheless, working toward self-sufficiency should still be the goal

Expectations for sharing of household chores. We saw how easy it was for Ben to let his mother do all of the domestic work that previously fell to Joan or to Brenda. The returning adult child should agree to his or her fair share of the chores (laundry, shopping, cleaning, yard work, cooking, vehicle maintenance, etc.). If the grandchildren are old enough to pitch in, they should be asked to participate. The potential for resentment will be greatly reduced if the new family members contribute to running the home rather than just flopping there.

Negotiation for any financial contributions (rent, food, childcare, etc.). This may seem harsh, but contributing financially will make your returning child feel less like a freeloader. You want to convey the message that you view your son or daughter as an adult who is working toward regaining his or her independence. Again, let your conscience be your guide. Obviously, if your child has come home because she is in dire economic straits, you don't want to add to her pressure by asking her to pay rent. But if she can, she should.

If your child is staying only a short time, a formal contract might not be necessary. If your returning child is particularly fragile, it is probably unwise to make too many demands in the beginning or it may appear that you are pulling up the welcome mat. Again, the goal is transition to independence.

•◀ *Why Do Adult Children Come Home?* ▶•

Typically, adult children come home because they need a place to stay and Mom and Dad's place is the last resort. You offer a safe haven from the harsh world that your child perceives has treated him unfairly. However, not all adult children return to the nest when their marriage ends, especially today when women are far more economically independent and society is far more accepting of single women with children living on their own. Kay Moffett and Sarah Touborg, authors of *Not Your Mother's Divorce* (2003), summarize the generational divide this way:

> *Until now, divorce was most likely something that happened to other people, people like your parents' friends or your friends' parents. But this is not your mother's (or mother's generation's) divorce. Partly because that older generation paved the way, there is much more acceptance and far less stigma than there ever has been toward divorce. In our post-feminist era, women have much greater social, economic, and*

political freedom, and this means that, despite the difficulty of the situation, you have many more choices and opportunities than your sisters of yesteryear.

Moffett and Touborg suggest that young divorcing partners in "starter" marriages — lasting less than five years and without children — recover quickly after a breakup. Does that mean your wounded generation X, Y, or Z offspring won't seek you out? Not according to the many parents I talked to who said even their financially solvent sons and daughters came home for a bit of tea and sympathy. Let's face it — marital failure still packs a wallop — whether it's a blow to the ego or a punch in the stomach. So don't be too surprised if your newly separated daughter, who has that big corporate job, jumps into her Beemer, drives hundreds of miles, and winds up on your doorstep, Louis Vuitton suitcase in hand. Like Margo, who announced that she and Jeremy had decided to call it quits after a year and a half, she'll expect complete understanding.

> *According to her mother, Margo was the buff bride who had the fantasy wedding with all the bells and whistles. When the decorator put the finishing touches on their apartment, the couple realized they had nothing in common and split.*
>
> *"We mutually agreed to end it," Margo explained easily. Her parents had divorced when she was in high school. "No one's to blame. It just didn't work out."*
>
> *Her mom hid her disappointment and said, "Come on home."*
>
> *Margo occupied the guest room long enough to rally, whereupon she registered with a roommate service, found new digs, and perused candidates for romance on Match.com. Three months later, she was in a new relationship, the marriage slate wiped clean.*

Adult children who come home for a short spell may just need parental support until they sort things out. One woman who lived with her partner for seventeen years went home after they had a bitter fight. "I stayed in bed for a week and realized, after looking around my old room and going through photo albums, I had made a terrible mistake and went back to Brian. I thank my mother for not plying me with questions and influencing my decision one way or the other," she said. Often a child's homecoming is simply down time. Try to guard against saying anything that might be used against you down the road. You never know how things will turn out.

●◄ *Here for the Long Haul Because...* ►●

Your adult child may need more than a shoulder to cry on, however. Let's look at some of the common reasons adult children come home.

Homelessness — The divorce statistics are quite clear: single-again women with children are the ones who suffer the most when the ex-husband is not living up to his financial obligations. The following is a common scenario:

Deprived of alimony and child support, and having no job skills, Tanya was forced to go back home, where she and her two kids lived in her mother's basement. Her mother was a compulsive housekeeper who constantly nagged the teenage boys about their slovenliness. The teenagers were so miserable living with their grand-mother, Tanya decided to send them to her ex-in-laws to keep the peace. "I hated to break up my family, but I had no choice. It was my mother's house, and I had nowhere else to go."

It's not only abandoned single-again women with children who suffer financially. Women who maintained a high lifestyle often discover they are cash-starved when the marriage breaks up because they are used to living off credit cards and now have no independent resources. Encumbered by debt, saddled with mortgages they can't afford, lacking skills to compete in the job market, they have only one way to solvency: taking up residence with family.

Protection from Domestic Violence — Another reason adult women, in particular, come home is because they and/or their children are victims of abuse and need the protection of family.

These victims may be reluctant to seek legal protection. They need continual reassurance they are safe. Parents and relatives can help by learning how to obtain a protective order against the abuser — a legal order issued by a state court requiring one person to stop harming or harassing another person. This is also called a temporary restraining order (TRO) or temporary protective order (TPO). These laws vary from state to state. The National Coalition Against Domestic Violence is an excellent resource for you in starting a search. Their hotline is 1-800-799 SAFE, and information is available online with links to other agencies in the various states that work with victims and their families to help bind wounds and protect victims. At minimum, a family member can contact the police to begin an investigation of a serious charge of abuse. (The local authorities may require that the victim herself report the abuse and/or agree to press charges.) Bear in mind that some statues allow the court to order the abuser to pay temporary support or continue to make mortgage payments. Many jurisdictions also allow the court to make decisions about the care of children.

Free Childcare — A third reason adult children come home is because they are juggling work and family, a feat that is difficult even in a two-parent household. Living with a built-in babysitter is the often the most convenient, cost-effective answer for your child. However, this is usually a short-term solution to a long-term problem because many parents today hold responsible jobs or have other commitments and cannot be full-time caregivers. (See chapter 9 — "Grandparents as Stabilizers.") Arthur Kornhaber, M.D. in his authoritative *The Grandparent Guide* (2002) notes there are many grandparents who love their grandchildren but are much happier contributing to the costs of daycare than actually doing the babysitting. If this is your situation, be direct with your child and work out an arrangement in which you are the backup, not the primary caregiver. Living together often presumes that you will take a more active role parenting your grandchildren; it does not mean you have to be there 24/7.

Solace and Comfort — Some adult children return to the fold because they seek familiarity of place and people when their world disassembles. In the words of Allan Gurganus, "You knew you were home because home knew who you were" (*Oldest Living Confederate Widow Tells All*). Family and home are healing antidotes to pain. Respect your child's needs to dwell for a bit in the past, when life seemed so much easier. Unfortunately, upon returning, your newly separated or divorced son or daughter may have unrealistic expectations or fantasies about home life and may be in for a letdown. If your child is depressed or too paralyzed to pick up the pieces of his or her life and envisions you as the miracle worker, you should suggest counseling.

•◀ *The Family Anchor* ▶•

While it is true that adult children have many external and compelling reasons to come home when the stresses, turmoil and practical exigencies are too much to bear, on a deeper level, they come home because they simply need the anchor of family. Try to remember that your children are redefining their role and restructuring their family system after the shattering experience of divorce.

You may recall that Nora was surprised when Ben decided to accept the assignment and come back east. She'd been misled by Ben's good reports when he was in Seattle. He kept insisting that everything was fine. It had been nearly a year since he and Joan parted. In the back of his mind, he was waiting for Joan to change her mind and take responsibility for the twins. But Joan was not over the trauma of the breast cancer scare. She was like a train rushing to an inevitable crash site, feeling as if life was passing her by and she had to grab it all in.

Meanwhile, Ben was experiencing what Craig Everett and Sandra Voigy Everett, authors of *Healthy Divorce* (1994), explain is the angst and re-stabilization associated with role redefinition now that he was a full-time father. The authors explain that typically the woman struggles with role redefinition when she realizes that she is no longer a wife, and in role-overload filling in for an absentee spouse. For the man, it is the realization that he is no longer a husband and spending more time alone or with friends and fewer hours with his children.

What can you do while your adult children are redefining their roles and restructuring their families? As the broader family system, you provide the framework, the emotional support, and the sense of security and continuity. Know that redefinition and restructuring take time, and this time could try your patience. Be on the alert for these problems:

- Disrespect of House (or Contract) Rules
- Parent-Child Role Regression
- Clashes in Moral Conduct
- Substance Use and Abuse
- Differences Parenting the Grandchildren

Disrespect of House Rules

Adult children are used to being heads of their own households. Now they are occupying your space and not with great enthusiasm. You may find yourself unwillingly sharing your kitchen, your computer, your car, your private space and balking at your son or daughter's standards of neatness. This is your home. You have a right to have your rules respected. Be clear about those rules from the beginning, and you have a better chance they will be respected. At the same time, be patient, loving, and forgiving. Your returning child and grandchildren are already feeling displaced and overwhelmed. Reassure them frequently they are welcome in your home and be prepared to make allowances for little ones who need lots of praise.

Parent-Child Role Regression

Mom's Complaint:

> *"Daniel never picked up after himself when he was living at home. I was always after him to put his dirty clothes in the hamper; to turn off the lights; to put his dishes in the dishwasher. It's the same old story now that he's back home. No wonder Judy gave him the boot."*

This Mom is fooling herself if she thinks Daniel's behavior is entirely his fault. (No, wife Judy did not stand for this, Mom. There were other more serious issues that had rocked the marital boat.) This is Mom's problem; she is responsible for her son taking advantage of her. She may be too willing to look the other way because she feels she needs to make up for his pain, disappointment, or whatever. It's her job to remind Daniel that she is not his slave. If Daniel doesn't shape up, she had best put him up in a motel! Your son or daughter will live up to your expectations if you treat him or her like a returning adult. You don't bind wounds by doing laundry.

Clashes in Moral Conduct

You and your offspring may be coming from entirely different places when it comes to sexual mores and standards of conduct. When Roger's son brought his latest girlfriend home to spend the weekend, Roger didn't mind — but he had a hard time explaining the sleeping arrangements to his ninety-year-old mother who lived with him and was sharp enough to figure out something wasn't kosher.

> *"Mama was not too happy that Gerald came back home to begin with because he competed with her for my attention. I had to tell my son that he couldn't bring anyone home to spend the night out of respect for Grandma. My son was furious. He packed his bags and left. Naturally I was upset, but what could I do?"*

Roger was caught between a rock and a hard place. He couldn't very well throw his elderly mother out on the street, and in this case, the grandson was being very immature in not respecting his father's awkward position. It's probably just as well the son moved out.

Substance Use and Abuse

The best advice is to stick to your guns if you don't approve of your offspring's relationship with drugs and alcohol. Like Connie, you may find tough love is the best and healthiest solution:

> *"My son's coke habit surfaced when he came back home to live. I suddenly realized that all the money I'd been giving him thinking I was saving his marriage was actually supporting his habit. My daughter-in-law never let on that this was what*

caused the problems in their marriage. Maybe she felt responsible. I don't know. I took Josh in when Cindy threw him out. I'm a lawyer. I have a busy practice, and Josh's problems took up a lot of my time. But I couldn't turn my back on my son. I insisted Josh get into rehab, and when he came out, my dad got him a job in his factory. I made Josh hand over his salary, and I gave him an allowance. I told him I wouldn't tolerate any slip-ups, and if he started using again, he was out on his ear. I know I treated him like a kid, but while he was staying with me, he was clean. Now he's on his own, and I just hope and pray he stays that way."

Connie not only gave her son a place in her home, she helped him turn the corner. In this case, the end of a son's marriage was his new beginning, and a mother's love and strength made it all possible.

Differences in Parenting the Grandchildren

Terry and her daughter Myra have been having a tug-of-war ever since Myra and the grandkids came back home to live. Fortunately, they air their differences away from little ears. Terry thinks it's okay to let the boys watch cartoons when they eat breakfast so she can sit and read the newspaper in peace and quiet before she drives them to school. Even though her daughter is already at work and leaves Grandma in charge, the rule is "No television in the morning." Myra also expects the children to buckle down and do their homework right after school. The children have been complaining, and Terry agrees they need a break. Since the children spend the morning and afternoon with Grandma, Terry and Myra worked out a compromise. There will be no TV in the morning, but the children may watch one hour of cartoons when they come home.

Moral of the story: If you are the caregiver, you should have some input. However, the final parenting decisions rest with the children's mother or father. This and other grandparenting issues are discussed at length in chapter 9.

•◄ *When You and Your Spouse Disagree* ►•

Often parents disagree when one of the couple is not in favor of an adult child coming home to live when his marriage dissolves. When asked about her experience, Martina offered this advice to other parents:

> *"During [his] divorce, my son knew he could depend on me absolutely. My husband is not my son's father and, although he was helpful, it wasn't the same. So my son feels he is not really "coming home" when he stays with us. My own divorce and the bad marriage that preceded it weigh heavily on my conscience. I couldn't just turn my son away. My current husband owns a two-family house. He asked his tenant to vacate the apartment when the lease was up so my son could move in — something my husband didn't like having to do, but family comes first. You have to protect your children."*

Martina's husband solved their problem by providing his stepson with a separate place to live. Martina was fortunate to have this option available to her. It's not always this simple. No parent wants to have to make a choice — "my child or my partner." If you think your son or daughter can handle a candid discussion, sit down together do some problem solving. Perhaps a friend's son or daughter is looking for a roommate or your sister has a spare room. Might your son be better off living with a sibling? If your child can find another solution, you might offer to chip in to pay the rent the first few months until the couple has hammered out their finances. Finances are generally the reason a child wants to sleep on Mom's sofa anyway. Also, keep in mind, if you and your spouse can agree on a specific timeframe as to how long your child will be staying (and you stick to that schedule), he might be more amenable to the "temporary" arrangement.

However, if you and your spouse are at an impasse over allowing your adult child to return home, it is probably a good idea for the two of you to sit down with a family counselor. (Your spouse may not want to go, and you'll have to live with that.) Face the fact that you may have to find another satisfactory solution for your child or run the risk of hurting your own relationship — which already might be at risk for other reasons. You need to step back and consider this from your mate's perspective. He or she married you for better or worse — but not for your adult child.

•◀ *Taking in the Ex-in-Law* ▶•

Occasionally, the former son-in-law or daughter-in-law occupies the guestroom. I've heard of a number of cases when ex-in-laws and ex-parents-in-law lived together amicably when the ex-in-law needed a place to stay. Generally speaking, parents are caught in their divorcing children's fray when the non-residential mom or dad is on the scene when the grandchildren are living with Grandma and Grandpa.

Back to Nora's story:

Even though Ben and Joan had come to some accord about their children, an undercurrent of friction continued to play out while Ben and the twins lived with me. One day I was upstairs doing laundry when the doorbell rang. I was surprised to see Joan. Without thinking, I invited her to come inside. It was strange seeing Joan in the house, although not that long ago this had been her second home. Now we stood side by side in the hallway, like two unmatched gloves. I was pleased to see how well she looked. It was an hour until the school bus dropped the children off, so we sat and chatted about her parents, the schools she was considering, and her part-time job at the law library back in Seattle. It was almost like old times, although I was cautious not to talk about Ben and his work.

While we were waiting, I suggested Joan make the twins' dinner — their favorite tuna casserole. Joan found an apron and made her way familiarly around my kitchen, putting the noodles up to boil and assembling the ingredients. Watching her, seeing her so at ease, bending down to pick out a mixing bowl, searching a shelf for the spices, knowing without having to be told which drawers held the silverware, the napkins, and the everyday china — it was hard to believe all that had transpired in the past year-and-a-half following the break-up.

The twins were delighted to see their mother, although a little shy at first. Joan left around six-thirty p.m. promising the children she'd be back to take them to the zoo over the weekend.

When Jake later told his father that Mama had been to the house, Ben froze. I could tell that he was furious she'd just popped in, a clear violation of their parenting plan, and that I hadn't rebuffed her.

My look was stern in return. It read, "Ben, this is your battle not mine. For the sake of my grandchildren, Joan has a place in my home."

In retrospect, Ben had every right to be angry because I should have called him first before letting Joan see the children. I'd been thinking about the twins and not the Parenting Agreement. Unwittingly, I put myself in the middle of their legal battleground.

•◀ *Learning from Nora's Mistake* ▶•

Part of achieving restructuring after divorce reflects the couple's ability to get past their anger and learn to co-parent for the sake of their children. It makes it a lot easier for grandparents when the parents have an amicable relationship, especially when one parent is living back home. I have spoken to grandparents who have slammed the door in the non-custodial parent's face, made the "enemy" parent sit in the car and wait for more than hour before they sent the child out. Some have even defied court orders and denied the mother or father access. Other grandparents are gracious and make the ex-in-law feel welcome in their home. It's not easy, but for the sake of your grandchildren who live with you, I suggest modeling good behavior by establishing as civil and cordial a relationship with the ex-in-law(s) as possible. Learn from Nora's mistake. Don't overstep your bounds. Take your cues from your child and learn the terms of the Parenting Agreement or the court order.

•◀ *What If?* ▶•

Suppose Joan had called in advance to let Nora know that she was coming to see the twins. The right thing for Nora to do, in that case, would be to ask Joan to inform Ben herself. If Joan refused, Nora should try to hold her off — find some excuse to call her back. (There's always the line: "Gosh, I was just on my way out the door and can't talk right now.") Nora's next step would be to call her son and explain the situation. No matter how she feels, Nora must be guided by her son's decision. Had Ben said, "Don't let Joan in," Nora should ask Ben to call Joan to avoid getting in the middle. If Nora can't reach Ben, she should tell Joan it would be better if she waited to see the kids since she wasn't free to act on her own. No one wants to be put in this predicament or caught off guard. It is a good idea to play out the "what if" scenario with whoever will be taking care of the children to relieve them of the burden of having to act on their own. I know of one case where a father pushed his way into his soon-to-be ex's house, terrorized the babysitter, and demanded to see his children. The babysitter locked herself and the children in the bedroom and waited it out. Fortunately, the angry father went away and no one got hurt.

If you suspect a parent might show up in violation of a court-ordered visitation agreement, you need a contingency plan. When there is possible endangerment to the caretaker as well as the children, it is necessary for the custodial parent to take legal action and file for a restraining order against the offender.

◆◀ *Homecoming: Celebration or Catastrophe?* ▶◆

You don't have to be told that your child and grandchildren are toting a lot of emotional baggage when they arrive at your doorstep. They are not only facing the failure of their marriage, they are dealing with the failure to pick up the pieces. Because parents are safe, you become easy targets for your child's emotionality. Because you are strong, you can duck. It's easy to tally up the potential losses when you agree to take your children in. There's the loss of peace and quiet, the loss of independence, the loss of privacy. There is the additional expense, the inability to tune out their problems. There are roller coaster rides with grandchildren who resent your "interference."

An older woman who went to live with her mother when her husband left her many years ago reminded me that there is that other end of the telescope. Children bear the guilt of burdening us with their problems when they move back and may feel eternally indebted. The woman told me that she never remarried. In fact, she admitted sacrificing her own happiness to take care of her mother, who became very ill. Was it worth the trade-off? She wasn't sure.

Now listen to the words of one mother who took her daughter and three granddaughters in when her son-in-law left his family.

"When Adriana came to live with me, I realized she needed me in a whole new way. She needed my strength. I couldn't take away her pain, but I could listen and be there for her. We became very close. I learned to respect Adriana for the way she came through the ordeal. She never berated the children's father in front of them. She was and is a wonderful mother. Today we are more than mother-daughter — we're friends.

When my daughter came home, she had no place to go. If I hadn't taken her in, she and the children would have been out on the street. They lived with me for five years while she went back to get her high school diploma and started college. She got a place of her own, worked, and continued going to school at night. We had to help out, but she graduated with top honors. I was never prouder of my daughter. I admit it was tough going because I was back doing all those things for my grandchildren I used to do for my own children. But I have to say that Adriana and the children are in much better shape today than ever before. The girls are all grown up. I get the most beautiful cards and letters from them, thanking me for all I've done. Don't misunderstand me. I love my other grandchildren, but these kids are very special because of what we've been through together."

As you have seen in the earlier chapters, your child's divorce causes emotional disequilibria for the entire family. Each stage triggers myriad feelings. While some parents welcome their child's divorce and see it as an escape hatch from a toxic situation and an opportunity for an unhappy son or daughter to forge a better tomorrow, more view it as a kind of family devastation. Many parents I interviewed talked about the ongoing emotional toll their child's divorce was taking in their personal lives. Feelings ranged

---

Parental Guideposts: Chapter Four

Mom, Dad . . . Can I Come Home?

- Be organized. The newcomers will probably appreciate routines after all the chaos in their own lives.
- Set timeframes for the length of the stay.
- Divvy up household chores.
- Negotiate any financial contributions from your adult child.
- Be clear in the beginning about house rules. Be reasonable.
- Provide a special place for the grandchildren where they can play and feel comfortable inviting friends.
- Make time for yourself and your spouse.
- Treat your child and family to a mini-vacation so you can have the house for yourself.

---

from anger and resentment to guilt and depression. I interviewed one woman who said she suffered from a depression so profound it took her a year of therapy to get back to normal.

The emotional intensity of the rescue period was very hard on these parents, who did not anticipate having this kind of stress at this time in their lives. Most of these parents were looking forward to retirement and having more time for personal enjoyment, not more involvement in their children's lives.

Mental health experts agree there is an inherent danger in parents continuing to play too active a part in their child's life after the rescue period is over. They also caution against being too involved emotionally in the actual divorce process. They explain that the rescue stage is supposed to be a transition period. It should not be prolonged. The sooner parents can pull back and establish healthy boundaries, the easier it will be to re-establish a mature adult-adult relationship with the divorcing children and guide them toward rebuilding.

✎ *Chapter Four: Workbook Exercises*

You may be ambivalent about your child's homecoming. It will help to acknowledge your concerns as well as the benefits you foresee.

1. Draft a homecoming "contract." Go over this with your child. Include timeframes, household chores, and any shared expenses.

2. Estimate the amount of time you are willing to commit to particular tasks such as babysitting, carpooling, grocery shopping, etc. Set limits. Share your estimates with your child.

3. Think about how you can best use your existing physical space to accommodate the returning family such as sleeping quarters and designated play areas.

4. Create a tentative list of house rules that address conduct, and order them in terms of your priority. Now look at the list from your adult child and grandchild's perspective. What items would you foresee them wanting to change?

5. Write two statements, one for your child and one for your grandchildren, expressing your delight in having them in your home. Use the statements as reminders to tell them often.

Part II

Dealing with Change

Your Child's Divorce:
What to Expect — What You Can Do

Chapter Five

Taking Sides

Even if you couldn't find a single good thing to say about your son or daughter's marriage, even if you maintained a safe distance the whole time the couple was together, you will be affected by the breakup. Some parents are prepared to go to battle for their wounded child. Others immediately retreat, not wanting to be caught in the crossfire. Whether you agree or disagree with your child's behavior, whether you view him or her as the initiator or the victim, the long and the short is that your child is your child forever. Your support is expected. Your son or daughter may not say it directly, but the assumption is there: "Blood is thicker than water." Nora learned this the hard way.

Nora's Story: Pushed off the Balance Beam

Right after Ben and Joan separated and Joan was diagnosed with stage I breast cancer, as a woman, I identified with Joan's plight. During her course of treatment, I journeyed through her labyrinth of fear. Afterward I sympathized with her inability to cope with the children. I loved Joan like a daughter. She was the mother of my grandchildren, and up until the separation, I had no cause to think of her in any other way. She and her parents had become part of our extended family. We had always shared our trials.

I had so hoped that we would continue to have a relationship after the divorce, although I no longer fooled myself into believing it would be the same. I'd spoken to enough friends to know there'd be that inevitable drifting away. Even when there are grandchildren to bind you together, ex-in-laws get married and start new families.

Like Ben, I kept waiting for the day Joan would come home. However, as time passed, it became apparent that Joan expected Ben to take full command. I then learned that recovery isn't just about the body; it's also about the mind. I'd read that depression is common in cancer survivors — not only is there the fear of the disease recurring, there is the difficulty adjusting to the withdrawal of the team of doctors taking responsibility for the patient's health. Joan felt the pressure of family and friends — waiting for her to resume life as usual, and it was too much for her to deal with.

I knew that Ben was willing to do his part and would be a support to Joan if she would let him. I found myself defending her behavior when anyone attacked her, hoping to buy her more time. I was always ready with excuses. *Joan will come around. She's not physically strong enough to cope with two active children. It's much better for the twins if Ben takes over now.*

I wasn't aware how my attitude was affecting my relationship with my son until things came to a head one day when our family was sitting around the dinner table, and my brother-in-law made some sarcastic remark about Joan's copping out. The twins were sitting across from me, and I saw Janice flinch. I turned to my brother-in-law and said he should give Joan some slack. Ben turned red in the face, threw down his napkin, and stormed out of the room. I got to my feet and ran after him. When I apologized for speaking out of turn, he cried, "How can you defend her? You, my mother!"

I explained that I was only trying to be fair by considering both sides of the picture. But Ben was too furious to hear me out. As far as he was concerned, I was in Joan's camp. "It's pretty awful," he said, "when you can't count on your own family for support."

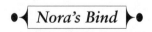

•◀ *Nora's Bind* ▶•

Nora learned the hard way that it is impossible to stay on the balance beam for very long. In defending her daughter-in-law, she came close to losing her son. Nora told Ben she was just trying to be fair, trying to see both sides of the picture. "*Fair* is a word for weather forecasters and umpires," quip Dorothy Gottlieb and her co-authors when discussing the parental dilemma when a son or daughter gets divorced. The reality, as their book *What to Do When Your Son or Daughter Divorces* (1988) makes clear, is that parents do get pulled into the fray and ultimately have to choose sides. "During those first, hardest months it is best to support the side of your child even though you know there's another side."

It's difficult to fault Nora for sympathizing with Joan, but she is at fault for not being more publicly supportive of Ben, who was grappling with all the changes in his life that had been thrust upon him.

•◀ *Sorting It Out* ▶•

There are many reasons parents have difficulty sorting out their loyalty when they first learn their child is getting divorced. Which of these can you relate to?

• *Your child's divorce is a double blow.* While trying to console an unhappy child, you're reconciling yourself to the loss of family as you knew it. Holidays and family get-togethers will feel different. You'll have memories of better times. It's only natural to feel angry, sad, or bitter about the breakup, and difficult to hold your feelings in check. If you have bottled up your feelings, you need to find a safe place where you can give expression to your emotions. You may want to talk to a counselor, or join a support group for grandparents or parents of divorced children. Think about organizing such a group if there isn't one in your community. Your place of worship is a good place to begin. Consider placing an ad in the local newspaper to drum up interest. (Some papers provide free space for community announcements.) Grandparents I've talked to participate in online grandparent chat groups, although I hasten to add, if you select this outlet you should be wary of giving out too much personal information.

• *Like your child, you are worried about the future.* While your son or daughter is worrying about finances and the best way to untie the knot, you are thinking about your future involvement in your single-again child's life. If this is a concern, it helps to acknowledge that concern. Begin by writing a list of possible changes you foresee and how you feel about them. E.g., *While I am happy about spending more time with my grandchildren, I am worried this will mean readjusting my own work schedule.*

• **You have a keen sense of responsibility toward your son-in-law or daughter-in-law.** For example, if you think your daughter-in-law has too much on her plate and feel the grandchildren are not receiving the care they need since their parents separated, you may need to deal with the problem directly, even if it means putting yourself out temporarily.

> *Jill didn't like the idea that her ten-year-old grandson was coming home to an empty apartment on the days her daughter-in-law worked late. Jill could not take off from work to be there when her grandson got off the school bus, but she found a friend's teenage daughter who was willing to tutor the boy on the days he was alone. Grandma made sure to call her grandson and check in at the same time everyday. She also prepared a batch of meals to ease her daughter-in-law's load, knowing she was too exhausted to shop or prepare healthy dinners until she settled into her single mom routine.*

Another case involved a father-in-law who helped his soon-to-be ex-son-in-law, who had gotten laid off from his factory job and whose unemployment was running out.

> *In desperation, Sal offered Jimmy a job in his restaurant. His daughter wasn't thrilled with the idea, but Sal said he would rather have Jimmy throw pizza dough than hang out in the unemployment office. "It's only temporary, just until he finds something else. I'm doing this for you and the girls." Sal felt conflicted having Jimmy at his elbow, but he was trying to make it easier on the family. If Jimmy wasn't bringing in a paycheck, guess who'd be carrying the freight?*

• **Your sympathies will lie with an abandoned spouse** who is going to have a tougher time recouping than your own child, who may be in a better financial situation or who has already moved on in a new relationship. A word of caution: Don't let your ex-in-law manipulate you into shouldering his or her problems. Find out if there are other support systems in place — friends, family, or social services — or you could be drained dry before you know it. If there are other resources, there's no harm in taking a back seat while communicating your desire to help in an emergency.

• *You feel strong-armed* into taking a hard-line position against a son or daughter-in-law with whom you had a perfectly good relationship prior to the breakup. You may see no reason to cut off communication, and even become furious with your own child who expects you to accede to his or her demands. Rather than engage in a tug-of-war with your child, express your feelings calmly: "I am sad that I cannot congratulate Shelly personally on her promotion. I'd like to send her a card." Your child may moderate his position if your behavior is not threatening your relationship with him.

• *You are receiving mixed messages from your own child.* It is likely that you will have difficulty backing your child if you are on an emotional seesaw — one day she rejects you; the next day she wants your help. Tough this period out and you will reap future rewards. Your child will appreciate your sticking by her side when she feels more secure and has a clearer sense of direction. Be patient.

• *Your child is the one who strayed* and you are having difficulty drumming up sympathy for your own flesh and blood. More about this struggle a bit further on. For the moment, let's look at the broader issue of loyalty and where you, as a parent, may have to draw the line.

•◀ *What Is Loyalty?* ▶•

In Western culture, sons and daughters are expected to transfer loyalty from the family of origin (parents, siblings, aunts, uncles, etc.) to the mate. If one of the couple is overly close with any member of the family of origin (a daughter is tied to her mother's apron strings, for example), this becomes what family therapists call a loyalty alignment triangle. "When a conflictual or toxic issue arises, such as money, the people who have the most influence over the husband may still be the family... Thus does the influence of the extended family and attachment to it take precedence over the marital relationship" (Guerin, et al, 1996).

◆◀ *Should I Say, "My Child, Right or Wrong?"* ▶◆

When your child was first learning to drive, you might have forgiven her for putting the dent in your new car's fender. Her adolescent prank was just a blip on the radar screen when the principal called you in for a conference. Now that your child is an adult, you expect her to take responsibility for her actions, and feel you shouldn't have to make excuses for her behavior.

Experts in child development tell parents that healthy maturation occurs when children learn to separate from parents, when they form their own identity. As I noted above, typically when a child gets married the old parent-child bonds are broken and new ones are formed with the spouse. However, when the marital ties are severed, when the child's marriage bursts apart, our divorcing son or daughter must now confront the reality of the past. This includes examining the past and present relationship with parents.

Most children approach their parents with trepidation when their marriage falls apart, especially if there is something in the marriage they are ashamed to admit. As Diane Vaughn explains in her book, *Uncoupling: Turning Points in Intimate Relationships* (1990), "Often for the first time in a long while, adult child and parent each glimpse who the other has become when they give and exchange information about the breakup." The outcome is unpredictable — the revelation of secrets can create or terminate bonds. If the child knows that the confrontation is going to be painful, he or she will most likely loosen or unhook all ties with the family of origin. Let's look at this extreme case when confrontation was particularly difficult for a parent who learns about his child's deception:

"I had no idea" Tommy laments, "that my son-in-law Lionel was taking money out of the till to cover his stock market losses. We'd been in business for many years, but it was only around the time my kids broke up that I realized what was

going on. To add insult to injury, my daughter knew all along and never came to me. Now she is begging me not to press charges for the sake of family appearances."

Tommy has to make a difficult call. He can accede to his daughter's demands and arrange some way for his son-in-law to repay him, or take legal action against him. The point is, parents may, when their child leaves his or her marriage, be privy to a lot of information they would not otherwise be aware of. The revelation and reaction to such disclosures will affect the parent-child relationship long after the marriage dissolves.

I assume that if you are reading this book, the last thing you want is for your child to detach from family. Your goal is to reestablish a healthy relationship with your wounded child and find it in your heart to forgive him or her for most transgressions. The best way to achieve this is to provide unequivocal support, especially in the early stages of the breakup when sensitivities are so raw. You can best do this by withholding judgment and simply listening. You do not have to come right out and say, "My child, right or wrong."

•◀ *Uncoupling: The Need to Go Public* ▶•

Know that it is not easy for your child to come forward and admit that the marriage is in trouble. Many couples make a valiant effort to keep their problems under wraps and are successful at putting up a good front, often for several years. That is why it may come as a shock when parents learn their children are getting a divorce. How much you are in the loop will depend on your relationship with your son or daughter before and during the marriage.

Going public is a necessary task of "uncoupling." Vaughn (1990) explains that going public is a way of validating the decision to end the marriage. The troubled relationship becomes officially troubled. "We cannot leave someone we like," says Vaughn, "so we come to terms with loss, and our possible contribution to the failure by making the loss acceptable and justify it to ourselves by dwelling on the negative aspects." By sharing secrets with a select audience, your child is lessening his or her discomfort. However, this process of disconnection can be particularly hard on parents, who will be pressured to take sides once the news is out.

Even if you had time to digest the decision, you will not be sure how to handle friends and family. What to say? How much information to share? Whether to back your child unconditionally (my child, right or wrong), or immediately grant concessions to an in-law with whom you had a special relationship, and who you may think is the victim. Then there is the issue of public mourning, another necessary task for your child and members of the family. Public mourning, says Vaughn, is as important as public declaration. The mourning also eases the pain.

Some parents feel they should put up a false front for the sake of their public image or as a way of defending their child. "Oh, we're just fine with the decision. It's something that probably will work out for the best." If these parents are suffering, they make sure to suffer in silence. Other parents are more prone to rend their clothes and tear out their hair. "How could Johnny do this to Mary? What will happen to the grandkids? Will my life ever be the same?"

Many sons and daughters, however, do not come forward because they are unable to accept the fact that the love relationship is ending. They wait it out, hoping the problems will sort out, either by themselves or in counseling. When the marriage fails, no one knows how the announcement will be received. There are bound to be repercussions: re-alignments with family, loss of friends, gossip, censure, questions, muckraking, and loss of face.

Now for this issue of supporting your child when you are riddled with doubt, when your child refuses to take any blame for the marital failure and is counting on your being in his or her corner. What should your position be?

•◀ *Alignments and Misalignments* ▶•

Right after the announcement of the split, alignments will form. The chips will fall in an unpredictable pattern. Longstanding friends may withdraw rather than take sides. A few friends you may have counted on for support will rally around the "enemy." Individuals whose own marriages are troubled will feel threatened and want out of the picture altogether. Couples often say that the toughest part of their divorce is abandonment by friends and family. That's why your loyalty is so important. It's easy to sympathize when Ben confronts Nora in the narrative and accuses her of desertion. It's hard to disagree with a wounded child who cries, "If you can't count on family, who can you count on?"

Co-authors Dorothy and Marjorie Gottlieb (1988) tell parents this is a rickety time. Parents shouldn't be fooled that they can just stand on the sidelines and not get involved. There is no such thing as neutrality. Neutrality is often misconstrued as treason. The first few months are the hardest on everyone. Even when there is doubt, parents should support their child for the sake of the child and the preservation of the family. It's not easy but probably a good idea to put the in-law on the back burner, they advise. In the next stage, when tempers cool and children can be more objective, parents can ease up and begin to look more critically at what happened in the marriage. "It stands to reason that you remain on the side of your child both at the altar for the wedding and for the separation and divorce.... There is a quid pro quo for backing up your child. You hope for some openness from her and perhaps for an unnegotiated tacit promise to stand behind you when you are in need."

Note that looking more critically at the marriage does not mean assigning blame. It means trying to understand what went wrong and trying to help your child face up to the issues (and if necessary, seek help so as not to repeat these mistakes). It also means helping your child face up to his or her responsibilities now that the marriage is over.

●◀ *When Family Members Take Sides* ▶●

There is an orbit around you of grandparents, aunts, uncles, nieces, nephews, sons and daughters, grandchildren, etc. who are watching your response and picking up cues. It is unrealistic to expect family solidarity. (Poor Nora discovered that when telling her story of her brother-in-law's lambasting of Joan in front of Nora's grandchildren.) Keep in mind that everyone is entitled to his or her own opinion. However, if you prove to be a strong supporter of your child, chances are the other members will follow suit.

If you sense division in the ranks, make it clear that your child needs allies and will recover more quickly if he or she can count on family backing. As a parent, you may hold up the banner: "Our Family Through Thick and Thin" or "United We Stand." Recognize that not everyone is willing to take up your cause.

Be sensitive to your grandchild who may side with your in-law right after her parents separate. Your grandchild may refuse to have anything to do with you as a member of the enemy camp. Children often side with the parent who they feel is the neediest.

Brenda didn't get along with her mother, who was a successful businesswoman driven by ambition. Yet when her father left them, Brenda's mother fell apart. Brenda took advantage of the opportunity to become important in her mother's eyes. The teenager became her mother's confidante and ally. To this day, Brenda does not speak to her father, who has tried to reopen the door many times. She feels her duty is toward her mother. They are bonded in their anger toward him.

Unfortunately, it's difficult to stand by and see young children take sides. They don't have an adult's perspective. They are often confused, anxious, and afraid of being abandoned. Let me bring this point home by citing a recent national study of 1,500 respondents from divorced and intact families. A poll was conducted by Elizabeth Marquardt and Norvel D. Glenn (*Institute of American Values*, 2005) asking adults ages eighteen to thirty-five, children from supposedly "good divorces," about stressors they experienced while growing up. There was a consensus that even though the children with amicable divorced parents had less conflict in their lives, they still felt less protected, less at home with each parent, and less likely to go to their parents for comfort. They also felt they had to play different parts with each parent, keep secrets, be more adult, take sides, and meet higher expectations in order to gain their parents' approval. ("Poll Says Even Quiet Divorces Affect Children's Paths", Tamar Lewin, *New York Times National*, Saturday, November 5, 2005, p. A13.)

Astoundingly, approximately three-quarters of a million American children experience their parents' divorce each year; many of them are not yet sixteen when their parents split. What does that mean for grandparents? It means you may well have young grandchildren who need all the comfort and emotional support they can find as their parents divorce. It also means you have to be more sensitive about what you are communicating to your grandchildren when you allow your biases to rule your words.

You cannot reconcile your children's marital situation. And you won't get far trying to demand they behave in a civil fashion, or lecturing them (especially when tempers are hot and wounds raw), or trying to take away their authority. What you can do is to model, through your own behavior, an appropriate attitude toward the ex-mate and the ex-in-laws.

I suggest that you trying catching your son or daughter demonstrating respect for the ex-spouse. For example, when Hal's son commented quite off-handedly that Melissa was a travel mom for his son's swim team and was taking time off from work to accompany the boy to a meet in Washington, Hal's mom took the opportunity to praise her son. "It's good for the kids to hear you say something positive about Melissa. I wish you'd do that more often." Now, maybe Hal's mother was about to get an earful, but in taking the risk she made a good point and was standing up for the youngsters.

Marquardt and Glenn concluded that children from intact families grow up in child-centered families. Children from divorce experience more stress, even though most of them grow up to be successful adults. When grandparents add to their burden by exposing them to their own hostility, they make recovery more difficult. You can play a part in helping your grandchildren recover. (More about this in chapters 8 and 9.) Keep in mind that it's not fair when children are forced to make choices and are pulled into the fray. Children should have the freedom to love both parents. You are the bedrock of your family. You can afford to be kind or more forgiving to the ex-in-law who is your grandchild's other parent — like it or not.

●◀ *Gossip and Backbiting* ▶●

Know that not everyone will accept the party line when you go public. You are not responsible for what other people say or think. If your sisters and brothers had close ties with the in-law, accept the fact your sibs may not back you. They might see things differently. Family members are entitled to their opinions, which doesn't mean they should be unkind or not sympathize with your feelings. Remind them you need support, too.

The first order of business is to set boundaries with those who would gossip or pry. Rather than cross swords with anyone who goes to "the other side," try to be civil and hear them out. Obviously, it's painful when close family members desert you and your child. However, as new information comes to the surface, attitudes are bound to change. They may even turn around.

You may discover that your other children are conflicted about their loyalties. Unlike parents, siblings will be more objective and more critical. Often a sister or brother may have more awareness of the underlying problems in your son's or daughter's marriage than you do. Your other children may withhold information to spare your feelings. For example:

Fanny was best friends with her sister-in-law before she married her brother. Fanny knew her brother was unfaithful but would never tell her parents. When the couple separated, Mom and Dad were furious that Fanny took her sister-in-law's side. Little did they know... or should they?

•◀ Why Can't I Sit on the Fence? ▶•

While divorce can be a blessing in disguise for the son or daughter who sees it as a second chance at happiness, it is too often a heart-wrenching experience for parents who have emotional ties to in-laws and grandchildren. Your child's divorce may require you to break off linkages with those you have learned to accept as family. Is it any wonder you may be tempted to defy your child who insists you let go?

Not every divorcing adult child understands that a parent can be in his or her corner and still have feelings for the ex-in-law. If you've been divorced, you probably have enough life experience to see the light at the end of the tunnel. Right now, your wounded child sees only darkness. You have learned that in time tempers cool, circumstances change, hardliners moderate. For the moment, however, your child may be too invested in his or her anger and too afraid of the unknown to let go and move on to the next stage of recovery. While your child is invested in anger, he or she will require proof of your loyalty. The reality is:

Parents cannot be in two camps at the same time.
In divorce, neutrality is treason.

●◀ *But I Can't Sever the Ties!* ▶●

The parents I spoke to agreed, with few exceptions, their first priority was their own child during and after the divorce. However, the reality is that many parents become blindsided by their affection for their in-law and find themselves wavering in their allegiance to their son or daughter. They feel guilty when they cannot sever ties. If you find yourself in this position, don't be too hard on yourself. It may be difficult to accept your child's interpretation of what went wrong. Closing the book on a marriage takes heroic effort, notes Judith Wallerstein in her book, *The Good Marriage* (1995). It takes heroic effort for everyone involved — grandchildren, siblings, and especially for you, the parents, when so much is expected of you.

For some parents, the handwriting is on the wall, and they discover early on that they cannot stay connected to the in-law. Here are some cases in point.

When It's Over, It's Over

Sandra's daughter-in-law made it clear that she wanted to blot out the past out and make a fresh start after her separation. She sent everyone in her address book an e-mail informing him or her she had gone back to using her maiden name. Sandra's parents-in-law were upset. It all seemed so cut and dry. They sent back a reply saying they were sorry things had turned out this way, and that when and if Sandra would like to contact them, they'd be pleased to hear from her. They are still waiting.

Frank was very fond of his son-in-law Glen. Right after the separation, Frank took his son-in-law out for a drink, intending to stay friends no matter what. But when the young man spent the entire evening badmouthing Frank's daughter, Frank got disgusted and walked out. He hasn't spoken to Glen since.

Refusing to Let Go

People react differently to change. Older parents may have a more difficult time detaching from an in-law they've known for years than younger parents whose kids walk away from starter marriages — marriages that last one or two years and produce no grandchildren. Listen to Hilda's story.

> *Hilda is seventy-three. Her daughter Calli and son-in-law had been married for thirty-two years when the couple decided to call it quits. That was nearly three years ago, but Hilda is still blaming Calli for the breakup. The relationship between mother and daughter has deteriorated to the point where Calli has left all the caretaking responsibilities to her brother and his wife rather than have anything to do with Hilda, who is now in ill health. Calli and her brother are no longer on speaking terms. Hilda's behavior is destroying her family.*

Closer Than My Own Kin

It is not often the case, but on occasion, for whatever reason, parents feel closer to their in-law than their own flesh and blood. Doris tells this story:

> *"My former daughter-in-law and I shared many interests. We both loved the theater, and once a month we used to go out for lunch and see a matinee. I was heart-broken when Gladys left my son, even though she was cruel in the way she broke the news. She left a note on the kitchen table saying the marriage was over and walked out. Unbeknownst to anyone, Gladys had already accepted a teaching job in another state. Needless to say, my son is very bitter. He has not gotten over the breakup. I know he always resented our friendship. He doesn't want me to have anything to do with his ex-wife. I haven't told him that Gladys and I still keep in touch. Recently my ex-daughter-in-law called to tell me she met someone and is getting remarried. I would like to send her a wedding gift but don't know what to do."*

Doris is playing with fire. Not only is she being disloyal to her son, she runs the risk of destroying any chance of their having a healthy relationship. One has to wonder why Doris is willing to overlook her ex-daughter-in-law's cruel behavior. She should not send a gift. In fact, she should respect her son's wishes and stop this collusion.

The Needy In-law

There are cases in which the ex-in-law makes it difficult for parents to detach. In both of the cases that follow, parents find themselves caught in a bind.

> *Rosalie is filled with guilt. Her son and his wife are embroiled in a very nasty custody suit. Rosalie's daughter-in-law, Kim, calls her every day and cries. She doesn't understand why she has to be cut out of the family just because she is separated from her son. "Kim is alone in this country, and we are her only family," Rosalie explained. "My son doesn't want me to have anything to do with her. He is not happy that she calls me. He wants me to tell her off. I don't want to hurt Kim or jeopardize seeing my grandchildren. The whole situation breaks my heart. I feel so torn."*

Rosalie needs to be firmer with Kim and establish some boundaries in terms of the continual phone calls. Rosalie needs to cool the relationship without breaking it off entirely and take measures to pull back without offending Kim. It's a tightrope, and no one said it would be easy. In terms of the custody issue, Rosalie does not know for sure that Kim will be awarded primary physical custody of her grandchildren. She might ask her son to attach a grandparents' rights clause to their divorce agreement. However, this attachment (even if Kim agrees to it) may not stand up in court if tested later. (More about this in Appendix A, a discussion of legal issues and grandparenting rights.)

•◀ *Staying Connected — It Can Happen* ▶•

Family bonds need not be broken when a child's marriage ends. I recently talked to a mother whose son insisted his mother call his wife to offer her support when they split.

"I felt awkward making the first move, but Jerry said my being there for Clara would make it easier on the children. So I invited my soon-to-be ex-daughter-in-law to lunch. I said Jerry asked that I help her any way I could. Clara was grateful, and although I was having a hard time with all this, my reaching out made it easier on my son."

Another divorced father of two admitted that he was pleased his mother and ex-wife remained friends even though he'd remarried. Whenever the extended family gets together, his mother acts as buffer between the former and current wives.

Some family ties that you think would be broken after divorce and remarriage can last a lifetime. Recently, I attended a funeral service where both the ex-son-in-law (who'd remarried) and current son-in-law delivered poignant eulogies about the deceased mother-in-law. In essence, they both said the same glowing things about the woman who maintained a loving relationship with both men in her daughter's life.

When parents-in-law become surrogate parents to an "inherited" child, it is particularly difficult to detach post-divorce.

Warren had grown up in a series of foster homes, so he formed a strong attachment to his wife's parents during their eight-year marriage. After his divorce, Warren felt the loss of Felicia and Rod more deeply than he felt the loss of his wife. Because their daughter was not threatened by their close relationship, the couple and ex-spouse remained close friends. Warren has since remarried. His ex-in-laws are part of his extended family to this day.

●◀ *For the Sake of the Grandchildren* ▶●

Aggrieved parents often ask if there is any situation when they can, in good conscience, defy their child's wishes and stay connected to their in-law. Child psychologist Dr. Arthur Kornhaber in his *Grandparenting Guide* (2002) emphasizes the importance of grandparents maintaining emotional ties with both parents when the marriage dissolves. "If you have a close relationship with your ex-son-in-law or ex-daughter-in-law, there is no reason to surrender that relationship because of the divorce. Your grandchild must deal with both divorced parents on a permanent basis. Understand and support your child's ex-spouse. Although you will most likely side with your child in the divorce, don't be over-zealous in judging the other party."

Family relations experts say it's also a good strategy to communicate your sympathy to the parents-in-law in the early stages of the separation. Begin to build bridges for your grandchildren, who need two sets of grandparents. The divorce terrain should not be barren of loving grandparents. If possible, work toward that goal early on.

Be alert: Your grandchild can easily become part of the divorce triangle when Mom and Dad play games and use kids as pawns, spies, scapegoats, or allies trying to get back at the spouse. Should you see this, be direct with your child and suggest (as diplomatically as you can) that he or she deal directly with the ex and keep the kids out of the line of fire. Your child may be unaware the effect all this is having on his children. Supporting your child also means being your grandchildren's ally and permitting them the freedom to love both parents. This goes back to my earlier point: If you can show respect and support for your former in-law while you are communicating your loyalty to your son or daughter, you will be contributing to your grandchildren's divorce recovery and, hopefully, helping your own child gain some perspective on his or her behavior.

Granted, it's a difficult balancing act. Is it any wonder that, like Barbara, it's so easy to stumble and fall?

Barbara lived a few miles away from her grandchildren, but since her son's divorce, she rarely saw them. In desperation, she called her son's ex-wife and invited her to come for lunch with the grandchildren. When her son found out, he jumped all over his mother. "Well, you gave me no choice," Barbara cried in self-defense. "When you have the grandchildren, you never bring them to see me, so I decided to take the bull by the horns and call Betty, who was very understanding. She brought the children over, and we had a nice visit." When Barbara's son realized how much his mother was longing to see her grandchildren, he promised to share them more often. In turn, Barbara agreed to ask his permission before she called Betty next time.

In chapter 4, we talked about the importance of consulting your child before making decisions about visitation and other issues that might be part of the divorce negotiations. You do not want to be violating a court order or interfering when couples are working out their settlement. Divorce is a sensitive time for everyone. It is better to err on the side of caution before overstepping those key boundaries. When it doubt, make a phone call and get permission, even when those heartstrings are pulling you in the direction of seeing grandchildren who are living with the custodial parent either full or part time..

When single-again parents are settling into the new arrangements, grandparents need to take a step back while everyone acclimates to all the changes. When you are permitted to visit, be sure to observe all the rules set down by the ex-in-law. Think of grandchildren as a privilege not an entitlement.

●◀ *Showing Support Without Going Overboard* ▶●

What if you currently have too many problems of your own to take on your child's burden?

One mother who had just been widowed and was still grieving, cried, *"My child expects a lifeboat now that she is separated, but I can only float a leaky raft."* Take heart. There are many ways to "float a lifeboat" without getting into the deep yourself. Here are a few practical suggestions:

• *Set boundaries with friends and relatives right away.* Don't give out too much information when your child goes public.

• *Discuss with your child what he or she wants said about the separation.* Make a list of the obvious questions, and some useful brief answers. People are bound to ask: *What caused the breakup? How are the grandkids doing? Has Rita gotten a lawyer yet, because it she hasn't I know this great barracuda . . . ?"*

• *Prepare a script beforehand. Thanks for calling. Yes, it's true Betty and Bob have decided to separate. It's a shame, but these things happen. Fortunately, they are both strong, mature people. I have every confidence they and the kids will pull through this just fine. After all, Jack and I are right there in their corner, doing all we can to help.* A bit vague on the details? That's okay. Think about how some of those Presidential press conferences are handled and take your cues from the press secretary. You're not required to answer the questions directly!

• *Do a spot-check around your house* and remove photos and gifts that might discharge unpleasant memories for your child, unless you think your son or daughter is okay with keeping their wedding portrait on the mantelpiece.

• *Avoid offhand references* about the estranged partner that might rub salt in the wound. Example: "Aunt Martha saw Jim at the playhouse with that girlfriend of his," or how about, "I read in the *Courier* that Mary took first place in the horse show."

• *Advise relatives to ask for permission* before inviting your child's soon-to-be-ex to family gatherings. Don't assume it's okay if Charlie goes to your niece's wedding even if he is sitting on the groom's side. It's embarrassing and not exactly Emily Post or Miss Manners, but Charlie may have to be uninvited if it means your own child stays home and sulks.

• *Encourage other family members to send the message, "We are here for you."*

• *Keep in mind that your child may not want to take phone calls* from sympathetic friends and family members. Encourage sympathizers to send cheerful e-mails that work just as well.

• *Include your child in family outings*, especially in the beginning. Weekends can be lonely, especially when the other spouse has the kids. Being with sibs and extended family helps bind wounds. Keep the outings upbeat — get tickets to a sporting event, take in a movie, or plan a picnic or a day at the beach, where the conversation focuses on something other than the split

•◀ *When You Can't Side With Your Child* ▶•

It is not always easy to be in your son or daughter's corner when you know your child has acted irresponsibly. What if you discover your son is delinquent in his child support payments or your daughter refuses to have the father come to his daughter's confirmation? It's not easy to hold your peace.

"I used to criticize my son for being over-indulgent and spoiling his kids," Timothy said. "Now he bitches that he has to pay child support, and he's giving his ex-wife a hard time about paying for summer camp."

What do you do when you know in your heart of hearts that your child is responsible for the failure of the marriage? In fact, your son or daughter was the dumper and the in-law the dumpee. How do you show sympathy for your child when the other party is so wounded? The answer is — there are no easy answers. It's better to keep an open mind. You don't really know what drove your child to act the way he or she did, and you may never know. Professionals in the field offer parents this advice if they want to re-forge a relationship with a child rather than cast blame:

- Your child is your child forever.
- It's worth searching in your heart to find forgiveness if your child has disappointed you.
- The in-law, a sympathetic and loving addition to your family, will move on.
- In the early stages of the breakup, when your child comes to you, he or she is relying on your unconditional support.

•◀ *When Your Values Clash* ▶•

Zach could not reconcile his daughter's divorce with his own religious convictions. Margot was distressed to discover her daughter left her husband for a female lover. Your child's divorce can be even more devastating to reconcile if there is some unsuspected disclosure — homosexuality, alcoholism, an addiction problem, criminal behavior, abuse, etc. If you find that you have ethical or religious issues with your child or that he or she has demonstrated behaviors or indiscretion that you cannot forgive and forget, it's time to seek counseling for the sake of preserving your relationship.

•◀ *Dealing with New Behaviors* ▶•

You may see a number of changes in your child's habits and behaviors that will upset you. Keep in mind that as a parent, you can do only so much. You don't want to turn against your child and create unnecessary friction. Still, there could be occasions when you feel you have the right to meddle. Here is some more practical advice:

• *Find an opportune moment when you and your child are alone,* when you are both calm and you can focus without interruption.

• *Do not overwhelm your child. Pick one issue.* Voice your concern positively. Remember you want to communicate your support while confronting a specific behavior. Obviously, this will call for some diplomacy. Try this tactic:

Begin by first saying something positive that you've noticed about your child's behavior. Next, suggest some action that might provide a remedy for the problem the behavior is causing. Examples:

> *Charles objected to the way his son allowed his kids to fade into the background when he got involved with a woman he met after his separation. Charles began his talk by telling his son he was glad he was dating such a nice woman. Then he reminded him that his oldest granddaughter had the lead part in the school play and that the girl was hoping her dad would attend. Charles gave his son a list of dates of the performances. He added that it would be nice if he, the girlfriend, and the grandchild could all go out for dinner or dessert afterward.*

Here is another situation:

> *Jack was upset that his daughter bad-mouthed his grandchildren's father in front of the kids. During halftime at his grandson's soccer game, he took his daughter aside and told her how proud he was of the good job she was doing single parenting. Then he said, "I know you still have a lot of frustration toward Jim. I can hear it when you talk about him to the kids. Why don't you save it for me? That way you can get it off your chest and I can really listen."*

●◀ *Put Down Your Dukes* ▶●

I would like to caution parents about crossing the line defending their child to the world at large. Two key points: Your child is an adult. This is his or her battle. Overcome your instinct to protect your wounded child. You will do more damage than good when you take it upon yourself to take on the in-law(s), for examples. Hold your emotions in check. If you need to explode, do it in private.

Marianne sat down and covered three pages in longhand, firing off every nasty thought she ever had about her son-in-law. She read her letter to her husband, and then put it in her safe deposit box. Thank goodness, she never sent it. Fifteen years later, when her grandson got married, guess who asked her for the first dance?

Remember — When you are smoking with rage:
- You cannot fight your adult child's battles.
- You only make matters worse when you stone the in-laws.
- Circumstances change. Wounds heal.
- Think about the grandchildren. Think about them again and again, and put yourself in their place.

•◀ *What to Do about Well-Meaning Friends and Relatives* ▶•

Tamara was reluctant to tell her mother that her favorite grandson had left his wife. She knew that her parents were hardliners for marriage and would insist that her son and daughter-in-law work things out. "Let me talk to Zellie," Momma insisted when she heard about the separation. "She and I always got along." Tamara said, "I know it was difficult for my parents to have to accept the failure of their grandson's marriage. They were very worried because the couple had a new baby, and they said the parents should stick together no matter what. But kids don't see it that way anymore. I had a hard time convincing Momma to stay out of their affairs."

Welcome your parents and well-meaning friends' support, but stand firm. Like you, they have to respect your child's privacy and not pry.

•◀ *A Final Word about Public Relations* ▶•

Once the news is out, your child's divorce is in the public domain. What are you going to say when you get all those phone calls? The best way to smother gossip is to affirm your allegiance to your child. Here are some guidelines when dealing with the paparazzi:

Script your responses to obvious questions.

- Don't make headlines by dumping on the in-law(s).
- Forget about private confidences. There is no such thing as "keep this under your hat." Hats blow off in the wind.
- Time your phone calls. Keep them brief. Same for e-mails.
- Return phone calls when you aren't angry or tired and likely to ramble.
- Make sure the spouse, partner, kids, grandchildren, etc. are on the same page in terms of what to say.
- Avoid daily updates.
- Switch-hit topics. Have a ready list. (Your uncle's hernia operation; that movie you saw.)
- Practice deep breathing. There's nothing like a long pause to get the point across: "I *really* don't want to discuss this any longer."
- My aunt has a great technique. If you have to talk to someone who is going to get your goat, keep a coloring book by your side and focus on staying within the lines.

When Can I Stop Telling My Child, "I'm On Your Side"?

When the sun stops shining. When there are no phases to the moon. Some adult children pick up the pieces right after they separate, convinced they made the right decision. Others are much shakier. They are continually looking for support. If your child asks you (for the umpteenth time), "Mom, do you think I'm right?" Smile. Give a hug. That says it all — for the umpteenth time.

Divorce is not the end-all. Many divorced individuals have found it to be a new starting point, and use the sad event as an opportunity for growth and renewal. It is also a time when you and your child can become closer if you can show your support early on and can get past your own emotionality.

Parental Guideposts: Chapter Five

Taking Sides

- Taking sides means saying: "As much as I care for ___, *you* are my priority.
- Remind other members of the family to send the message, "We are here for you."
- Set boundaries with friends and relatives who may be quick to criticize the decision and blame one of the parties.
- Temporarily put your daughter- or son in-law on the back burner.
- Be compassionate with the other side for the sake of your grandchildren.
- Let your child fight his own battles.
- Model family loyalty through your own example.

✎ *Chapter Five: Workbook Exercises*

1. What underlying issues, if any, might prevent you from giving your child 100 percent backup?

2. Write a letter to your child's ex-spouse expressing your feelings. *Don't* send it.

3. Use this scale to determine where individual family members and friends stand in their allegiance to (1) your child (2) to his ex-spouse.

   Completely side with him (her)
   Somewhat side with him (her)
   Do not side with him (her) at all
   No opinion

4. To better understand each position, try to find reasons for this stance.

5. Consult your child about what to tell people who ask about the divorce. Script some pat answers to standard questions such as:

   What went wrong in the marriage?

   How are the children taking it? What are the plans now?

   Did you have any idea there were problems?

6. Consider each of the following and the impact it has on family solidarity. What advice would you give those involved?

> *Helen knows her brother has been unfaithful to his wife. Having been down the same road in her marriage, she turns against him and sides with her sister-in-law.*

> *Jerry's mother never liked his wife. When Jerry announces his separation, she harangues him for marrying her in the first place.*

> *Sheila is angry that her younger sister is unwilling to stay in her marriage. She sides with their parents, who have strong religious convictions against divorce, and tells her sister she should just stick it out.*

Chapter Six

The Road to Your Recovery

The path to family renewal, according to Joan Schraeger Cohen (1994), begins with you. She writes, "If we do not attend to our pain and become whole, what can we accomplish for the good of [our] beleaguered family?" Admittedly, it is not easy to get back on track, especially in high-conflict situations. It is especially difficult when there are complicated financial and child custody issues. There is an unfortunate amount of sludge in divorce — anger, resentment, bitterness — that parents must wade through. Like Nora, who is at the end of her rope, parents look forward to the day they can pick up the pieces and just go on with their lives. In this chapter and the next, we will explore the steps along the path to your recovery and your family's renewal.

Nora's Story

Ben and the twins returned to Seattle when his work project in New Jersey was completed. Because we'd become so close while he and the children were living with us, it was even more difficult to separate emotionally from our son's marital difficulties. The divorce dragged on and on, and so did our involvement. Ben was convinced that Joan was having second thoughts about his being the primary residential parent and looking for excuses to clog up the divorce proceedings to buy time.

Since Ben and Joan's separation, I'd had no peace of mind. I'd heard Ben harangue about court delays and the cost of lawyers until I could quote him chapter and verse. Nevertheless, I would no more think of turning off my cell phone and not taking his calls than deny a dying man his last rites. As time wore on, I found myself sinking lower and lower into despair. Ben's problems followed me everywhere. Even on Gary's birthday — we were looking forward to enjoying a leisurely dinner and going to the opera. Just as we entered the theater, Gary's cell phone rang. We had ten minutes until curtain time. Gary stood in the lobby with the phone pressed to his ear. His mouth was taut. I pointed to my watch. Gary waved me on ahead, but I stood by his side while he talked to Ben through the Overture to *La Bohème*.

"Well," I asked stonily when Gary finally clicked off. "What was that all about?"

"You won't believe this," Gary said. "While he was away, Joan let herself into the house and removed the children's computer and all their video games so Jake and Janice would have something to do when they stay over at her place. Joan told the kids their father is in a better financial position than she is and can replace them. Ben is so furious he's threatening to charge Joan with breaking and entering."

"Oh, no," I said.

"It's okay," Gary whispered, taking my arm and leading me down the aisle to our seats. "I calmed him down and said if he did that, he'd only cause another delay in the settlement."

As hard as I tried, I couldn't keep my mind on the opera. *When would this fighting ever end?* I asked myself. *When would Gary and I get our life back?* Is it any wonder that, as the curtain closed, I wept more copiously for poor Mimi than I'd ever intended?

The truth is I didn't realize the degree to which Ben and Joan's problems were affecting me until almost a year after Ben and Joan separated. I was sitting in a restaurant, and I glanced over to see a young couple with a set of twins sitting at the next table. The next thing I knew, I was crying. Though my intellect had accepted the fact that the marriage was at a dead end, a part of me was still in denial. It took me months to remove Ben and Joan's wedding picture from the table where I displayed all the family photos. I realized that I needed to talk to someone if I was to get past this period of mourning.

•◄ *Nora Moves On* ►•

Let's face it. Like Nora, at some point, you are going to get tired piloting the family boat. There will be days your divorcing child is going to test your patience. You might feel manipulated, consumed by his or her neediness. You may disapprove of a decision, wish your child would ask for your advice, and get tired hearing one more complaint about a former spouse or a difficult grandchild. As much as you would like to, you hesitate to turn down yet another request to babysit or make an emergency house call, run an errand, or prepare a meal.

Your life is in a holding pattern now that your child is single again. Wouldn't you like this divorce mess to be over? Is it on the tip on your tongue to say, "It's time to move on so I can get my life back"?

Many children going through divorce cannot break through the maelstrom of self-pity. Mental health professionals say it takes more than a year for most divorced adults to move past grieving, although there is no set timeline. A lot has to do with the emotional strength of the individual, his or her level of maturity, the duration of the marriage, the circumstances of the breakup, the support systems in place, and the willingness of the individual to actively work the key steps of emotional recovery from divorce (Fisher & Alberti, 2000). The more you can exhibit through your behavior the expectation that your child will get through this crisis, the greater the likelihood your son or daughter will fulfill the prophecy. It is essential that you give yourself the boost that will also elevate your child out of the doldrums of divorce.

Let's see how Nora fared.

Nora's Story Continues

I decided to answer an ad I saw in our local newspaper for a grand-parenting support group. I arranged a meeting with Beth, the facilitator. Beth explained that many of the grandparents had joined because they were in overload taking care of their grandchildren. A few had divorced adult children. She asked me about my motivation for coming to the group.

"I just can't be there for my son anymore. I can't get past the sadness of his marriage breaking up. "It's the ricocheting," I explained. "Sometimes I feel sad, sometimes angry. I still think my son could have done more to save his marriage. I am angrier with my son than I should be since Joan's health crisis. I'm worried about her. Ben is certainly not responsible for Joan's medical problems or the fact that she can't cope with the kids right now. I don't know who to side with."

"Who do you want to side with?" Beth asked.

"My daughter-in-law," I said quietly, and began to cry.

Then Beth asked me about my own family history.

Oh, no, I thought. *I didn't come here to dredge that up.*

She explained that to get some perspective on my reactions to my son's divorce, I should examine my feelings and attitudes about my parents' marriage and then my own

After a minute, I began to describe my family history. Thirty minutes and several tissues later, I was starting to see a bigger picture, and a pattern.

The more I talked, the more I began to realize that I was identifying with my daughter-in-law, who resented being home with the twins while Ben pursued his own career. After all these years, I was still carrying around resentment that I'd stayed home with my children while my sister, for one, was making her mark in corporate America. My mother encouraged me to be a stay-at-home Mom. I felt I had no support back then.

We talked about the guilt I felt for Ben and Joan's failed marriage. On some level, I believed my mothering was inadequate. Beth let me go on and on, wallowing in self-blame. I told her that Gary and I felt we had failed Ben in some way. We should have been able to repair the damage, fix the problem the way we had when our children were younger, when we had control . . . .

That was when Beth stopped me. "There's that word again, Nora. 'Fix,' and the other one — 'control.'"

I took a deep breath. "The other night Gary compared Ben's divorce to a spinout! It reminded me of the time I was the designated driver after a party at my cousin's house. Gary was dozing in the front seat and Ben, Joan and the kids were in the back seat. I hadn't been drinking, but I was groggy from the big dinner, and the hour was late. Suddenly the car hit a patch of black ice. Try as I might, I couldn't prevent the spinout into the opposite lane. Fortunately, the oncoming car saw us and pulled over to avoid the collision. I know there are better drivers than I am, but since I was responsible for my family's safety, I blamed myself for taking the more precarious, dark, back road instead of the highway. Gary's comment brought back those feelings of blame, helplessness - that lack of control that just makes us both so miserable."

Beth and I talked about the changes in my own marriage since Ben and Joan separated. It was true that we'd allowed Ben's problems to dominate our life. Prolonged mourning for the death of my son's marriage was not only hurting my relationship with my husband, it was affecting my relationships with my other children.

I realized then that it was time to do some soul-searching as well as take some steps onto the path of healing for my own marriage and myself. I started by acknowledging that Ben's divorce was not the end of my world, and that it was time to stop blaming myself for any mistakes I might have made in my parenting or for things Gary and I should or should not have done when Ben was younger. Instead of continuing to mourn the loss of my family, I resolved to become my family's healer.

•◄ *Getting Back on Course* ►•

In *The Shelter of Each Other: Rebuilding Our Families* (1996), author and clinical psychologist Mary Pipher, Ph.D. writes:

When children are troubled, we ask, "What have these parents done wrong?" Our professional language traps us into blaming families.... We have overemphasized early development and given families of origin too much responsibility for the lives of their members. We have overlooked how much people learn as adults — especially from their love and work. Personalities can be changed by adult experiences. Many of us have had an experience stepping in when we needed help, a mentor teaching us what we needed most to learn or a family member carrying us love that enabled us to go on in rough times.

After talking to Beth, Nora realized she had to work on her own recovery. It was not fair to Ben or Joan, or to Gary to carry the burden of the divorce on her shoulders. Nora had to learn to distance herself from her children's pain and to take care of herself so she could be available when they needed her.

•◀ If You're Not Okay, I'm Not Okay ▶•

"I was caught in the maelstrom of self-pity."

"I felt paralyzed. There were days I didn't want to get out of bed."

"It's like the bottom had fallen out of my life. There were a million decisions to be made, and I couldn't make a single one."

These are the voices of divorcing adults describing what it felt like in the early stage of their marital breakup. Unsuspecting parents have very similar reactions when they first get the news that their child's marriage is in trouble.

There is no question that difficult days are ahead for the whole family. However, as parents, you are expected to keep up a good front for the sake of the wounded children. Your job is to maintain a steady course for as long as it takes your children to recover.

•◀ The Parent's Road to Recovery ▶•

The parent's road to recovery after a child's divorce is paved with many bricks, including setting boundaries, limiting self-sacrifices, not building resentment, prioritizing goals, relinquishing control, getting back-up, focusing on other relationships, taking time out, listening to your body, and tuning in to your emotions. The road to recovery is going to take time and patience — patience with yourself and patience with your child.

Set Boundaries

Imagine an old-fashioned switchboard, aflame with flashing red lights. You are the operator, fielding questions from in-laws, relatives, and friends who just got wind that your child is getting divorced.

You've answered all the calls. Things quiet down. Now there is only one light that is continually flashing. Need I tell you it's your child? You've gone from staffing a switchboard to answering an emergency hotline.

During the rescue stage, your child needed constant reassurance and support. You responded to every call and, naturally, your ears were fine-tuned to every whimper, every sigh. You may have also noticed in those early days that the "crisis" evaporated rather quickly. It was just a matter of talking your child through his or her fears or giving your input.

If you are still getting these calls four and five times a day, there is no shame in setting some limits. How about for starters, "Dad and I have decided you should call us in the morning when we're fresh" or "We're too exhausted after nine o'clock to take calls."

Nora might have avoided the phone call that ruined her evening at the opera by forewarning Ben that she and Gary were going out for his father's birthday. Without offending Ben, who obviously had a need to talk, she might have said, "Dad will be turning off his cell. Leave a message and we'll call you in the morning if you need to talk."

It's much easier to fade into the background when you know in your own mind that the circumstances surrounding your child's separation and divorce have gone from red to yellow alert. Based on your history together, you can have faith in your child's ability to recoup from the marital crisis. While it may very well be that the same kid who for years survived in the wild suddenly wants Mom and Dad back in the picture — big time — you can make some fairly good predictions as to how much you're really needed and comfortably decrease your involvement accordingly. To determine your child's level of dependence/independence, honestly answer the following:

- How independent was your divorcing child when he or she was living at home?
- Did your child live on his or her own before getting married?
- Did he live alone or with a roommate?
- How often did you see or hear from your child during that period?

- How close were you with your son or daughter before/during the marriage?
- How dependent was your child on his/her spouse?
- Who usually initiates the telephone calls now? You or your child?
- How many times a week on average do you speak or see each other since the separation?
- What is the substance of your conversations? How often is it for some specific need? Or, does your child just need a sounding board?
- Is there a pattern to the calls (particular time of day? after talking to a lawyer? spouse? child?)

You should be able to draw some conclusions from your answers to the questions you just answered about your child's level of dependence/independence in the past and about what current behaviors might be signals that you need to step in and set some boundaries.

One more suggestion: If your child is using your time and energy primarily to badmouth the ex, you should limit the amount of time you spend listening to the gripes. Consider pointing your child in the direction of a support group or counseling where he can get his share of "air time" — and you can get some sleep.

Limit Self-Sacrifices

When I asked parents what effect their child's divorce was having on their own lives, those who lived near their child talked about the amount of time they spent helping their child and how that took so much time away from themselves. Those who lived long distances from their child said they were more than willing to pitch in when needed, and had been traveling more than usual to do so. Parents who could afford it had worked out supplemental financial arrangements if their child requested help, but most parents provided some in-kind support: babysitting, grocery shopping, running errands, or airing out the guestroom. The majority of these parents assumed these would be temporary measures, just until the child could get back on his or her feet. A few realized they would be playing a much longer-running starring role and were willing to make the necessary sacrifices when there were grandchildren.

There are always those parents who feel locked into their children's problems following separation and divorce. Jeanne and Brian are parents who couldn't say no and felt put-upon.

Jeanne, a cheerful widow in her sixties, was used to eating out three or four times a week with friends when she suddenly found herself back in the kitchen, cooking meals — even grocery shopping — for her daughter and grandchildren. In the beginning, she didn't mind pitching in, but after a while she began to resent the time it took away from her social life.

Brian became his single-again daughter's handyman-in-waiting. More than once, she called him — sometimes in the wee hours — when her car wouldn't start or the security system went off. To save her expenses, Brian mowed her lawn in the summer, raked her leaves in the fall, and in the winter, he shoveled snow off her driveway. He blew off his weekends to be available for his daughter and was too tired to pick up the phone to call his buddies to arrange a golf game or go out for a beer in the evenings.

Key Point: If you are giving up your time to be help your child out, ask yourself whether you are enjoying this role. Whatever you decide to do to help your child out, make the decision to do it for you. Do it without asking for anything in return.

Don't Build Resentment

It's no shame to admit that having to be there for your divorced child may not be your first choice at this stage of your life. You spent many years parenting, and then got used to your independence after your children finally got married. It's natural to resent having to give up that independence. Some parents refuse to be a lifeboat when they disapprove of the child's decision to end the marriage. One young woman who got divorced for the second time recalls her mother's words when she needed help: *I told you not to marry that guy. It's your bed; now lie in it.* I'm not sure I agree with that parent's attitude, but at least this mother was upfront. Many parents look back rather than forward when their children ask for help.

Know that resentment is a two-way street. When you go the extra mile for your children, your efforts may be misinterpreted. Guard against sending the message that says, "I'm doing this for you because you aren't capable of handling the situation on your own." Your child will resent your taking control. It is much better to offer temporary assistance until your son or daughter feels secure enough to take over the reins. Keep in mind that a lot of guilt is associated with your child's request for help. Divorce is in many ways demeaning. It is admitting failure. Your adult child may resent having to ask for help and may feel obligated to you afterward as in Betty's case, when she was caught in a bind because her father insisted on paying her rent:

> *"My ex was deliberately late with my living allowance. Dad knew how crazy I got at the end of the month when I didn't have enough money to pay all my bills. I wanted to get a job, but Dad said if I stayed home with the kids, it would make the judge more sympathetic, and I'd get more in the settlement So I gave in to him, but now I'm sorry that I listened to Dad. In the end, I didn't get more money, and I know I would have preferred carrying my own weight from the very beginning."*

Some divorced adults are made to feel indebted to their parents long after their divorce.

> *Dolly's mother bailed her out of an abusive marriage. The payback was that her mother expected her daughter to care for her when she became an invalid. Dolly never remarried and now resents sacrificing her own happiness on the altar of her past mistakes.*

Set Priorities

More than one parent approaching retirement has had to put his or her plans on hold when a child gets divorced.

> *Jerry was sixty-five when his daughter Tara and her husband split up. Even though Jerry had a lucrative offer from a buyer interested in taking over his insurance company, he decided not to sell until his daughter and three grandchildren were back on their feet. His divorced family was his priority.*

Flora, a former schoolteacher, was all set to sell her house and buy a condominium in Ft. Lauderdale when she found out her daughter and son-in-law were separating. She decided to wait another year. One year stretched into two, two into three. The opportunity passed her by although her daughter had never asked her to put aside her retirement plans.

Some might argue that Jerry and Flora were too accommodating; that it is not selfish for parents to want to fulfill their dreams. On the other hand, many parents say having responsibility for their child and grandchildren has given them a second lease on life. One grandmother told me she'd never been so energized. Taking care of her grandchildren was more fun than going to the local senior center and hanging out with the "codgers." She was spending more time with younger women she met at the grandkids' nursery school and was enjoying "going back in time."

Establish your priorities and make sure they mesh with your child's. She may have no idea you are making these adjustments to satisfy her needs.

Suggestion: Make two lists: your goals and your child's needs. Prioritize them. Then ask your child to take a look at your list. Don't be surprised if your child has a completely different spin on what you consider uppermost.

Relinquish Control

Initially, your child may be too shaky to make his or her own decisions and therefore wants your input. It is not always a comfortable spot to be in, especially if your child is trying to avoid responsibility and starts making it a habit.

When her daughter kept coming to her, Kenya was very forthright about wanting her to stand on her own two feet and figure things out for herself. She told her, "When I got divorced, I made a big mistake letting Mama take care of me. I never learned to make my own way. Well, a lot has changed since my time. I don't want my baby following in my footsteps."

It can be a relief when children turn to friends for advice, and are not solely dependent on family. In many instances, adult children *prefer* that support because friends will tell them what they want to hear. Recently I was in a coffee shop and overheard two young men discussing their divorces. It was clearly a situation of misery loving company. The friend, who was apparently an old hand at divorce, was advising his companion to move on. "This is your time, buddy. Just forget the f—ing wife and kids." I doubted that the young man's parents would have offered advice in just that way.

Get Back-up

Grace's daughter went back to school to get a nursing degree and dropped the kids off at her parents' house every morning. Grace fed them breakfast and drove them to school. In the afternoon she picked the grandkids up and took them to their after-school activities and stayed with them until her daughter came home around 6:00. She found the routine invigorating in the beginning and loved spending all that time with the grandchildren. Later, when she realized she had taken on more than she had bargained for, she called the other grandmother, who was only too happy to share the duties.

Call for reinforcements when you find you are bearing too much of your child's burden. Support, by the way, has no gender. There was a time when men let women pick up the slack when it came to family. Today's grandfathers would have to be hiding in some dark cave not to be aware of the pressures on their single-again daughters and the emotional needs of their grandchildren. Your divorced children should expect as much support from their fathers (many of whom are children of divorce themselves) as they do from their mothers. I recall chatting happily with a grandfather at a fast-food chain restaurant while our grandchildren were tumbling together in the outdoor play area. This grandfather was bragging that since his daughter separated from his son-in-law, she had gone back to school in addition to holding a full-time job, and while it was hard on him taking care of his grandson in the evenings after work, he knew his daughter was working toward a goal. I meet more and more grandfathers who find that fulfilling the role of an absentee parent provides greater enjoyment than when they raised their own progeny.

Focus on Your Other Relationships

Speaking of spouses and partners, many widowed or late-in-life divorced parents remarry and want to devote the bulk of their time to their new partners — not their adult children. In addition, many new partners resent having to share space and financial resources with their spouse's single-again son or daughter and children. One older gentleman who took a late-in-life second trip to the altar was straightforward:

"When I agreed to love, honor and cherish, I didn't count on love, honoring and cherishing Bernice's daughter and her three kids."

Guard also against your child's divorce spilling over into the time you spend with friends.

Kiran noticed that his son's problems dominated his conversation whenever he and his wife got together with friends who wanted news about the couple. "It was impossible to have an evening out without talking about our kids' divorce. My wife and I made a pact not to answer more than one or two questions when we went out socially. Our friends got the hint pretty quickly that we wanted to spend a relaxing evening getting away from our kids' problems.

Take care your child's problems aren't pulling you and your spouse in different directions.

Amanda went to see a marriage counselor, fearing her own marriage was headed for disaster. She began to notice that she and her husband, Jack, were sparring more than ever since the kids split. The latest incident had occurred when she overheard Jack criticize her son's lawyer. Amanda bounded into the living room and accused her husband of undermining their son's confidence. Before they knew it, Amanda and Jack were engaged in a screaming match while their son stood helplessly on the sidelines, wishing he had kept his mouth shut and not asked his father for advice.

This is the time your child needs the strength of both parents if he or she is lucky enough to have the two of you for support. Not all parents see eye to eye as to how the divorce should be handled. Agree to disagree in private. It's not fair for your child or grandchildren to have to tiptoe around the folks whenever the subject of the "big D" comes up. Make time to invest in your own marriage for the sake of those who are depending on you to pull the team ahead.

Take Time Out

Part and parcel of your own recovery is finding enjoyment with friends and family. Healing takes place when you can do for others. If you've stepped away from community life, make the time to get involved again. You can volunteer, become involved in your church or synagogue, join a club, or take part in an educational or recreational activity — do things to get your mind off your child's divorce.

If you are not able to take time out, chances are you are feeling overextended and overwhelmed. Too many parents are buried under the weight of "ought to" and wind up exhausted or resentful when it comes to meeting their child's needs. Try to be realistic when it comes to the amount of time you can spend and how much energy you really can invest into the situation. Decide what it is you truly wish to achieve to help stabilize your family, and prioritize towards that goal. You can't do it all, and shouldn't have to.

Listen to Your Body

The road to personal recovery includes taking care of your health. Parents admit to being so frustrated and emotionally drained by their divorcing child's problems that they lose interest in sex, they overeat, and they drink too much. One mother said after spending a marathon session with her son listening to all his complaints about the ex, she went out and bought a pack of cigarettes, years after kicking the habit.

Has your child's divorce drained you physically? Today more and more parents are taking on the role of active grandparenting when their children separate or get divorced. They help with carpooling, take the kids to dentist and doctor's appointments, attend school events, and arrange play dates, squeezing all this into their busy schedules. One grandmother told me she agreed to watch her toddler grandson five days a week and was running herself ragged. I met her

> ## *Parental Guideposts: Chapter Six*
>
> ### *The Road to Your Recovery*
>
> - Establish boundaries.
> - Limit self-sacrifice.
> - Don't build resentment.
> - Set priorities.
> - Relinquish control.
> - Get back-up. (Support knows no gender.)
> - Focus on your other relationships.
> - Take time out for yourself.
> - Listen to your body's physical and emotional needs.
> - Seek counseling if you can't get past the emotionality.

in a grandparent support group. When it was her turn to speak, she said she was lonely, depressed, and burned out. "Why do you keep up this routine day after day?" I asked Jane. "I'm too ashamed to tell my daughter that I can't do this anymore. She has so many other worries." Most of the other grandmothers in the group agreed with her. Rather than own up that they were exhausted or frustrated, they were playing the role of martyrs.

The instinct to protect and do for our children is strong - whether they're unhappy infants or hurting adults. Franco was unaware of the stress his son's divorce was causing until he went to the dentist:

"The last time I went to the dentist, he asked me if anything was bothering me. I said my kids were in the middle of a divorce, and I asked how he knew there was something wrong. "Well, at this rate you're going to need all new fillings," he told me. "You've been grinding your teeth down to stubs."

Staying balanced is important during stressful times. Your body is quick to send you signals to slow down, get more rest, eat right, and exercise regularly. If you fall apart at the seams, you won't be effective in rebuilding your family!

Tune in to Your Emotions

When you become emotionally overwrought, you can't be there for your other kids or your mate. If you want to get your children through tough times, if you want to preserve your family, you can't allow their anger and pain to become *your* anger and pain. When you cannot get past all that emotionality, it's time to seek help. Nora found a helpful counselor and support group. Others can get help from their clergyperson, caring and supportive friends, or from a human resource counselor at work — larger organizations often provide such employee assistance free of charge. The exercises at the end of this chapter will help you do some soul-searching about your feelings and reactions to your child's divorce. I suggest you take a few minutes and read them. Just thinking about your answers is a first step on your road to recovery.

✎ *Chapter Six: Workbook Exercises*

1. Take a minute to answer the following questions to understand your emotional and physical response to your child's divorce:

   - What are some of your emotions when you think about your child's divorce?

   - Describe any occasions that trigger these feelings.

   - Note any change in feelings between when you first got the news your child was getting a divorce and how you currently feel about the breakup.

   - What kind of support are you presently giving your child? Will you be withdrawing any of this support?

   - Are you suffering from any new physical ailments since your child's divorce? Have you sought help from a doctor, dentist, chiropractor, etc.?

   - What plans, if any, have you put on hold because of your child's divorce?

   - When can you go forward with these plans?

2. You will find this exercise helpful in understanding your response to your child's divorce. Describe what you believe are the similarities and differences in your marriage and your parents' marriage. Do the same for your marriage and your child's marriage. Can you draw any conclusions?

3. Begin Your Recovery Plan

Dr. Mary Pipher in her book *The Shelter of Each Other: Rebuilding Our Families* (1996) suggests that families that have experienced trauma such as a sudden death of a family member can design "healing ceremonies" to help move them forward. Parents of divorced children can facilitate their own and their family's recovery after the trauma of divorce by bringing family members together who would support one another. Birthdays, family picnics, trips to the theater or beach, a mini-vacation to a cabin or ski lodge, a day of shopping, a visit to an amusement park, etc. are excellent opportunities to get your family together.

> Take a moment to plan an event that your family would enjoy doing together. Work out the details and decide your guest list.

> What are some of the obstacles to having this kind of get-together?

> Are there ways to overcome these obstacles?

Chapter Seven

Supporting Your Child Post-Divorce

Nora's Story

It had been nearly two years after Ben and Joan's separation, and I was still on an emotional merry-go-round.

"I try to be supportive whenever Ben wants to talk," I told Beth, the leader of my grandparent support group, "but I thought that once the divorce was over and done with I'd be able to fold my tent and walk away."

I'd spent another sleepless night after Ben's last phone call. I jumped on one of the other members in my group who had this "perfect" relationship with her son and was complaining about her difficult daughter-in-law. Her issues seemed so trivial compared to mine.

"A divorce takes on a life of its own," Beth said. "Your son is just trying to hold his day together. Unless you've been through it yourself, it's hard to understand."

And I didn't understand. It seemed to me that by now the situation in Seattle should have improved. Ben and Joan had negotiated a joint custody arrangement, which meant they had equal say in any decisions affecting the children's welfare. I felt sorry for the twins, who were being jockeyed back and forth between parents. They spent one night a week and alternate weekends sleeping over at their mother's house. Their holidays were split down the middle. This year it was going to be Christmas with Mom, Easter with Dad. Joan had the children three weeks during the summer. She was already planning a trip to Paris, knowing she'd be too busy to take the trip she'd dreamed of once she was in law school. My ten-year-old granddaughter was thrilled at the prospect of seeing the Eiffel Tower, but her brother was angry he'd be missing the last session of soccer camp. "Who wants to visit some dumb country where no one speaks English?" he'd complained. Conflict; always conflict.

Joan was waiting for the results of her law school admission test. She'd always been a good student, and I had no doubt she'd have her choice of schools. The question on everyone's minds was where she'd go and how that would affect the twins. The most practical solution was to have the children live with their dad full-time. Everything was still up in the air, which made things that much more difficult for Ben.

I remembered when my son called to say the divorce was signed, sealed and delivered, Gary and I broke out a bottle of champagne. We should have left it on ice because it didn't take long for new storm clouds to gather.

Post-divorce there were new disagreements: inconsiderate last minute changes in the visitation schedule; Joan refusing to pay her share for repairing the roof before they sold their house; hard feelings that Ben was getting the oak desk and not the matching file cabinet; all the tales carried back and forth by the children that Mom said this or Dad said that. Would this ever end?

●◀ *Welcome to Reality* ▶●

Nora is now experiencing the next phase of her son's divorce. Just when she thought the dust had finally settled, a new windstorm begins to blow. Rather than fold up her tent, Nora realizes she must move it to a new location on the battlefield — back behind the lines. It's time for her to extricate herself from the situation. Ben is in the process of rebuilding his life, and Nora needs to understand that much of what he is experiencing is fairly predictable.

California psychologist Dr. Constance Ahrons (*The Good Divorce*, 1994) calls this phase the "emotional" process of divorce: the grueling disruptions in everyday life; the stress, ambivalence, power struggles, and contradictory feelings after the initial crisis has passed. It's when the reality of the divorce hits home.

Therapists Bruce Fisher, Ed.D. and Robert Alberti, Ph.D., in their popular book, *Rebuilding: When Your Relationship Ends* (2000), point out "There is an adjustment process after divorce — with a beginning, an end, and specific steps of learning along the way." The steps to rebuilding are like climbing a mountain, and for most divorcees, it is not an easy journey. You are likely to be barraged with the whining and complaining that accompanies this uphill battle. It's good to be prepared with the right response.

I've numbered the complaints that follow for the sake of convenience, but their order is arbitrary. I'm sure you can add to my list, but let's begin with the ones I've heard from the many parents of divorced children who were kind enough to share their stories.

Complaint #1: "I'll never recover from the financial devastation of my divorce."

This complaint has to do with the real fear of loss of economic power that women, in particular, experience when they get divorced. It is likely to be one of the first complaints you will hear, and the one that is most likely to draw your sympathy and require a response. While it is true that your daughter will be more likely to experience a decline in her standard of living if she had been financially dependent on her spouse, your son will also worry about money. The reality is that today many married couples survive on two incomes, and when partners split, there are financial adjustments on both ends. Men complain about losing their kids, their house, and a substantial chunk of money, and feeling harnessed by their future financial obligations, especially when they remarry and support two families. They speak passionately about being thrown into debt because they cannot keep up with court-ordered child-support payments (in some states, they can run thirty percent or more of gross income.) and of being hauled into court time and time again by ex-spouses seeking more money.

Nevertheless, it is largely true that divorced women with children hit the wall financially when fathers renege on their financial responsibilities. Susan Dominus reported in the Sunday *New York Times* (May 8, 2005) that "although child-support payments have crept up in recent years, in 2001 only 52 percent of divorced mothers received full child-support payments . . . . Fathers' rights groups have a tall order explaining those statistics, convincing judges — and the country at large — that if fathers skip town, or refuse payments, it's a function of how unfairly family courts treat them rather than the very reason that the courts treat fathers the way they do."

The issues of parental financial responsibility were discussed at length in chapter 3, but it bears repeating since so many parents are pulled in post-divorce and still struggle with their financial obligation. If that is where you find yourself, and unless you plan to be in the game long-term, remember Lao Tzu's old Chinese proverb: *"Give a man a fish; you have fed him for today. Teach a man to fish; and you have fed him for a lifetime."* As much as you may want to, know you cannot iron out the wrinkles of economic inequity. You'll only add to the problem if you create a long-lasting financial dependency. It's not your place to even out the score. What you want to do is help your child acquire the skills to become more competitive in the job market and more budget conscious at home.

> *When Wyonna's daughter complained she wasn't making enough money as a teacher's aide, her mother suggested she consider selling real estate. Delta always had an eye for property, and she was good with people. Wyonna babysat while Delta went to school, and she pitched in on the weekends after Delta got her agent's license. Wyonna's reward wasn't the fancy dinner when Delta closed her first deal; it was the pride on her daughter's face that she'd come this far after her divorce.*

What if you're convinced your child got the short end of the stick in the divorce settlement? What if you know in your heart that his or her woes about finances are justified? It's a bad idea to keep harping on the inequities of the financial arrangement, and, worse yet, to compare your child's and the ex's lifestyles. Why rub salt in the wounds? Often the costs of going back to court to reopen the case are not worth the gains (lawyers usually come out ahead), and the decision needs to be your child's, not yours.

Experts in the field of marital counseling say that divorced partners often engage in an economic power struggle as a way of staying attached. Don't be surprised if your son or daughter is still haggling over some relatively valueless item acquired during the marriage — a shag rug that neither one liked. You might remind your child of the emotional energy expended reclaiming a spoil of war. Know, too, that an ex will withhold money to punish a former spouse. Rather than get involved, if it's your child who is at fault, remind him or her who is really getting hurt. You might also point out the legal consequences for this kind of behavior. Then cross your fingers and hope for the best.

Complaint #2: "My life is in shambles"

Expect that your son or daughter is going to experience a dramatic shift in identity, especially if the marriage began when the couple was very young. Your daughter is no longer a wife; your son is no longer a husband. More than likely, your child is orienting himself or herself back into the singles' scene. Friends and family will treat your child differently. Married friends may cut her off, thinking she is a threat now that she is back in circulation. The ink on the divorce decree isn't dry before Aunt Alice mentions (rather casually) when your son is sitting at the dinner table that her secretary is also newly divorced. Imagine that! What a coincidence.

As a parent, you may observe your child "morphing" before your eyes. You may not be terribly pleased with what you see. That steady-as-a-rock son chucks his job to pick mangos in Madagascar. That shy, retiring daughter is suddenly notching her garter-belt with sexual conquests.

I'm going to call this the third individuation. (The first one had to do with the "terrible twos" and the second with adolescence.) Look at this third personality shift occurring after the trauma of divorce as a period in time when your child is struggling with self-concept. Rebellion can be troubling for parents who worry about the effect all this is having on grandchildren who need a stable role model. The best advice is to be patient, wait it out, and hope your child comes back to his or her senses. In the meantime, you can be that role model for your grandchildren and a source of reason and comfort for your child.

Shifts in identity may also have to do with disclosure about some well-kept secret about your child when he was married. Disclosures may have to do with drug addiction, mental illness, love affairs, domestic violence, sexual orientation, etc. Let's look at one such situation:

> *After she announced her separation from Lloyd, Miranda told her mother that she was planning to move in with a female companion. She explained that for years she'd been struggling with her sexual identity but was afraid to reveal it because she knew her mother loved Lloyd. Miranda's mother was a pastor. She counseled many gay men and women in her ministry and was sympathetic to their plight. She'd long suspected there were problems in her daughter's marriage but was surprised to learn Miranda was a lesbian. In the end, Miranda's mother maintained relationships with both her daughter's partner and her ex-son-in-law.*

Despite society's growing liberal attitudes, parents may have problems reconciling homosexuality with their religious beliefs and feel threatened, guilt-ridden, or embarrassed by their child's disclosure. If you find yourself in this position, there are support groups, such as Parents and Friends of Lesbians and Gays (PFLAG), where you can discuss your issues with others in similar circumstances. Seek advice from professionals who can answer your questions and help you understand your attitudes and biases. If you can, reach out to your child, who values and needs your acceptance, even if you can't give your approval. Know that your children may choose many roads. If you can journey with them, your family will not lose its way.

Complaint # 3: "I've lost my kids."

Your son or daughter may become a disenfranchised parent. If the former spouse is granted full physical custody or is intentionally making it difficult for the nonresidential parent to have a relationship with his or her kids, your child may very well be cut out of the family picture. Once the divorce is finalized, your daughter may become the full-time caretaker, exhausted by the responsibility and, most likely, coping with a disgruntled child who misses Daddy. On the other hand, if your son is the weekend dad, he will feel as if he has lost access to his own children and will resent having to get permission to see them. You can best support your child by understanding this parental role shifting and the guilt and pressure it causes.

The experts say it is beneficial to children (they make a better adjustment) when both parents are involved (married or divorced). In some states, joint custody has become the predominant form of child custody after divorce, accounting for nearly half of child custody awards. While the number of fathers gaining custody of their children has risen from 7.5 percent in 1995 to 15 percent today, and there is a trend toward so-called equal or "shared" parenting, the courts still overwhelmingly favor maternal custody, according to C. Haley's *Dads Today Divorce Series* (*www.dadstoday.com*). Your son may be a father who is very involved with his children post-divorce, spending and enjoying quality time with them since the breakup. Today, an increasing number of fathers are advocating for a 50-50 custody split and are awarded joint physical custody. Be aware, however, that even with joint physical custody, if the mother controls the amount of time the child spends with the father (perhaps even defying court orders and creating obstacles in the way of visitation), she will typically also assume the role of primary authority and make most of the daily decisions affecting the child

It is possible that your son will voluntarily decrease the time he spends with his biological child if he remarries or moves out of state or there are circumstances pulling father and child apart. According to the American Academy of Matrimonial Lawyers, in their treatise, *Stepping Back from Anger* (1998), "Roughly one-third of the children of divorce lose contact with one of their parents, depriving them of years of adult guidance, support and love."

According to the 2000 U.S. Census Bureau Current Population Survey, twenty percent of children have no contact with non-residential fathers or see them only a few times a year; only twenty-five percent have weekly visits. Another study reported by the Children's Rights Council in Washington D.C. (May 20, 2005) notes: "Sadly, most children of divorce see their non-custodial parent only four days a month, which is not enough whether that parent is a mother or father." Custody issues are complex. Have a look at Appendix A for a walk-through about the various custody arrangements and the associated terminology. It is important to understand some of these definitions as custody arrangements can affect your access to your grandchildren.

Successful co-parenting is a skill not all divorced couples acquire. Nothing causes more dissension in a family than when parents are adversaries and children are caught in the power struggle. Your daughter may tell you that the children's father spoils them or fills them with junk food when he takes them out for the day. Your son may complain that the ex-wife puts him down in front of the children. You might gently remind your child that this same dad who stuffs the kids with junk food didn't quibble about paying for the new hockey stick; and the mom who puts him down is learning how to coach soccer. Tread gently, however. If you overplay your hand, you may be accused of "going to the other side."

Here are three tips to help support your child who is single parenting:
- Don't get in a situation where you are "triangulating" — getting between your child and the grandchildren, or between your child and the ex. Let the parents work out their issues.
- Support your child's authority.
- Don't disparage either parent when you are with your grandchildren.

Complaint # 4: "I'll never trust another man (woman)."

If your child has been betrayed, you can predict there will be a fear of intimacy and commitment. Sara noticed that her recently divorced daughter spends all her free time surfing the matchmaking sites on the Internet but never sets up a date. On the flip side, her other divorced child, Andrew, flits from flower to flower like a honeybee.

People react differently when they have been "dumped." One child may be gun-shy of any future involvement. Another plays the Casanova, over-compensating for having been hurt. It takes time to re-establish self-worth. Be patient. The best strategy is to offer the safety net of a loving family where your child doesn't have to put on a public face.

Complaint # 5: "I'm lonely."

The experts say that loneliness is one of the most difficult adjustments post-divorce. They also say that loneliness can be healing. Sound like a contradiction? According to Dr. Bruce Fisher, who conducted divorce process seminars for over twenty-three years, an important step in rebuilding when a relationship ends is learning to be comfortable in one's own skin. Loneliness makes space for self-discovery. "A mentally healthy person maintains a balance between being with others and being alone" (Fisher & Alberti 2000).

You may notice that now that your child is divorced, he or she is filling every waking hour with busyness or work.

Tamara joined two health clubs, enrolled in three adult education classes, volunteered to head a town committee, and filled her Palm Pilot with luncheon and dinner dates. Sidney gets into the office by 7:30 a.m. and leaves around 10 p.m. He buries himself in work on the weekends. It's a wonder he takes time out for his children.

Overloading with "things to do" is one way to shut out loneliness. Leaping into a serious relationship right after divorce is another. Neither is a good strategy.

The high divorce rate in our society produces a very large pool of eligible divorce(e)s. Most of them are willing to risk remarriage. The U.S. Census Bureau's divorce and remarriage findings (2002) are that most remarriages after the first divorce take place within five years. The median number of years for males (generally age thirty-four) is 3.3 years between first and second marriages, and for females (median age thirty-two years) is 3.1 years. Not surprisingly, the remarriage rate for women (particularly younger women without children whose marriage was of a short duration) is leveling off while they take their time choosing the next mate and building careers.

The implication in all this data is that you, as a parent, should prepare yourself to meet that next "special someone" at some point. How will you handle it? My suggestion: Be open — even if you are still mourning the loss of the former in-law and not thrilled with the co-habitation arrangement that is so popular today. Chances are, if your child is hesitant to commit to another relationship, he or she may opt for a trial period with someone, and you will have to decide how to handle that situation as well

While it is certainly reasonable for you to object on moral and religious grounds, there is danger in putting up too many roadblocks. Your child may take another route — far away from family. I'm not proposing that you go against your principles and accept the "living-together" arrangement. I am suggesting that it's in your best interests to have a frank and loving conversation with your child, rather than have her think you don't like her new boyfriend.

Unfortunately, right after adjusting to the realities of a child's divorce, parents may have to reconcile themselves to behaviors they deem unacceptable. (I mentioned some of these in chapter 4.) As the parents, however, you set the standard about what goes on in your own home.

One mother I talked to said she was perfectly comfortable telling Christina, "What you do on your own time is your business. But when you are in my home, I expect you to respect my rules." Mom made up the bed in the guest room so it was quite clear that she would not tolerate any hanky panky under her roof. By the way, the daughter was in her mid-forties and the boyfriend a successful Wall Street mogul. (More about this in chapter 10, "When Your Child Remarries.")

Admittedly, your children can create some confusion in your life. Here is another example:

> *"A year and a half after his divorce, my son moved in with April and her two children. Recently they bought a house, but the couple does not show any signs of getting married. I know nowadays that parents are supposed to look the other way. On one hand, I understand that neither my son nor his girlfriend wants to rush into anything, but I think this is terribly confusing for my grandkids. My problem is this: My husband and I have talked about taking everyone to Disneyland, and my grandkids are disappointed we keep putting the trip off. We don't know what to do."*

In this situation, Elena and her husband should let their consciences be their guide. If they think that by paying for a vacation they are stamping "approved" on an arrangement they don't, in fact, approve of, it's probably best to put off the trip to Disneyland for the time being.

It's a tough call — how to support your child when you don't approve of his or her behavior without jeopardizing your future relationship when and if the couple should marry. Again, it's best to be upfront about your boundaries without being unnecessarily critical of the arrangement. Your son or daughter has a right to order his or her own adult life, but not yours.

Complaint # 6: "Maybe I would have been better off if I hadn't got divorced."

More than one adult child has called a weary parent in the middle of the night to say she or he made a terrible mistake. If that happens to you, try to reason with your son or daughter who, after reliving the past before and after the divorce, is convinced he or she made the wrong decision. Listen to Tina's story:

> On the day that would have been her twelfth wedding anniversary, Tina came to her parents and said she never should have divorced Ira. Her parents were horrified, having lived through the avalanche the divorce had caused. They were still paying off the lawyer's fees. Tina's father reminded his daughter that her husband had been unfaithful and mentally abusive. He enumerated all the problems she had had in her marriage. Tina was inconsolable.

What this befuddled father didn't understand is that the bonds of marriage do not necessarily fall away with a divorce decree. Time whitewashes a lot of graffiti.

According to Dr. Constance Ahrons (1994), the ambivalence about the decision to divorce can linger for years, even when a relationship had been very bad for a long time. Years later, an event, a gift, a photograph, a special occasion can trigger memories of a pleasant time. Bubbles of sentimentality rise to the surface, even in the worst divorce scenario. Even if adult children want to let go of the past, they cannot when the couple has offspring. They are constant reminders of the marriage.

Ahrons counsels: "At first...divorcing couples — in their ambivalence — may deny any good memories about their ex. Although this wards off the pain of the immediate loss, it also requires shutting down other emotions. Anyone who relies on denial as a major form of psychic protection limits his or her ability to form healthy relationships in the future — the very ability needed most of the time."

Parents who are not embittered can create balance by acknowledging the good as well as the bad in their child's past marriage. One mother told me that she introduced her son's girlfriend to members of the family by showing her photos in an old family album.

> *"There were photos taken at my son's wedding I hadn't removed. I was embarrassed at first. My son came over, looked at some of the guests, and began to tell funny stories about the wedding. We actually laughed our heads off. It was all very natural."*

Complaint #7:" I will never see the light at the end of the tunnel."

The end of a marriage (or ending of any significant relationship) is bound to trigger a natural grieving process for you, your child, and other family members. Many divorce counselors use Elisabeth Kübler-Ross's five-stage paradigm developed in her seminal study working with terminally ill patients (*On Death and Dying*, 1969), which parallels the emotional passages leading to rebuilding after divorce. Kübler-Ross's well-regarded though not universal stages (they would be different in some other cultures) include: Denial, Anger, Bargaining, Depression, and Acceptance. The sequence is not necessarily linear. Often stages overlap. Let's take a closer look at what these emotional passages look like.

Stage One: Denial

In the beginning, it is hard to control emotions, especially if the breakup comes as a surprise. Typical reactions are shock, fear, and a sense of isolation. "This can't be happening! What am I going to do?"

Stage Two: Anger

It's natural to feel cheated and disappointed with the state of affairs. After all, the family is disassembling; the future looks bleak or frightening. Anger may have many targets. Your child may be furious that he didn't read the handwriting on the wall sooner. You may be angry with the in-laws or any friends you hold responsible for the marital problems. Perhaps there is a problematic child or a spouse's demanding job that gets the blame. Even Fate! Expressing anger is healthy as long as the person does not lose control and can move past the anger. In your child's case, moving past anger may begin when he or she assumes some responsibility for the breakup.

Stage Three: Bargaining

In this stage, we look for a way to push away the pain. People engage in bargaining by entering into some kind of agreement with themselves, the Deity, or with the ex-mate. Bargaining is a way to try to postpone the inevitable. Your child may hasten to "fix" the problem, in a last ditch effort to save the marriage. "If I change my spending habits (... lose weight, ... spend less time at the office, ... agree to move to New Zealand, etc.), I just know we can get back together."

Stage Four: Depression

Even if your child initiated the breakup, he or she may experience a profound sense of loss when it is no longer possible to deny the fact that the marriage is over. Many people experiencing separation and divorce admit to having "crazy," even suicidal feelings. Fortunately, most people get past depression. However, when the depression interferes with normal daily functioning, professional help is called for. Be aware of uncontrollable mood swings, crying jags, serious eating problems, sleeping disorders, physical ailments such as headaches, ulcers, backaches, and other stress-related symptoms. These can be managed if the individual is willing to work through the depression and move on to the next stage.

Stage Five: Acceptance and Rebuilding

This final stage calls for objectivity and the awareness that experience is a teacher. With acceptance comes a sense of freedom — of being able to put the past behind and get beyond the loss. Rebuilding begins with learning to feel comfortable with oneself before jumping into the next relationship.

Not all individuals experience all these stages or manifest them in the same way. The timeline is different for everyone. A lot depends on the individual's attitude about the breakup and coping ability as evidenced in the following story:

> ## *Parental Guideposts: Chapter Seven*
>
> ### *Supporting Your Child Post-Divorce*
>
> - Acknowledge your child's issues related to finances, shifting roles and parenting.
> - Allow your child to vent conflicting feelings about the decision to get divorced.
> - Look for signs of healing.
> - Begin to disengage after the rescue period.
> - Keep track of where you, your child, and members of the family are in the stages of emotional recovery.
> - Be patient. There is no set time for recovery. If your child is stuck, suggest he or she seek help.

Lucille called me from out-of-state to share her story. She told me that her daughter Amy had been married for two and a half years, divorced for ten years, and during her marriage had suffered major physical ailments. Lucille thought that Amy had been waiting for her to give permission for her to leave her husband, which Lucille did, once she realized how ill and unhappy the girl had become. The mother told me that Amy had not dated much since the breakup. I could tell from the way she was talking about her daughter that Lucille felt Amy was too "gun-shy," but she wanted her to meet someone. Mom said Amy was too picky. She'd recently encouraged her to join a computer dating service. It was fairly clear to me that Amy and Lucille had a very different concept about rebuilding after divorce. Mom saw it in terms of remarrying; Amy saw it in terms of living on her own, working, and just dating.

As an observer, you may be able to monitor your child during the grief process, picking up any signals that your child is stuck and needs professional help. You will also want to acknowledge the progress you are making toward your own recovery. It might be a good idea, at this point, to go back and see where you and your child are on the emotional reaction continuum. (Do the same for your grandchildren, your spouse, or any in-laws.)

Although you cannot be responsible for your child's healing or growth, you *can* create an environment that allows that healing and growth to take place. Make the effort to understand where he or she is emotionally, and do what you can short of turning your own life inside-out.

In the next two chapters, we will look at the special issues facing grandchildren, and explore the role you can play providing the support and comfort they need as they journey through their parents' divorce.

✎ *Chapter Seven: Workbook Exercises*

1. These are typical complaints family counselors hear from clients who are at different points in the emotional stages of grief. Identify each person's stage:

   a. *My daughter never goes out. She just stays in her room and mopes. I tell her it's time to get out and meet people.*

   Daughter is at stage _____
   Mom is at stage _____

   b. *My son is getting married to a woman who isn't half the person his Mary was.*

   Mom is at stage _____
   Son is at stage _____

   c. *I had a blow-out with my father because he won't go to his granddaughter's graduation because my ex is going to be there.*

   Daughter is at stage _____
   Father is at stage _____

   d. *I just know that my kids would rather spend Thanksgiving with their father and his ex than be with me.*

   Kids' mother is at stage _____
   Kids are at stage _____

2. Indicate which of the following are concerns for your child. Describe the specific problem(s) from his or her vantage point.

   a. Finances

   b. Parenting

   c. Friendships/Social Status

3. Use this scale. How conflicted do you think your child is about the decision to get divorced?

Not at all conflicted . . . . . . *Very unhappy about the decision*

10 9 8 7 6 5 4 3 2 1

4. If you have been very involved in helping your child, it may be time to pull back. Think about the specific kind of withdrawal actions you need to take and the best way to accomplish this without showing a lack of support.

Part III

Strengthening Family Bonds

Your Child's Divorce:
What to Expect — What You Can Do

Chapter Eight

Grandchildren in Crisis

Nora's Story

The most difficult part of being a grandparent after Ben and Joan split was putting up a good front and hiding my pain. I'm sure I was as transparent as glass. The twins' radar picked up that things were different now. There was that empty chair when we sat around the dining room table, the missing wedding photo album I used to display in the study. To protect me, Jake and Janice never talked about their mother, and I avoided bringing up her name, thinking I was protecting them. We never spelled it out, but the letters D-I-V-O-R-C-E flashed on and off like a neon sign whenever our family got together.

Ben and Joan had done the best they could to reassure the children that the divorce wasn't their fault. Nevertheless, I could tell that something was going on in those two little heads. During a trip I took out to Seattle, I noticed subtle changes had occurred in their personalities. Jake, in particular, was moodier, balky, and quick to anger. Janice was clingy. She'd developed some nervous habits like twisting her hair into knots and biting her nails. I was upset about the changes I saw in my grandkids. Ben said they just needed time to get used to the idea that he and Joan were never getting back together.

As time and life went on, the memories of the divorce began to fade. I had put aside the agonies of the crisis stage and started to focus on rebuilding. I assumed Jake and Janice were doing the same, but I was very much mistaken. This is how I knew that they were still dealing with the fallout.

It was school break. Ben was away on a business trip, and Joan had exams, so I volunteered to watch the twins at Ben's place. I was folding laundry and could hear Jake and Janice squabbling in their room. Then there was a sudden crash, and I went running to see what happened.

"What's going on here?" I cried out. A night table was up-ended next to the bed.

"Janice hid the last piece I need to build my Transformer," Jake said angrily.

I turned to Janice, who was rubbing her leg and sobbing. "He hit me because I changed the channel, and I bumped into the table and the lamp fell on me."

"She deserved it," Jake said sharply.

"No one deserves to be hit," I said checking the lamp. The base had survived the spill, but the shade was now an odd elliptical.

I sighed. All week I'd been playing referee. "You know, you're much too grown up for all this fighting." Then I added, "Big people don't hit each other. You never see Uncle George hitting Grandpa when they disagree, do you?"

Jake grinned, picturing my six-foot-three brother-in-law taking potshots at my five-foot-nine husband.

"Momma hit Daddy, and that's why he went away," Janice said quietly. Her bottom lip was quivering. She tossed a missile, the missing toy part, which landed at Jake's feet.

I took a deep breath and said carefully. "I'm sorry you had to see that. Sometimes adults lose control when they're very angry, and they say and do things they don't mean. It's sad, but that's not the reason Daddy left. Mommy and Daddy just fell out of love. It's hard to explain, but the main thing is now they won't be so angry at each other since they don't live together."

Jake picked up the missing piece. "Bullshit," he muttered and threw it across the room.

That night while I was combing Janice's hair, I brought up the subject of what had happened earlier in the day. It was difficult, but I asked Janice if she wanted to ask me any questions about her mom and dad in case there were other things she had seen or heard that disturbed her. Janice shook her head. Then she said, "If Mommy is really sick, maybe she'll die. Then Daddy will be sad. When someone dies you cry, and you can't be mad at them any more."

Naturally, I was upset that my granddaughter was harboring such thoughts, even though I knew that in her childish way, Janice was trying to resolve her parents' conflict - trying to make things better. I gave her a hug. "Your mommy doesn't have to die for Daddy to get over his anger. It's just going to take more time for them to learn to get along."

•◀ What Can be Learned from Nora's Experience? ▶•

Grandchildren Grieve Differently from Grandparents

Adults and children grieve differently. Nora realized that months after Ben and Joan's divorce, her grandchildren were many steps behind her on the road to rebuilding. For Nora, the crisis stage was over and she had put the pain behind her, but she was not finished grieving. There are flashbacks — she is aware of the empty chair at the dining room table when the family gathers for dinner, and the missing wedding photo album in the study. She is also aware of her grandkids being aware. Nevertheless, she is coping well with the changes. Jake and Janice, however, are still angry and confused and reliving the past.

The incident when the lamp fell over surfaced unexpected aftershocks for Nora. You'll recall that when Jake hit Janice because she'd changed the TV channel, Janice blurted out that once "Mommy hit Daddy." Nora was caught off guard. Fortunately, she rose to the occasion. For the first time, she explained that the real reason Daddy left Mommy was because the two had fallen out of love, and she quickly smoothed things over by saying that Ben and Joan would improve their relationship now that they don't have to live together. (Notice she did not say they would get back together or love one another again, which would be untruthful and unfair to say to the children.) Of course, Jake saw right through his grandmother. Kids often do. It was obvious his parents were still fighting, so moving apart hadn't changed a thing.

Grandchildren Cannot Sustain Long Periods of Grief

What's happened here? Grandma has moved on, but the kids are stuck. Child psychologists who specialize in bereavement explain that not only are children's grief patterns different from adults', but children's capacities to cope are limited. Because of this, their grief resurfaces at irregular intervals.

A Grandchild's Grief Is Triggered by Unexpected Events in Unexpected Ways

Grandparents need to be aware that a grief trigger can surface at any time.

> Gladys took her granddaughter, Suzy, shopping to buy her a dress to wear for her cousin's wedding, but Suzy wanted to leave the mall before they got what they came for. Unbeknownst to Grandma, they'd gone into the same store where Suzy and her mom had bought her prom dress last year. Suzy and her mom aren't on speaking terms since her mom and her dad separated. Or this case: Billy's granddad gave him a hundred dollars for his birthday to take tennis lessons. Granddad didn't know that Billy had decided to give up playing tennis because that's his dad's favorite sport, and his dad had just moved out of state.

If it's tough for adults to make these connections or understand these behaviors when they happen, imagine how tough it must for the grandchildren who are personally experiencing these flip-flops in mood and behavior.

Grief Can Cause Mood and Behavior Swings

Nora hopes that time will be the great healer in the case of her grandchildren. She is moving toward rebuilding and wants the same for Janice and Jake. Bereavement counselors explain that a child's grief often extends into adulthood. There have been a number of longitudinal studies of children of divorce that talk about the fallout in the kids' lives long after their parents split. Problems include their inability to commit to a relationship; their fear of marital failure when they finally tie the knot; their estrangement from the parent they fault; the guilt they harbor that somehow they were responsible for their parents' problems. Let's return to Nora's story and see how she intervenes to comfort Janice and stabilize her flip-flopping behavior and confusion.

I brooded about this incident for days. I decided to take Janice out for ice cream when Jake was at soccer practice so we could be alone. Once again, I brought up Ben and Joan's situation. I acknowledged how difficult it must be on the twins, all this moving from place to place. Janice nodded this time. She didn't like the new school and missed her best friend. I said that I understood if she felt angry about having all these changes thrust upon her, that it must be upsetting seeing her parents in such turmoil. I told her that, under the circumstances, I thought she was handling the situation very well, and that I was proud of her.

Janice said she was sorry that she had talked about Joan dying. "It wasn't a nice thing to say." She twisted a strand of hair nervously.

I held her free hand. "Being upset with Mom and Dad doesn't mean you don't love them — even talking about them dying," I tried to reassure her. "It just means that your feelings are all mixed up right now. You probably feel sad, angry, hurt. You might think and say and even do things you don't really mean when you feel this way." I stressed that, in time, these feelings would be replaced by much happier feelings. I encouraged her to come and talk to me if ever she felt particularly sad or uncomfortable, and that if she preferred, we would find someone else she could talk to. She'd stopped seeing a counselor right after the divorce was finalized.

They Need Time to Work Through Their Grief

Nora thought she was protecting her grandchildren by not talking about the divorce or her former daughter-in-law. She believed she was helping them avoid pain and even masked her own feelings, putting up a false front. However, children are perceptive — Janice and Jake were intuitive enough to know that Grandma had been affected by their parents' divorce.

Children need the freedom to talk about their feelings, knowing they won't be judged if they say things they don't really mean or will regret and feel guilty about later. A good example of this is Janice telling her grandmother that if her mom were really sick, her dad would have to get over his anger. Ashamed that she would talk about Joan dying, she retracts that thought. "That wasn't a nice thing to say."

Nora was wise. She picked up on the thought and used it as an opportunity to tell Janice that people have many mixed-up feelings when they are angry or disappointed. She told Janice that she could come to her anytime when she feels "uncomfortable" with her thoughts, or if she prefers, talk to a counselor. Children are often referred for professional help during their parents' divorce. If the divorce is contentious, it may be necessary for them to continue in counseling.

Grandchildren Process Divorce Differently from Adults

The other point bereavement counselors make about processing grief is that adults and children react differently to loss. Adults experience shock, disappointment, anger. Children, on the other hand, are more likely to experience feelings of abandonment. E. M. Hetherington and J. Kelly interviewed more than a hundred children of divorced families in their 1980 longitudinal study and learned that children who find out their parents are separating ask questions such as — *Who will take care of me? Where will I live, go to school? Where will we get money? Where are my parents going to live? Will the other parent leave, too?*

Grandkids Need to Blow off Steam

It's not easy to be sympathetic with a grandchild who targets the parent who is your own child or puts you on the chopping block, too. Bonnie yelled at her grandmother, *"I know she's your daughter, but I hate my mother. She's the reason my father left us."* Her grandmother's knee-jerk reaction was to come to her daughter's defense. Instead, she bit her tongue and said, *"I understand that you feel that way now. A lot has gone on to make you angry with your mother. In time, perhaps you will be able to forgive her."*

Notice that this grandmother did not try to explain why Mom or Dad had cause to end their marriage, or how badly either parent was behaving since the separation. Instead, she tried to maintain a neutral position and validate her grandchild's feelings. It is helpful to know that your grandchild feels like a victim even when taking sides. Child psychologists explain that these violent feelings dissipate in time, and that, in the meantime, a child needs to vent. Allow your grandchild to blow off steam. Know too that by blowing off steam he may be testing you while looking for allies.

•◀ *Dealing with Your Grandchild's Anger* ▶•

A good grandparent-grandchild relationship calls for openness, unconditional love, support, honesty, patience and flexibility. Try to put yourself in your grandchild's shoes. Try not to triangulate or take sides when dealing with your grandchild's anger, as doing so will only add fuel to the fire.

Your grandchild may be old enough to understand that life is not a fairy tale. This is a great opportunity for a "teaching moment." You can help the child to learn that some of the anger he or she is feeling is the result of unrealistic expectations — especially about how moms and dads are "supposed" to behave, about life being "fair," and about happy endings.

Here are the key concepts you may be able to teach your grandchildren about their anger:

- Life is often not fair.
- Adults, like children, don't always act the way you want them to.
- It's normal to feel angry when things don't work out the way you want them to.
- Being mad about something is different from being mad at someone.
- *Feeling* angry doesn't mean you have to *act* angry.
- It's not healthy to shout, hit, or kick things or people.
- Anger can be expressed in healthy ways. Here are some good ideas:
  (a) Relax, take some deep breaths, and count to ten.
  (b) Run laps, swim, play soccer, or do some other physical exercise to work off your angry energy.

(c) Talk about your angry feelings with someone who will listen to you.

(f) Remember that your anger comes from you. Nobody can "make" you angry if you don't allow it.

(g) Work out a compromise with the people you're angry with.

(h) Forgive the people you're angry with.

(i) Remind yourself that your angry feelings will go away in time.

•◀ *Grandchildren Need Comforting* ▶•

Dr. Arthur Kornhaber (*The Grandparent Guide*, 2002) tells grandparents that it is important to monitor and understand what their grandchild experiences. When parents separate, they cannot always be there for their children. They may be too overwrought to provide the comfort and security their children need.

Grandparents cannot replace parents, but they can be a source of solace. Here are some guidelines to help you when your grandchild needs comforting:

- Be reassuring.
- Give your grandchild permission to say whatever is on his mind.
- Refrain from disparaging either parent.
- Hold your own emotionality in check.
- Listen. Do not pry for details.
- Assure your grandchild that he or she is not to blame for the parents' behavior.
- Use simple language when explaining things.
- Calm fears.
- Above all, respect your grandchild's confidences.

It is also important to validate your grandchild's feelings. For example:

When Joey complained bitterly to Papa Bill that his father wasn't coming to his birthday party, Papa Bill said, "I know you're upset that your father won't be there, but he said something about taking you to a ball game for your birthday. It won't be the same, but your dad loves you and is trying to make it up to you."

•◀ Behavioral Changes in Children ▶•

When your grandchildren are mourning the loss of an absent parent and dealing with all the changes in their environment, they will have a storm of feelings: rejection, humiliation, feeling unlovable, powerlessness, and guilt. They may behave in ways you may not understand or will have trouble accepting. Some children will act out to get attention. *I used to be good, now I'll cause trouble.* Others will withdraw, turn their anger inward, and become sullen and depressed. You may observe your grandchild throwing tantrums, developing nervous habits such as nail biting or hair twisting, eating compulsively or rejecting food, wetting the bed, etc.

It's perfectly normal to worry about your grandchild's emotional well-being. It's difficult to stand by if you think the parents are not doing enough to solve a problem you've detected. My suggestion is to be diplomatic about the way you bring the problem to your child's attention, or you may do more harm than good, as in the situation where one grandfather was convinced his grandson had developed Attention Deficit Disorder (ADD) after the parents separated. He read up on the condition and convinced his son that the boy needed medication. The grandfather was not wrong to speak his piece, but his relentless interference sparked more conflict between the parents.

•◀ Children's Reaction to Divorce and Family Disruption ▶•

Professionals in the field of child psychology have compiled a list of predictable reactions that occur at specific developmental stages. Note that children move at different rates in their development and that the ages in each category are approximate. This is a partial list of behaviors from Claudia M. Fetterman's *Participants Guide Putting Children First — Skills for Parents in Transition* (1999) available from the Connecticut Council of Family Services Agencies. Use it as a guideline for evaluating behaviors you see in your grandchildren.

At birth to eighteen months, children may be nervous, fretful, and exhibit some delays in development. They need cuddle time, consistent routines, and a feeling of security. Warning signs: failure to gain weight, diminished growth, or unresponsiveness.

Toddlers (eighteen months to three years) may appear moody, withdrawn, fearful, and become even more attention-seeking. They may exhibit unusual changes in sleeping and eating patterns. Toddlers need verbal and physical assurance, routines, and consistency. Obvious signs of regression are bed-wetting and tantrums.

Preschool (three to five years) children do not understand the concept of divorce and may feel responsible for the situation. They may express fears unrelated to the divorce and will not want to separate from parents, fearing that one or both will not return. Again, they need reassurance the parent will return. You can read age-appropriate books to them about divorce and help them verbalize their feelings. (Check Appendix B.)

Elementary school-age children (five to eleven years) will feel torn between parents, may take sides, and engage in magical thinking, believing they can control the outcome and bring their parents back together if they behave a certain way. At this age, children will experience feelings of loss, anger, guilt, rejection and sadness. They may have difficulty sharing possessions and want to control situations. Adults should allow the children to express their feelings, not offer false hopes, set structure and routines, avoid power struggles, and encourage the child's relationship with the other parent.

In *middle and junior high school (eleven to fourteen years)* children turn to peers for support. They worry how their own life will be affected, may become protective of a parent and play the role of the absentee parent. You may observe a child engaging in negative acting-out behaviors, and being critical of the parents' dating/social/sexual behavior. At this age, children need to express their feelings appropriately. You should encourage outlets such as exercise and sports. Children should have some input into visitation plans and be given permission to act like a child.

Older children of high school age will be concerned about money, resent the fact that their lives have been disrupted, may be afraid of intimacy, and be embarrassed by their parents' behavior. They can be capable beyond their age level and have the ability to understand and adapt with structure and guidance. Not all high school age children, while articulate, are able to reason like adults, however. Parents need to continue to maintain parental control, give permission for children to love both parents, and develop an adult support system so the child can be free to be his/her age.

•◀ *Does My Grandchild Need Counseling?* ▶•

It will be comforting to know that many experts in the field of child psychology do not think it is a good idea to jump on the family-counseling bandwagon right after the parents' separation. One social worker told me, "Everyone can profit from some help in times of stress. But sometimes we go overboard and even put the dog in therapy."

Be patient. It may take longer than you think for your grandchild to process the changes in his or her life. Some children, however, profit from short-term, problem-centered counseling and adjust rather quickly, especially if they have left a toxic, abusive, or violent situation. Because divorce is so prevalent, more and more school personnel are trained to identify families that need help and will make referrals. Some public schools offer divorce workshops for children as young as kindergarten. However, do not assume this is true in your case; don't leave it to the school to catch the problem. Too often, children slip through the cracks. Be alert to these signs that your grandchild is having difficulties: lack of interest in school, excessive absences, sliding grades or problems getting along with other children.

Keep in mind that the decision to seek professional help is not yours. You can be an advocate for your grandchild, but your grandchild's parents have the ultimate authority. If you do have the go-ahead, there are resources in your community you can turn to: social service agencies, your grandchild's school counselor, referrals from Human Resource or Employee Assistance departments at work, counseling centers in local colleges and community centers, pediatricians, churches or synagogues, professional societies of psychologists, clinical social worker and marriage and family therapists. Check telephone directories, community help lines such as

Info line, and the Web for listings in your area for professional counseling services. (Also, check Appendix B for a listing of professional societies of psychologists, clinical social workers, and marriage and family therapists.)

●◀ When the Courts Step In ▶●

In high-conflict situations involving custody, a case manger and/or child psychologist may become involved in the divorce proceedings. If a child is deemed at risk, the court will appoint a *guardian ad litem* (GAL), an attorney or other individual who renders an opinion on the children's best interests. Once the attorneys and all the professionals assigned to the case have given testimony, the judge will render a decision. Once the case is decided, the process of family healing must begin. This is where you come in.

Often the courts recommend short-term therapy for children in high-conflict divorce cases during negotiation. Short-term therapy is problem-centered. Not every child is disturbed or has a diagnosable mental health problem, yet he or she may still need a safe place where he can express himself and get guidance. Very young children cannot speak for themselves, and a trained professional can engage them in play therapy.

●◀ Facing the Grandchild Challenge ▶●

I've spoken to grandparents who say they wouldn't have a clue how to raise their grandchildren if they were put in that position. Grandparents are bewildered and overwhelmed by teenagers who've been brought up in the technology age and who know more about sex and drugs than they do. Some grandkids are simply too challenging to take on. Rosie was thrown into a tailspin when her fourteen-year-old stepgranddaughter came to live with her and her husband. She explained it this way:

> *"My daughter recently separated from her second husband, who is serving time. I agreed to let Lilia stay with me because she and my daughter don't get along and there's no one else*

who was willing. I keep getting calls from school that Lilia's skipped, and more than once my husband caught her going through my purse. I hate to give up, but what am I supposed to do with this child? I am thinking of going to the Department of Children and Families. Maybe she'd be better off in foster care."

It's not unusual for grandparents who have the best intentions to discover they are way out of their league. Clearly, Lilia needs a firm hand. If she stays with Rosie, the girl may be at further risk. Rosie should not let the situation ride. She needs help. Foster care might be the solution, but before taking this step, Rosie should contact a community social service agency and consider family counseling. If Rosie is reluctant to go outside, and sees this as defeat, she might begin with her clergyperson or consult the youth leader of her house of worship. The school guidance counselor who alerted Rosie might be able to refer her to a child psychologist for Lilia.

Let's take a minute to examine this case. There are many reasons children behave the way they do, especially when they are removed from their home environment. Perhaps Lilia is stealing because her grandparents do not give her enough spending money or do not understand her needs. In addition, she is being bullied at school, so she skips to avoid being taunted. There are reasons for Lilia's behavior that are not obvious. The grandparents need to take the time to sort them out. Should Rosie alert the Department of Children and Families, a caseworker would be assigned to the case to evaluate and be obligated to do follow-up. Lilia will be in "the system" for a long time. Placing her granddaughter in foster care is much more than the situation warrants. In all likelihood, going the distance by working on the problem will be worth the effort.

On the other hand, it is not a disgrace to admit you cannot honor your commitment. Some children may simply be too challenging. There are hosts of other issues that come into play such as a change in your health, your work, or family demands. If that is your situation, be open and bow out as gracefully as you can. Work with your child to find other options for your grandchild.

•◀ *We're on Different Planets* ▶•

Sometimes it's not a question of finding a child too challenging, but a matter of cold feet. Dolores was finding it difficult to communicate with her fifteen-year-old grandson, who spoke street-slang and dressed the part as well.

For the sake of your grandchild, it's probably worth trying to get past the tongue and nose rings. I love watching the movie *On Golden Pond*. Grandfather (Norman) and his stepgrandson get off to a rocky start, then in the end forge a beautiful bond. If you haven't seen the movie, I recommend you and your grandchild view it together.

If you and your grandchild are not connecting, there could be a variety of reasons, and as many ways to improve the situation:

• *You and your grandchild did not have much of a relationship prior to the divorce.* It takes time to build trust. Find opportunities to be together or schedule a set time when you telephone your grandchild to keep in touch. Begin slowly. Keep conversations light. Do not overwhelm your grandchild with your attention or try to make up for lost time. Your goal is to show interest in his or her current life, not to pry or burden your grandchild with your own problems.

• *Your grandchild resents your filling in for the absentee parent.* Explain that you are not replacing the parent; you are just helping for a while, and it can be a chance to get to know your grandchild. If possible, specify how long you expect to be in the picture. Be positive and upbeat by saying something like: "I'll be pitching in for two weeks until Mom finds a new place for you guys to live. I was hoping during this time you and I could play some tennis, finally get to see that movie, read the latest Harry Potter book, go shopping, etc."

• *Your rules and standards are very different from the parent's.* Try not to deviate too much from your child's routine. Discuss and negotiate necessary changes.

For example:

Granny Sarah hates the thought of ten-year-old Tommy riding his bicycle on the main roads to and from school. She insists on driving him while she is in charge. She asks her grandson to consider her feelings. "Sorry to be such a nervous ninny. You can ride your bike in the park where there isn't so much traffic and go back to riding to school when Mom takes over again."

If you show respect for the rules your child is used to and do not go overboard enforcing your own, you stand a better chance of having your rules accepted.

• *Your grandchild has heard you say negative things about the other parent and knows you are one-sided.* Find something nice to say even if you have to dig deep! But don't overdo the turnaround — they'll see right through you. Your grandchildren do not expect you to be in your ex-in-law's corner, but they don't want you wearing boxing gloves either.

• *Your grandchild consciously or unconsciously blames you for his parents' problems.* If you can, find out what's behind this perception. While you don't want to come off being too defensive, you may have to justify your behavior. Understandably, this requires diplomacy. Let's use this example: Your grandson has overheard you criticize his father to your daughter about your ex-son-in-law's fiscal mismanagement. He blames you for making his mother cry. You might explain that your primary concern is your grandson's welfare. "That's why I got so hot under the collar when Dad missed the last payment. I'm sorry I spoke so harshly and upset your mom."

• *Your grandchild sides with your ex-son or ex-daughter-in-law; therefore, you are the "enemy" by association.* You cannot be responsible for how your grandchild feels about your child. Hopefully, in time, your grandchild will feel differently. Make it clear that you are a separate person from your child, and then demonstrate your love and support. Myra has her granddaughter and ex-son-in-law over for dinner one night a week. Her daughter left her family, moved in with her lover, and rarely sees the girl. This grandmother cannot make up for her daughter's behavior, but she can work on building a relationship of trust with her granddaughter.

• *You've maintained a "Great Silence" and deliberately avoided talking about the divorce or mentioning the ex-in-law's name, which makes you unapproachable.* Break the Great Silence. Begin by finding positive things to say about that parent that deal with the here and now. "I saw your mom yesterday when I was at your soccer game. She was really proud when you scored that goal."

• *Your ex-in-law has poisoned your grandchild against you.* This can be tough. The best advice is to be yourself and try to mend broken fences the best way you can. Send cheery notes; remember a special day; try to stay connected.

Case in point:

Freda was devastated that her grandsons wanted nothing to do with her or her husband when they were growing up. When one of the grandsons was away at college, his grandparents sent him an invitation to attend their fiftieth anniversary party. He delighted them by showing up. "It's a shame we lost so much time," the grandparents said sadly. They still do not see the other grandson, but they have not given up hope.

• *Your grandchild is acting out when he or she is with you, and it can be difficult to maintain a relationship.* This can be especially true with young children who are hearing mixed messages from parents who must honor visitation agreements.

Case in point:

Margaret was devastated when her eight-year-old grandson yelled, "I don't have to listen to you. My mommy says you're a witch, and I hate you." Margaret talked to her son. She asked him to talk to his ex about not setting her grandchild against her. Her son did not want to get involved, so Margaret wrote her ex-daughter-in-law a note expressing her love for her grandchild. She explained that it was in everybody's best interests if family could be there for one another. Meanwhile, Margaret did little things to show her grandson how happy she was to have him visit. She cooked his favorite foods, went to the library and borrowed videos they could watch together. Margaret understood that her grandson was conflicted. She hoped that there would come a day when he did not feel that he was being disloyal to his mother by enjoying his grandmother's company.

While many children say they bear the legacy of divorce into adulthood, there are as many who claim they had better lives when

Parental Guideposts: Chapter Eight

Grandchildren in Crisis

- Allow your grandchild to talk openly, even if you disagree with his or her feelings. Point out the difference between healthy and destructive behaviors if your grandchild expresses feelings inappropriately.
- Calm fears. Provide comfort. Be optimistic about the future.
- Reassure your grandchild that he or she is not to blame for the parents' divorce.
- Keep any personal hostility towards ex-in-laws in check. You don't want to burden your grandchild with your issues.
- If possible, bolster the parent who, after all, is probably trying his or her best. Even if that's not the case, don't further disparage the parent. Your grandchild knows the score. Why add to his or her emotional discomfort?
- Avoid making the divorce (or one parent) the cause of all family difficulties.
- Respect confidences. Do not pry for information when your grandchild visits the ex-in-law.
- Do not ask your grandchild to manipulate either parent into getting material things.
- Acknowledge how hard your grandchild is trying to please both parents while caught in their "tug of war."

their parents left a bad situation and finally found happiness. The verdict is still out in terms of the subcutaneous scars. I suggest grandparents err on the side of caution, since the after-effects are still unpredictable; however, you can anticipate that there will be disruption in your family while you all get your bearings.

In the end, your grandchildren may forget the pain, but long-term they will not forget your love. Grandparents can make a world of difference during the crisis of divorce. Perhaps your role is even more important post-divorce, when the storm subsides and you move toward family renewal and stabilization.

✎ *Chapter Eight: Workbook Exercises*

Read each of these sentences and think about what the statement is communicating to the child. Next, reframe each one so that the sentence is more positive.

(1) "If your parents had stuck it out, maybe your brother wouldn't be getting into so much trouble."

(2) "I understand you spent a week with your mother and her boyfriend. What's he like?"

(3) "You know your mother can't afford to buy you a new computer. Why don't you ask your father? He's sitting in the big house with that new wife of his."

Sentence (1) is faulting the divorce and the parents for the brother's problems, and just adding to the child's anger and bitterness about the split.

Sentence (2) is asking the child to be the bearer of tales. The child feels further conflicted about whether to tell all or keep secrets.

Sentence (3) is manipulating the child to get material things from the parent who is better off. It only adds to the guilt of the child wanting something out-of-reach from the parent in reduced circumstances, and taking (or being bought off) by the parent can afford the luxury item.

Try these alternatives for making the negative more positive and communicating respect for both parents.

(1) "I know that your mother is doing all she can to help your brother. I'm going to talk to her about seeing his school counselor. Maybe they can arrange for some tutoring...

(2) "Did you have a good time with your mom? What fun things did you do?"

(3) "I know that you are dying for a new computer. You might put that on your Christmas wish list if your dad asks you what you want."

There are bound to be occasions when you are going to slip up. It will not always be easy to find the right words, but you'll find it rewarding to keep a positive outlook when dealing with your grandchildren.

Chapter Nine

Grandparents as Stabilizers

Nora, like so many parents, could hardly wait to have grandchildren. She looked forward to having "all the privileges without the responsibilities." It doesn't take a whole lot to be a standout grandparent. According to Age Wave Communications, a market research company, the five best things grandparents can do to make most grandkids happy are: take them out to eat, let them sleep over, go shopping, play games, and watch TV together. It's a cinch, and a whole lot easier than parenting your own kids was. By the time you have grandchildren, you hope you've learned from your mistakes. Generally, you are a lot less ego-involved this time around.

Did I say it was a cinch? Well, it should have been up until your grandkids' parents got divorced. Then, like Nora, your role shifts, and you can find yourself becoming friend and confidant, mentor, rescuer — or foe, depending on how you play your cards.

Nora's story

When the twins were living with me during Ben's temporary assignment in New Jersey, I noticed that Janice complained of stomach aches and would burst into tears when I tried to get her to eat her breakfast. Jake was fine at home, but the bus driver reported a number of incidents when Jake was rowdy on the way home from school. Since Ben was busy with work and Joan was packing up to move East, I decided to meet with the school psychologist (after getting Ben's permission, of course). The psychologist talked about the predictable developmental reactions children have to family disruption. She explained that while extreme changes in a grandchild's behavior should be followed up, many of these symptoms are temporary and predictable reactions to stress. "Give the children a feeling of stability by sticking to routines and provide some relief from the tension between the parents," she suggested.

Acting on her advice, Gary and I decided to take the children on a camping trip to Liverpool, Pennsylvania. During the fall, the campground was quiet and peaceful. Our site was right on the water. We could sit by our campfire and watch the fishermen go up and down the Susquehanna River in their boats. The trip had a calming affect on all of us. I remember watching the twins feed bits of their leftover hot dog buns to the ducks, the wildlife whipping around them, flapping up sound bites of laughter. Tears filled my eyes. It was the first time they'd been this joyful since their arrival.

●◄ *Multiple Roles* ►●

Dr. Arthur Kornhaber — grandfather, physician, researcher, medical writer — reminds us that a grandparent plays many different roles in a grandchild's life irrespective of marital conflict (2002). You can be a buddy, a hero, a historian, a mentor, a nurturer, a spiritual a guide, a teacher, a student. When your child gets divorced, your grandparenting role becomes more focused. Your task is to provide:

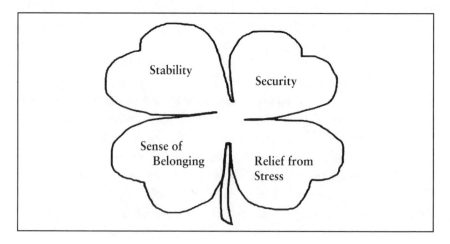

Leaf One: Stability

As I have mentioned several times, children going through divorce are experiencing a lot of change. Often they are shuttling back and forth between parents. Many are uprooted. They may have changed schools, said goodbye to friends and neighbors. They may have left prized possessions behind. Even those children who stay in the same surroundings experience a change in their environment. I think you will find that when you go to your child's home, the place will have an entirely different feeling because of separation or divorce.

Your domicile should be a war-free zone. It should offer familiarity and regularity.

When Leigh's grandchildren come for the weekend, she makes sure they sleep in the same room and has a set place for their clothes and toys. She told me that the kids use their "special" cereal bowls, which they fill with their favorite cereal. She keeps these on a shelf the kids can reach themselves, so she can get some extra shut-eye in the morning. Leigh takes them out for dinner on Wednesdays, when their mother works late. They like to go to the same pizza parlor and always order extra cheese and sausage. Right now, the kids need a lot of sameness, and she provides it.

You may not have to be this concrete with older grandchildren, but they, too, find familiarity is comforting. For example, Virginia finds herself hanging out in the mall because her granddaughter likes to shop. *"I stand by and she makes all the decisions. The point is, we're together."*

Whether it's shopping, playing a computer or board game, trying out a new recipe, watching a favorite video, or looking through a photo album that brings back happy memories, these activities will show your grandchildren that some things never change.

Leaf Two: Security

It goes without saying that children who have been exposed to domestic violence need a great deal more comfort and support than most. If your grandchild has been a victim or witnessed abuse, he or she may exhibit a host of symptoms including anxiety attacks, nightmares, insomnia, withdrawal and depression, and self-destructive or aggressive behavior. You should seek professional help for your grandchild and offer as much reassurance as possible that your home is a refuge. It's important to listen to your grandchild's fears and to offer your protection on that long road to recovery.

Even children who have not been exposed to physical danger will suffer emotional trauma if they are victims in the power struggles between embittered parents who use them as pawns, messengers, spies, scapegoats, or bargaining chips. If you can intervene in your grandchild's behalf and provide respite from the crossfire, you will be instrumental in your grandchild's recovery. Seeking help for the parents should be a goal also, although you may not always be successful.

Leaf Three: Sense of Belonging

No matter how hard you try, you cannot fill the role of the absentee parent. A grandparent offers another kind of kinship that grandchildren need in times of disequilibria — the feeling of belonging to a larger family system. You are the historians of the family, passing down the clan's traditions, the "rituals" and lore that tie members together. When the nuclear family disbands, children need a foundation for rebuilding. Grandparents can provide that foundation even if they have also branched off by remarrying. Grandparents are still the roots of the tree. Your grandchildren look to you for guidance and wisdom because of your life experience. Chances are you have weathered and survived other crises. You cannot let them down now.

Leaf Four: Relief from Stress

Your grandchildren need joy in their lives. You can provide joy by planning family get-togethers or substituting when parents can't be there for the child. A couple I knew went to their grandson's college football weekend because the parents had recently separated and were too embroiled in their own problems to fly out. Needless to say, the grandparents and their grandson had the time of their lives. Many grandparents include their grandchildren in vacation plans during the first year of separation. During times of stress, you and your grandchildren can benefit from being together, enjoying the beauty and tranquility of nature like Nora and Gary did on the camping trip. The Sierra Club, the Grand Travel agency, and the Foundation for Grand Parenting offer special intergenerational vacation packages that have grown tremendously in popularity. Elderhostels and organizations for learning vacations for seniors offer more than 3000 vacations for kids and grandparents. (See Appendix B for information about intergenerational camps and adventures.)

A tip: If you want to make sure your grandchild has a good time, and you're up to it, encourage the child to invite a friend.

•◀ *The Caretaking Grandparent* ▶•

Today more and more grandparents are taking care of their grandchildren on a full-time basis. According to the U. S. Census Bureau (2000), more than two million grandparents are raising a staggering 4.5 million children. "Gray Power" is the muscle behind legislation to improve medical benefits and financial assistance for grandparents, many of whom have assumed responsibility for their grandchildren due to the large number of divorces in our nation. Senator Hillary Clinton of New York is among the legislators who proposed the Kinship Caregiver Support Act S. 2706 (2004), which would create an outreach program linking grandparents and other non-parent family caregivers to support services such as respite care, housing, health insurance and childcare benefits.[1]

Many grandparents who have the responsibility of raising their grandchildren thrust upon them are not sure they are up to the task or want the responsibility, having raised families of their own. There will be innumerable adjustments should you become your grandchild's primary caregiver. Among the changes are decisions about work, commitment to other family members, and the potential drain on finances. There is also the effect on your health and energy level. While grandparents today are fitter and younger than when their parents became grandparents, (the average age according to one report is forty-seven, and this generation can expect between thirty and forty years of grandparenthood!), taking care of children is exhausting. Even grandparents who are in excellent condition find it difficult being full-time caregivers, especially if they are running after toddlers or constantly on call, carting around teenagers.[2]

It's a question of attitude, researchers will tell you. You can see the pitcher half empty or half full. Ronald Lee, a professor of demography at the University of California at Berkeley, claims that grandparents taking care of their grandchildren are significant contributors to the longevity and long-term survival of the human race. "Fitness isn't just about bearing offspring," Lee claims. "It's about investing in each offspring." As reported in the *Ottawa Citizen*, Researcher Sunmin Lee from the Harvard School of Public Health and Harvard Medical School looked at the other side and found in her study that women providing care to grandchildren for more than nine hours or more a week have a 55 percent greater chance of developing heart disease.

•◄ *Will I Ever See My Grandchildren Again?* ►•

This is a question that plagues grandparents as soon as they hear the announcement, "Mom, Dad, . . . I'm getting a divorce."

While there are no pat answers, sociologists Cherlin and Furstenberg (*The New American Grandparent*, 1986) say that grandparents are more likely to maintain or even enhance their relationship with their grandchildren if their daughter's marriage breaks up. If it's a son's marriage, their relationship with their grandchildren is likely to be diminished in quantity and probably in quality as well. This seems likely to be the case if the mother is awarded sole physical custody. According to Kaplan and Weitherheimer (1988), even with joint custody, the paternal grandparents are usually the ones who suffer unless the couple has worked out a very equitable split.[3]

Obviously, how often you see your grandchildren hinges on your relationship with your son- or daughter-in-law during and after the divorce. Let's face it. The parents, whether or not they are married to each other, are the gatekeepers to your grandchildren. You may find that you've grown very close to your child, who is counting on your emotional and physical support during separation and divorce. Your bond with your grandchildren may become even stronger.

•◀ *Don't Assume You're Not Wanted* ▶•

The newly single parent may have to work longer and harder hours post-divorce to make ends meet. There is going to be all that added pressure on both sides. The residential or custodial parent will worry what is going to happen to the children when there are school vacations and neither parent can take off time. Or who will cover in an emergency when the babysitter doesn't show or quits?

Here's when you — the grandparent on the side of the non-custodial parent — can take up the slack if you are available and willing to help. Even if you live great distances from your grandchildren and cannot go to them, you can arrange for your grandchildren to come to you. Airline personnel are very experienced at dealing with kids flying solo, or with only a sibling, given that there are so many young children of divorce jockeying back and forth on their own for long-distance visitation, unaccompanied by an adult. Call ahead to find out the cost (usually there is an additional fee) and how the trip can be arranged so that children travel safely.

Your former daughter or son-in-law may appreciate the extra time you spend with the grandchildren, even look to you as an additional back-up. If you have a good relationship like Phil and Rita with your ex-in-law, you can take the initiative to be helpful.

When these grandparents learned through their son that his ex, Ellen, had won a trip to Cancun for being top salesperson in her company, they called to congratulate her and offered to stay with their grandchildren. Ellen's mother was not in good health, so she was pleased to have the offer from Phil and Rita. Ellen arranged for the children to fly to Indiana, and spent a worry-free week soaking up the rays. Just because the marital bonds are broken doesn't mean you can't be there for the ex - if you're wanted and your own child doesn't object.

Two Sets of Grandparents Are Better than One

Many ex-sons- and daughters-in-law agree that it only profits their children to have two sets of loving and caring grandparents who can provide continuity and stability when the nuclear family dissembles.

The trend today is joint legal custody — both mom and dad are equally involved with their children. Subsequently, both sets of grandparents are more likely to have access to their grandchildren. Some states — Connecticut and Iowa are examples — oblige divorcing couples with children to enroll in parent effectiveness courses such as "Putting Children First." These workshops stress the importance of the extended family and encourage partners to maintain ties with grandparents. You might consult your state's divorce requirements to find out whether there are similar workshops for divorcing parents. (Check Appendix A and B for references about locating state requirements.)

Participative grandparenting has become a way of life in some families who have experienced divorce. I've spoken to many maternal and paternal grandparents who work out a schedule and take turns carpooling, having the kids over for dinner, and babysitting. Even grandparents who don't get along may overlook their differences for the sake of their grandchildren.

Get Off on the Right Foot

While there is no assurance you will have access to your grandchildren, you will better your chances if you begin on the right foot. Family therapists advise both sets of grandparents to do the following:

- Maintain civil and open communication with the ex-in-law and his or her parent(s) right after the breakup.
- Don't let negative feelings get in the way. Bite your tongue. Accept the fact that, in order to keep the peace, you may have to overlook things the ex-in-law says or does.
- Be upfront and discuss your grandparent visitation concerns frankly with your child and ex-in-law. Let everyone know that, above all, your interest is maintaining a positive relationship with your grandchildren, and that you will do whatever it takes to assure that relationship continues.
- Do your best to make visitations in which you are included stress-free, increasing the likelihood that you will be invited to participate more often.
- Give the custodial parent lots of advance notice if there are special family occasions (such as weddings, birthday parties) to which grandchildren are invited.

- Don't come on too strongly. If a recently divorced in-law feels that your weekly visits are a strain, settle for a more flexible schedule. Once the family is stabilized, you can request more time.
- Adhere strictly to the visitation timeframes. Don't arrive too early or keep the grandchildren out later than agreed. Call as soon as you know that something may interfere with the original arrangement — especially if you are going to be late.
- Be considerate. Make your visits easy on the ex-in-law by offering to pick up and drop off the grandchild.
- Abide by the ex-in-law's rules, especially when it comes to meals, treats, television viewing, and video games.
- Discuss with the parent movies, shopping trips, and toys you'd like to buy your grandchildren to get his or her approval. Your taste and standards might be quite different from the parents'.
- Show your appreciation for having that special time with your grandchild. Be pleasant both coming and going. Even if you've had a hard day with your grandchild, say something positive to smooth the way for the next visit.

If you want to gild the lily, send home a token of appreciation after spending the day with your grandchild. One ex-mom-in-law sends the rest of the home-baked cookies she and the kids made with a note saying what a great time they had, and she includes the recipe.

Something to Remember: Seeing Your Grandchildren Is a Gift, Not a Given.

•◀ *An Ounce of Prevention...* ▶•

If you've been denied access to your grandchild, you have good cause to grieve (See Appendix A, Legal Issues, Grandparenting Rights). Sadly, many states do not offer protection for grandparents. The best insurance that this won't happen is to maintain as good a relationship with the custodial parent as possible. Many more ex-in-laws are sympathetic to grandparents and do not want them cut out of their children's lives. Nevertheless, there is the inevitable distancing when custodial parents remarry or move away.

A number of grandparents I interviewed got A+ for their creative solutions aimed at keeping the doors open:

- *When I e-mail or send a note to my grandchild, I also include a kind word to pass along to the ex-in-law, knowing she is going to read what I sent.*
- *I send holiday cards to show good will, and I usually include a photograph I've taken of the children when we've been together.*
- *I go through the back door by staying in touch with my ex-daughter-in-law's parents, who are very sympathetic to my cause. We swap news and photographs of the grandchildren. They make sure their daughter lets me see the kids.*
- *I don't like my ex-in-laws and blame them for many of my daughter's problems, but for her sake, I'm cordial when we get together at my grandson's sporting events. I try to think about my grandson and not myself.*

In keeping with that last point, there is one story I would like to pass along, told to me by grandparents who were determined not to fan the flames of family conflict. Here is Adele and Mitch's story:

My husband and I were very insulted that we were not asked to participate in the service or the candle-lighting ceremony at our grandson's bar mitzvah. His other grandparents were paying for the whole affair, and we've never had a good relationship with them. I knew they were using this as a chance to lord it over us. I wanted my son to say something to my ex-daughter-in-law, but I decided it would only cause more hard feelings, so Mitch and I suffered in silence and just held our heads high.

It sounds like the ex-in-laws were running the show. Adele and Mitch were wise to turn the other cheek although they were deeply hurt. Rather than burden their son, ex-daughter-in-law, or grandson with their complaints, they appreciated the fact that they were at least at the bar mitzvah.

●◀ The Worst Scenario... Seeking Legal Recourse ▶●

Roberta and I have never gotten along. I just know she is going to cut me out if she gets custody.

If your ex-law(s) makes it difficult for you to see your grandchildren, you may have no recourse but to seek legal assistance. Many states have precedents for grandparents to demand visitation. If you are convinced you are going to be denied access, your child can specify grandparenting visitation rights in the divorce agreement.

Since the mid-1970s, grandparents' visitation rights have been debated in state legislatures across the country. Grandparents can petition courts to continue seeing their grandchildren. If this is your situation, the best advice is to seek a specialist in family law. Contact a local grandparenting group (check the Web and Appendix B) that can fill you in about precedents and rules in your state. Be aware that this can be a costly and uphill battle. In many states, parents have the final say as to whether or not grandparents can see their grandchildren, even if it is in the best interests of the grandchild.

> Advice: Before you go to court, ask a mutual friend or relative to advocate in your behalf. Another option is to have all parties meet with a family counselor, who can act as a mediator.

•◀ *Long-Distance Grandparenting* ▶•

When I was growing up, we sang, "Over the river and through the woods, to grandmother's house we go." Today our grandkids are more likely to sing, "Over the clouds and through the sky to grandmother's house we fly," as more and more branches of families spread out across the globe.

What does that mean for grandparents who want to reach out to their grandchildren when their parents divorce? It's comforting to know that in the age of technology you are only keystrokes away, and that cell phones, email, instant messaging, faxes, digital cameras, and audio tapes can communicate your support. Some families have their own Websites, where they post stories, share jokes, and scan photos. Maybe you can get that computer-savvy grandchild to create one for you!

No matter what device you use, it is important for you to have an ongoing relationship with your grandchildren. One gentleman relies on good old snail mail. For years, he's been sending a letter a week to each of his nine grandchildren.

"I cherish every letter they send me in return, and I keep them in an album, so when we get together, anyone can look back and see all those changed handwritings and the topics we wrote about."

This grandfather has created a history for his grandchildren. It's a lovely idea that you might think about replicating in your own way.

●◀ Today's Grandparents Are a Whole New Breed ▶●

Grandparents today play many roles and are a growing force in our communities. They represent a large segment of the population and, as more Baby Boomers enter grandparenthood, the segment is getting even larger. According to a study conducted by AARP and reported by Age Wave Communications, a California-based company that tracks the mature market, the number of grandparents is expected to grow from 72 million in 2005 to 80 million by 2010. Since the average life expectancy today is 76.5 years, sixteen percent of today's families have four or more living generations. Therefore, not only are grandparents willing and able to lend a helping hand with their grandchildren, but great-grandparents can also be involved.

The growing involvement of grandparents has been just as dramatic a change in the American family life as the unraveling of the nuclear family. Grandparents, who are now living longer, have a chance to accumulate wealth and have become an important resource for family support as well as family stability. Today's grandparents are not only helping with child-rearing, many are keeping their families afloat, financing their grandchildren's college education, paying for camp, daycare, vacations, and assisting children and grandchildren with real estate down payments. "For many Americans, multigenerational bonds are becoming more important than nuclear family ties for well-being and support over the course of their lives," says Vern Bengston, a sociologist and gerontologist at the University of Southern California, who was quoted in a recent *New York Times* article (Lewin).

Prior to the baby boomer generation, it was usually Grandma who became involved with the grandchildren, because she was a stay-at-home mom, and that was the expected role. Look around next time you are at your grandchild's sports event or eating hamburgers at a fast-food or "family" restaurant. You will notice almost as many grandfathers as grandmothers in the stands or wiping ketchup off sticky fingers. Like their sons, many of today's grandfathers know how to change diapers and prepare formula. Granted, they still spend more time on the ballfield than in the nursery, but in general, grandfathers are a lot more involved with their grandchildren than their own fathers were. This positive male role model is a great resource for families trying to find their way during divorce.

•◀ *What Lies Ahead?* ▶•

Our worth as parents and grandparents is measured by how we bind our families' wounds and preserve the values and traditions that give meaning to the next generation. As someone once said, when our families break down, there is still family — albeit reconfigured, blended, reconstituted. In chapter 10, we will look at the shape of the modern family. It is likely your child is going to meet a new special someone and form a new partnership or remarry. This will be the last stage of your divorce journey. You need to be prepared for the next turn of your family carousel.

END NOTES:

[1] Summary of the Kinship Caregiver Support Act, S. 2706:
On July 21, 2004, Senators Clinton (D-NY), Snowe (R-ME) and Daschle (D-SD) introduced the Kinship Caregiver Support Act (S. 2706). The bill takes three important steps to assist children being raised and cared for by grandparents and other relatives. The Act: (1) establishes a Kinship Navigator Program; (2) establishes a Kinship Guardianship Assistance Program to provide federal assistance to states to assist relative caregivers and their children; and (3) ensures notice to relatives when children enter foster care. Introduced on July 21, 2004. Status: Read twice and referred to the Senate Committee on Finance. 7/21/2004 Referred to Senate committee, where it remains as of the date of this book's publishing.

[2] Source article: "Simply Grand: Generational Ties Matter and Grandparents are Finding New Ways to Play Starring Roles in the Lives of Their Grandchildren," *Time Inc.* Oct. 11, 1999 | By Megan Rutherford

[3] Women being maternal and generally spending more time with the children post-divorce tend to be the kinship-keepers. They are said to be better at maintaining connections with ex-in-laws than men, who, when they remarry,

tend to show their loyalty to the new spouse by severing relationships with the exin-laws. (Hetherington, Marvis E. and Kelly, John. 2002. *For Better or For Worse: Divorce Reconsidered* N.Y.: W.W. Norton & Company.) If we accept this finding, then one conclusion is that maternal grandparents will have to work harder at keeping the doors of communication open with the former son-in-law if he gets custody of the children. Even if the father is not the custodial parent, it is much easier on children if grandparents support parents who remarry, especially in the early stages, when the newly evolved family is so vulnerable. According to Hetherington, it generally took five to seven years for the tensions of stepfamily life to decline to the point where the couple's stress level matched that of a husband and wife in a first marriage. Why does it take so long? A lot has to do with the ages, gender, and behavior of any children in the new constellation. In particular, when second marriages involve difficult adolescent children (especially girls,) there will be more pressure on the family. The early stage is a period of destabilization, while members learn how to compromise, get past their personal rivalries, and define their own space. Why seven years? It may take that long for adolescent children to mature and leave the house, at which point tensions subside.

Parental Guideposts: Chapter Nine

Grandparents as Stabilizers

- Make the time you spend with your grandchildren a respite from the problems in their home.
- Give your grandchild a sense of belonging to the larger extended family.
- Avoid disparaging former in-laws in front of your grandchildren.
- Demonstrate your willingness to cooperate with "the other side" for the sake of the grandchildren.
- Seek professional help if you are the designated caretaker of an especially challenging grandchild. Consider other options that may be best for everyone in the long run.
- Only take on the amount of caretaking responsibility you can realistically handle. Be ready to revisit your participation as the situation stabilizes.
- Keep the doors of communication open with both parents. Respect their rules and show appreciation for the time you have with your grandchildren. Keep in mind that spending time with your grandchild is a gift, not a given.
- Refrain from court battles. Ask a mutual friend or relative to advocate in your behalf if you are having difficulty gaining access to your grandchild. Make the legal route the last resort.
- Play a role in your grandchild's life. Create long-lasting bonds with letters, phone calls and e-mails.

✎ *Chapter Nine: Workbook Exercises*

Think about these three cases and your responses in each:

Case A. Your ex-daughter-in-law has canceled the last two visits you were supposed to spend with your five-year-old grandson. You decide to have a heart-to-heart with her first, and if that doesn't work, you will call her mother and find out what this is all about.

Plan what you will say to your ex-daughter-in-law.

What will you say to her mother?

Case B. Your son has joint custody of your two grandchildren, yet you rarely get to spend time with them. Your son says his time is too limited to share them with you.

What can you do to entice your son to spend some of his visitation time with his kids at your place? (Plan a video-movie night, a sleepover, a scrap booking party.)

What can you offer to do at his place during their visit that would both be helpful to your son and allow you time with your grandkids too?(E.g., offer to cook dinner for them and bring it over; offer to take the kids shopping for school clothes; offer to help with a homework project)

Case C. This is the first year your son and daughter-in-law are separated. You and your husband live in another state and have not seen the grandchildren since their parents' announcement. When you call to talk to the grandchildren, their mother is very cold. Often she says they are not home or makes excuses why they can't come to the phone. A month ago, you sent one of your grandchildren a CD player for his birthday, but you have not received any acknowledgement.

What should you do?

Chapter Ten

When Your Child Remarries

Can anyone blame you for being apprehensive when your child announces that he or she has met that special someone — again?

Establishing relationships with each member of a new blended family can be both daunting and gratifying. The roots of the extended family created through divorce and remarriage stretch far beyond the tree trunk. They include — in addition to the new son- or daughter-in-law — your grandchildren, any stepgrandchildren brought into the marriage, other grandparents, perhaps an ex-son or daughter-in-law and his/her extended family, and other strangers who suddenly become relatives.

Like Nora, you may be feeling uneasy — if guardedly optimistic — about the next stage of the divorce journey. Is it any wonder that you have questions about how the pieces of the puzzle are going to fit together and what your role is going to look like? Will you be an "insider" or an "outsider"?

Nora's story

While I looked forward to the day my son Ben would remarry, I wondered what effect that would have on our family. I was especially concerned about my grandchildren. The twins already had a mother and might resent sharing their father with a stepmother and new sibling(s) being thrust upon them. Ben, Janice, and Jake were a tight threesome. Joan was an omnipresence who, on occasion, upset the balance for Ben and the children. Generally, the disputes focused on visitation or money. The real issues were about control and retribution. Divorce wounds are subcutaneous — they take a long time to heal.

Gary and I tried to avoid getting in the middle of these disputes, but every once in a while Ben would call and sound off about something my former daughter-in-law had said or done. I'd managed to re-establish a civil relationship with Joan, and I didn't want to jeopardize our fragile link. When Ben complained, I advised him to pick his battles carefully for my sake as well as the twins'. Most of the time, the dust settled and we all went on with our lives.

Naturally, Gary and I talked about the possibility of Ben remarrying. We thought he'd be happier if he had someone to share the day-to-day responsibilities of caring for two active children. "Wouldn't that make life easier?" In some ways yes; in other ways no.

Two-and-a-half years after his divorce, Ben fell in love with Ruth, a thirty-five-year-old divorcee he met in St. Jo's emergency room when Jake broke his arm playing soccer. Ruth was sitting across the way, comforting fourteen-year-old Faith, who'd sliced her cheek sliding over a skate blade while playing ice hockey. Ben and Ruth later said that their kids' pain was their gain.

The first time I met Ruth, I knew she was going to be my next daughter-in-law. I liked Ruth and was happy for Ben, but I thought they were plunging into marriage a bit too quickly. They'd known each other only three months before they announced their engagement. I took a risk and told Ben I thought the twins needed more time to get to know Ruth and her daughter. I also let him know that I was against the two families just living together because it would send the wrong message to the children.

Ruth and Ben waited another three months until they made it official. They had a simple wedding in a friend's house, surrounded by the three children and our immediate family — so different from the splashy first wedding that had been planned for more than a year by my first daughter-in-law. Gary and I held hands while Ben and Ruth made their vows. With our fingers interlocked, both of us uttered a silent prayer, "Please, let this one last."

I knew that most children who lived in blended families lived with their biological mother and stepfather, and that it was far less common for children to live with their stepmother and biological dad. My twelve and a half year-old twin grandchildren would be living with Ruth. While I believed she would never want to replace their mother, she would be a strong influence in their lives, and I was concerned that she might be biting off more than she could chew, building a stepfamily while establishing a relationship with Ben.

In the first place, Ruth had been a single parent for twelve years. She was very independent and had her own ideas about parenting. Tom, Faith's father, was one of those long distance fade-out dads, who'd remarried right after his divorce, letting his new family take center stage. Other than spending a week during the summer or an occasional holiday with Tom, Faith had little to do with her father. She and her mother were very close. I had no idea how Faith would like sharing her mom with two younger stepsibs. Or having a new live-in Dad.

I was concerned about Joan's potential interference. While Ruth and her ex had little contact, Ben and Joan were very connected, since they shared custody. Even though Joan was the non-residential parent while she attended law school, she had a lot of input about her children's welfare. I knew that Ruth was going to have to consider Joan's opinions before she made decisions affecting the children. That would be difficult since Ruth was spending so much time caring for them. She needed some authority if the twins were going to toe the mark.

As I had predicted, there were plenty of rough spots. When Jake was having trouble with one teacher and wanted to switch out of her class, Ruth was willing to talk to the principal. Joan was adamantly opposed to his changing teachers. She stood firm and said Jake had to learn to get along with all kinds of people. When Janice wanted to quit piano, Joan insisted she stick it out for six more months.

"It's all well and good for Joan to lecture from her ivory tower," Ruth complained. "But I have to deal with the fallout." I sympathized with Ruth, who was trying to do her best with two testy children. Despite complaining about Ruth, I could see that the twins were growing attached to their stepmother.

There were other issues, mostly having to do with parenting styles. Ben had never been much of a disciplinarian, especially when he was so focused on work and his divorce. The twins were used to getting their own way. Ruth was much stricter. She objected to the twins staying up late to watch television and complained about their lack of responsibility around the house. Ben, she said, wasn't firm enough, even when it came to Faith, her own child, who was taking full advantage of her mom being otherwise occupied with two fractious stepchildren.

Ruth was not the only one struggling with parenting issues. Ben was overly cautious when it came to Faith. He preferred having a buddy relationship rather than being seen as an authority figure. Of course, the twins were quick to pick up the injustices. "But you let Faith do that!" they reminded him when he took a stand with them and let Faith get off breaking a rule.

Because the two parents could never agree on the rules, the children kept getting mixed messages. Remarriages are difficult in and of themselves. Stepchildren make the adjustment that much more difficult.

Meanwhile, Gary and I wanted Faith to accept us. I made a point of bringing our new stepgranddaughter little gifts when we visited. I kept trying to draw her out. In retrospect, I think I over-played my hand, being too attentive. Janice resented all the time I spent with her stepsister, and Jake, who was used to having his sister to himself, complained that the girls shut him out. He'd become the third wheel.

There were many dark patches that first year. However, by Thanksgiving, it seemed to me that Ben, Ruth, and the children had finally settled in together. I remembering watching my family gathered around the dining room table. Jake said something funny, and everyone was laughing. I don't know how it happened, but just then, it clicked. It seemed so natural, all of us being together.

•◄ *Remarriage Issues for Your Child* ►•

Once the honeymoon is over, your child and new in-law will have to do a fair amount of reshuffling. The first task is establishing a strong couple relationship, the foundation for remarriage. The second task, assuming one or both partners bring children into the new union, will be learning how to co-parent the stepchildren, who may be living full or part-time with the couple. The third is delineating stepparenting boundaries and negotiating with former spouses who may or may not be sharing custody.

Learning to co-parent means adjusting individual parenting styles so they do not come into conflict. Delineating stepparenting boundaries can be a difficult dance when biological parents have an adversarial relationship and use their children as pawns. Too often stepparents are caught in the crossfire. The real difficulty in remarriage is learning to stepparent while simultaneously cementing marital bonds.

According to the website of the Stepfamily Association of America (www.saafamilies.org), the U.S. Census Bureau 1988-1990 reported that about 65 percent of divorced parents bring children into a second marriage. The biggest source of conflict in second marriages is children — and their prepackaged problems. It helps to know some of the basic co-parenting issues your child is going to face:

Deciding whether to be a pal or an authority figure. A lot depends on the age of the stepchild, his or her receptivity to the new parent, and how comfortable your child feels laying down rules.

Getting through the testing period. It takes time and patience to win over a child who comes into the marriage resenting the stepparent from the get-go.

Learning to co-parent. Some parents are not willing to give up their authority over their own child.

Struggling with kinship issues. There are going to be times when your child will be blinded by his own child's faults, will be overprotective, or will over-compensate and not take his own child's side.

Being fair. It's hard to treat all children the same. Children are quick to pick up signs of favoritism, especially when they are competing for attention and attempting to triangulate. It's important to recognize that "fair" and "equal" are not the same thing!

Accepting a different parenting style. All of us have been raised differently from one another. Each of us tends to carry what is familiar forward and parent our own children accordingly. Your new son-in-law might be from the old school: "children should be seen and not heard." Your new daughter-in-law may be freewheeling and encourage debate.

Resolving ethnic or religious differences that affect the children. *Julie expected her husband's kids to go to Christmas Mass. Aaron was fine with his sons decorating the tree and exchanging presents, but he drew the line at going to church.*

Dealing with former spouses who have their own ideas how much influence a stepparent should have over the child(ren). If the ex-in-law resents the new mate, the stepparent will have a more difficult time parenting.

Dealing with a history of such problems as drug addiction or truancy. Trying to make a difference and turn things around may not be possible. Have realistic expectations.

According to E. Mavis Hetherington's research (2002), it generally took five to seven years for the tensions of stepfamily life to decline to the point where the couple's stress level matched that of a husband and wife in a first marriage. Why does it take so long? A lot has to do with the ages, gender, and behavior of any children in the new constellation. In particular, when second marriages involve difficult adolescent children there will be more pressure on the family. The early stage is a period of destabilization while members learn how to compromise, get past their personal rivalries, and define their own space. Why seven years? It may take that long for adolescent children to mature and leave the house, at which point tensions subside. Grandparents often act as buffers when there are problems between parents and stepparents, but they need to watch their boundaries.

●◄ *If You Want to Help Your Child* ►●

The best advice is to applaud your child who is making the effort to create a "more perfect union." It takes courage to take on someone else's children. Today many kids come into a remarriage with a lot of baggage related and unrelated to the failed prior marriage. Teenagers can be particularly difficult to win over. If a child has a behavior problem, self-esteem issues, problems with drugs or alcohol, etc., your adult son or daughter will be working twice as hard to build a relationship with the child to make this marriage work. Do what you can to support that effort.

One suggestion you might pass along to the new couple: Many couples prepare for remarriage by attending stepparenting groups. The Stepfamily Association of America, Inc. is an excellent place to begin if you are looking for local chapters. There are many other resources in your community. Check the telephone directory for social service agencies that can point you in the right direction. Use your Internet browser to surf some of the stepparenting Websites and online chat groups. Appendix B lists general reference materials you can find in bookstores or in your library. Again, *Strengthening Your Stepfamily* (Einstein & Albert, 2005) is a valuable resource. If your divorced child doesn't read much, there are audio tapes available on the subject of co-parenting and raising children in stepfamilies. To help the children sort things out, get a copy of *Jigsaw Puzzle Family* (MacGregor, 2005).

•◀ *Remarriage Issues that May Involve You* ▶•

Even if you are tickled pink that your child is rebuilding his or her life, you have reason to be concerned if you observe the following:

You see the couple rushing headlong into remarriage. This is Nora's first concern. You may recall that she stuck her neck out and advised Ben and Ruth to take more time. She anticipated that blending two families would be a complicated business. Robert E. Stahmann, Ph.D., professor of family sciences and head of the Marriage Preparation Research Project at Brigham Young University, was quoted in an article on the *Psychology Today* website: "[Couples] need to know each other individually and jointly. This means time for bonding as a couple because the relationship will be under stress from each partner's various links to the past..." i.e.

their heritage, past marriages, and children. The timing of a remarriage has a major influence on its success or failure. In the case of blended families, when children enter the picture, the couple needs additional time to coalesce relationships. "The vast majority of children, especially those who have been prepared for the new marriage and have had prior contact with the prospective stepfather, eventually view the move positively if the marital relationship is good and the stepparent is warm and supportive," advise Hetherington and Kelly, who studied nearly fourteen hundred post-nuclear families to determine how remarriage affected the parties. Boys (particularly adolescent boys) will have a harder time adjusting to the changes than adolescent girls, who will nonetheless be wary. Children need time to get over their jealousy, suspicion of and rivalry with the new person. In light of the fact that approximately 60 percent of second marriages fail, and that the leading issue is problems with children, you should encourage your son or daughter to spend time getting to know the children before rushing into remarriage.

You notice the couple is much more focused on themselves than on their children. According to some relationship experts, couples who remarry often become so focused on their own happiness they fall into the trap of thinking their families will merge seamlessly. As one college student whose mom remarried commented, "Just because your parent is ecstatic doesn't mean you're going to be thrilled with the arrangement."

Barbara LeBey, author of *Remarried with Children: Ten Secrets for Successfully Blending and Extending Your Family* writes from personal experience as the head of a blended family. She notes that very often the expectations for bonding two disparate units are too high. Couples need to be realistic about the amount of time it will take for everyone to find their place in the new unit. Grandparents can help by making their home a neutral gathering place, where new and prospective family members can get to know one another. It worked for this woman:

Lucille invited her son's girlfriend and her two children over for lunch. She brought out Monopoly. In no time, her grandkids and the two younger guests were competing to buy Park Place.

You realize that everyone is pushing too hard. I think we can sympathize with Nora, who was frustrated that she could not win over her stepgranddaughter. She decided to back off, realizing she was overplaying her hand. Faith was just not that receptive, and Nora's own grandchildren resented all the attention their grandma was paying their new stepsister.

There are a number of issues to consider before showering stepchildren with attention. First, children need time to adjust to new family members. Just as they need time to process their parents' breakup, they need time to process a remarriage. Grandparents are part of the territory they may not want to explore. Second, since most children are shy of strangers, even loving children will be suspicious if someone else's grandmother comes on too quickly — or is too distancing, for that matter. Third, divorce can effect disengagement from the family. During separation and divorce, the child's peers may become more important than family members; teenagers, in particular, may avoid new family contact. Last, by overcompensating, you risk making your biological grandchildren jealous.

•◀ *Your Attitude Can Make the Difference* ▶•

Like Nora, you may be standing on the sidelines observing the changes in your family. You may like what you see, or you may disapprove. Not all parents are as supportive as Nora was when their child remarries. Many are still mourning the loss of the past or unhappy with their child's new choice of a spouse. It goes without saying that in order to help rebuild your family you must be willing to accept the changes. It will help if you understand the dynamics of the new constellation and the adjustment issues that are involved. Once again, the book *Strengthening Your Stepfamily* (Einstein & Albert, 2005) is an excellent resource which will help you understand your grandparenting role.

Grandchildren — and stepgrandchildren — may be unwilling participants in their parents' newfound happiness:

Doris knew that her daughter had been struggling with whether or not to marry Cliff. "It was my grandson who pushed her into finally saying yes," she told me. "Gregory wanted to be like all the other kids. He desperately wanted a father. I'll never forget the day my grandson called and yelled, 'Grandma, Guess what? We're getting married.' I was so happy for Greg; I just burst out in tears. My new son-in-law has three biological children from two previous marriages. I was concerned about whether or not this marriage would work out with that kind of track record. But Cliff is a fantastic stepdad. My daughter is so happy. I wish she'd found him ages ago, but then Greg wouldn't have this instant family, would he?"

It's not only your sons and daughters who are looking for happiness; so are your grandkids. Grandparents can make it easier for them. Let's take a look at how You can help.

●◀ Tips from Seasoned Grandparents and Stepgrandparents ▶●

In gathering material for this book, I talked to many grandparents and stepgrandparents, who were only too happy to pass along their advice:

- Don't expect immediate affection from the stepgrandchildren. Try not to come on too strongly in your effort to get to know them. Give them space. Kids are cautious. You are a stranger adding to all the other pressures on them to fit in.
- Treat your stepgrandchildren and biological grandchildren fairly but make distinctions. Give comparable not the same gifts — "fair" is not "equal." Individualize. For example, if you give one child a bicycle, you can give the other a portable DVD player.
- Remember to send a card on birthdays and special occasions to your stepgrandchild to show you care. E-mail a hello every so often if the child is away at school and you want to establish some relationship. However, take your cues from the child. Don't push too hard.

- Make an effort to get to know each stepchild individually. Find out special interests, skills, hobbies, etc.
- Discuss what stepchildren should call you. Older children may want call you by your first name. If you feel comfortable in the very beginning, say, "Call me Grandpa Pat," but don't be hurt if the child just sticks with Mr. Brown for a while. One day he might surprise you and introduce you as "Gramps."
- Read up about stepgrandparenting. There are many excellent books listed in Appendix B. There are many Internet sites that you can visit for additional help — this is a very popular topic. You might even engage in a chat group and discuss your issues with other stepgrandparents. Take care, however, to maintain your confidentiality.

●◀ *Those Teens and "Tweens"* ▶●

As I noted above, any teenage grandchildren you inherit may have a more difficult time accepting you than younger children, especially in the early stages of the remarriage. Hetherington and Kelly noted in their study that one reason young boys have more difficulty in adjusting to divorce is that they get less emotional support from their overstressed mothers, who find single-parenting boys more physically and emotionally demanding than single-parenting daughters. The loss of a male presence and a boy's attempt to stand in the gap may further complicate the boy's adjustment and cause him to be less accepting of a rival when his mother remarries. Young girls, the authors found, adjusted more readily to divorce. In general, they were less vulnerable to the absence of a male authority figure, which doesn't presume they readily accepted competitors for their mother's attention.

Older kids will be cautious and seem more aloof than they really are. Keep in mind that everyone is looking for acceptance. Don't overwhelm older children with your affection. Show them respect and some distance. Learn what the teenager in your new family is all about — ask his or her parent about the child's interests and goals. Eventually this stepchild will be more approachable. If you are patient and keep a respectful arm's distance in the beginning, you have a greater chance of becoming fast friends in the future.

Another word of caution: If a grandchild or stepgrandchild resents the remarriage, you are automatically a target for his anger, just on general principles. The best strategy is to keep trying, but not pushing. Use some humor. If everything fails, you may have to back off until the child has sorted out his issues. It will take time for the defensive child to figure out that this marriage is a done deal and you are part of the package.

●◀ *What about the Unlovable Stepgrandchild?* ▶●

Let's face it: some kids are lovable, and some are not. More than one grandparent has inherited a stepgrandchild with purple hair and body piercing. Stepchildren come pre-packaged. Look beyond the tattoos if you can — remember that adage about beauty being only skin-deep. Smart grandparents find a common meeting ground.

> *Clark was mortified by his stepgrandchild's terrible table manners and sloppy appearance. He told his son in no uncertain terms that no way would he be seen with this kid in a restaurant, but Clark did take the young man to a baseball game, where manners and neatness were of less importance. Clark and his stepgrandson could let their hair down at the game (granted the boy's hair was a lot longer than the elderly gentleman's was!) and enjoy each other's company.*

Remember that your stepgrandchildren are learning about you while you are learning about them. There's usually a good reason why kids behave the way they do, so why not give the newcomers some slack? If your stepgrandchildren see how well you get along with your grandchildren, they will probably want to know what you're all about and want find out what they are missing.

A word to the wise: One surefire way to wreck your child's chances for marital happiness is to complain bitterly about a stepgrandkid. More than likely, your son or daughter already has an inkling that there's a problem and will appreciate your tolerance.

The experts, including Dr. Arthur Kornhaber, whom I have cited throughout this book, predict that at least one-third of all grandparents will eventually have a stepgrandchild, due to the changing norms and definitions of marriage in today's society.[1] Dr. Kornhaber also reminds stepparents and stepgrandparents that they can play a significant loving and protective role in a stepchild's emotional well-being, especially if that child has been neglected or abandoned in the past. Some may be harder to reach, but it's worth the effort for the sake of healing and rebuilding the family.

►◄ Remarriage Issues for the Grandchildren ►●

Children are deeply affected by their parent's remarriage. Many have not fully processed their parents' divorce when they are thrust into another situation over which they have no control. It is easy to overlook the many sacrifices children make. Carlos's story is a good example.

> *"The thing is, I didn't know my stepfather very well when my mom got remarried. I'd met Enrico a couple of times, and all of a sudden here was this guy laying down the law and telling me what to do. My mom sold our house, and we moved in with my stepfather because his place was a lot bigger, and it was set up for his other kids, who used stay over on the weekends. It was a madhouse when we were all there. I had to transfer to a new high school in the middle of my junior year, and it was tough making new friends. I didn't do well in school that year because I was pretty miserable. I moved back in with my dad, but he was always working or going out somewhere, and I was alone a lot. Holidays were the real pain. My folks wanted me to split them down the middle. Half the time I never knew where I was supposed to be. That first Christmas I went to my mother's, and just about everyone there was from Enrico's side. I felt very uncomfortable. I mean, it was Christmas, and I was with all these strangers. When I went away to college, I wound up staying at school during school breaks or going to a friend's house to avoid the hassle of going home."*

You can see how difficult it was for Carlos. Here are some other issues children struggle with when their parents remarry. You might want to check the ones you think your own grandchildren might face when and if one of their parents remarries.

- Sharing the biological parent with the new spouse and stepsiblings.
- Competing for attention with younger or older, more outgoing, more accomplished stepchildren.
- Experiencing a change in status and position in the family — going from the (youngest, middle, oldest) to the (youngest, middle, oldest).
- Making physical accommodations — moving to a new home, town, state; changing schools; sharing a room; leaving friends, a pet.
- Moving farther away from a biological parent and having fewer visitations or difficult visitation arrangements.
- Not having sufficient time to get to know the stepparent or stepsiblings before the remarriage.
- Not having sufficient time before switching from one house to another.
- Trying to meet the expectations of a parent who is over-anxious that the child makes a good impression and fits well into the new constellation.
- Having engaged in magical thinking that the absentee parent would return or the parents would get back together, and now facing the reality of that impossibility when the stepparent steps in the picture.
- Feeling guilt because one parent has achieved happiness and the other one is still single.
- Feeling guilt that there is so much financial inequality now that one parent has married and the other parent is still struggling to make ends meet.
- Being caught in the middle of the biological parents' tug of war because the remarriage has intensified their antagonism.
- Being caught in a rivalry between a stepparent and the biological parent.
- Knowing other members of the family don't approve of the remarriage and are not supportive.

•◀ Can You Help an Unhappy Grandchild? ▶•

While you cannot perform miracles if your grandchild or stepgrandchild is truly unhappy with the new arrangement, you can be empathetic and positive without going overboard. It might help to acknowledge how difficult it is for your grandchild if he is struggling to fit in. Be the adult who notices how hard she is trying. You might say something like, "I'm very proud of you for sharing your room with Vinnie," or "I know it's not easy moving in the middle of the school year, but I think it's great that you're getting good grades (you're making new friends, you've joined the soccer team, etc.)"

Be empathetic if your stepgrandchild comes to you with a complaint. But be careful of boundaries. Your role in the new family constellation can be tricky — you are almost like an invited guest when it comes to the new in-law's child. Keep in mind that in order to develop a relationship with the stepchild, you must also earn the respect of his or her parent.

•◀ Why Do Some Kids Do Better than Others? ▶•

According to the experts, children between ten and fourteen years old usually will have the most difficulty adjusting to their parent's remarriage. Younger children are more flexible. Assuming there is no stress and they have time to get to know the partner, they will be more accepting. Older children can always look forward to leaving home or choose to live with a biological parent if they are unhappy.

•◀ The Flip Side: Happy Stepkids ▶•

Up until now, the focus has been on the difficulties children have adapting to the new family when their parents remarry. Let's not forget that there are many situations when children are thrilled their parents have found a new mate. Remarriage may mean more financial security and less pressure for the previously single-parent household. It is often a very happy occasion for a child whose life has been disrupted by divorce. Many appreciate the fact that their parent is not so stressed and that the family feels more complete again.

Children in remarriage report having more family time as well as another adult to go to for advice.

Judith Wallerstein (2001) offers these words of hope: "As children of divorce move into their late twenties and thirties, relationships with their parents change unexpectedly. Both generations have another chance to reexamine their interest in one another. Each developmental stage in adulthood offers the potential to grow as a person, to enhance one's closest relationships that have gone awry, and to correct past mistakes and poor judgment...." There are countless stories of children who have eventually formed close bonds with their stepparent and have even been adopted by a stepparent. Blood is not always thicker than water, in spite of what people think. Listen to Jeanette's story:

> *"My son was seven and Jason's daughter was three when Jason and I got married. I made it my life's mission to offer my stepdaughter, Teri, a positive role model and to rescue her from turning out like her mother, a co-dependent who had grown up in a dysfunctional family. My intentions were naïve, and my efforts often backfired. Generally, though, I thought I was succeeding. Teri struggled with the wide disparity in rules between her two homes, and with never living in one place long enough to make lasting friendships. Her mom exacerbated her problems with her incessant phone calls to our house, crying and complaining about her daughter's neglect of her and her "loving Jeanette more" when she was living with us. To make a long story short, Teri and I had a major fight one day and, when she went back to live with her mother for good, I was devastated by my failure to keep her happy and with us. Years went by and we rarely saw Teri. It was hard on my husband, but he wasn't willing to go head-to-head with his ex over anything, including his own daughter. After Teri started college, she moved out of her mom's place, and could communicate freely with us without the "oversight" happening. Our relationship took on a new dynamic. I could chat with her about college stuff, and she came to see us often. The wonderful finale occurred after her graduation ceremony,*

when we were all out to dinner. Teri announced to the family that she had something to give me. She took off one of the stoles she was wearing over her graduation gown. It was the university's traditional "stole of gratitude," something that's typically given as a gesture of appreciation to someone who had most inspired or encouraged the graduate during his or her time there. She placed it over my head and thanked me for my support, letting everyone know how much my help had meant to her. I guess I had done something right! The tears of joy I shed that night and the incredible miracle of that moment made all those other tears I had shed in frustration, anger, doubt... all worth it."

●◀ You're Going to Get the Whole Package, Too ▶●

Whether you like it or not, when your child remarries you will inherit a bunch of new relatives... and their problems. Let's face it: Remarriage is difficult enough without parents creating more complications for the new couple. I have heard all kinds of stories about in-laws who made life unbearable for the new couple. The parents were dropped like hot potatoes. Unfortunately for them, they lost out on watching their grandchildren grow up.

Your relationship with your child is largely up to you, and the first step for rebuilding your family is your willingness to accept change. It's a question of *attitude*. The remarriage can be your opportunity to strengthen bonds with your child, or it can be the wedge that finally drives you apart.

Obviously, you will be less positive about the remarriage if you think your child jumped into the second marriage too quickly. So-called transitional — rebound — relationships (right after divorce) are a very poor foundation for another marriage. It takes time for your children to accept responsibility for the failure of the first marriage.

And you may be unwilling to give your stamp of approval to the second marriage if you think the new spouse was the cause of the breakup. "I will never accept that home-wrecker as my child," one mother stormed. Maybe if this mother knew the reason why her son found comfort in the other woman's arms, she would be more accepting. Chances are she will never know if she slams the door in the new woman's face.

Clearly, you will have trouble accepting your child's new spouse if you are still mourning the loss of the last one. You may feel disloyal building an attachment to the woman who is not the mother of your grandchild. Perhaps you and your former in-law had a great deal in common as in this situation:

Fabian's son-in-law shared his love of opera. They had season tickets, and Fabian always looked forward to the evenings they spent together. His new son-in-law is far more comfortable with his head underneath the car hood than following a libretto. Fabian misses his ex-son-in-law and just can't seem to get on the same wavelength as this one.

Think about it. Why has your child chosen someone completely different from the last spouse? Could it be that he or she was afraid of making the same mistake twice and was intentionally looking for someone completely different in personality? Alternatively, could it be that your son or daughter may have discovered delightful things about himself or herself that this new partner brought out? Rejoice in variety, and in your child's happiness. Move on.

What is Family?

The Background

Family or kinship used to assume blood ties resulting from marriage with the adults responsible for childcare. In Western society, kinships were monogamous and between men and women. The traditional family of the 1950s, (the so-called "Ozzie and Harriet" generation) was the "intact nuclear family" composed of the husband (the breadwinner), wife (the caretaker) and the couple's biological or adopted children. Today there are many alternatives to the intact family due to cohabitation, single parenting, merging families, and same-sex unions. Statistically, as women divorce or choose to have children without marrying, more and more families are headed by single females.

There are a number of explanations for this dramatic turn of events. Sociologists point to the ideologies of self-fulfillment, entitlement, personal freedom, and self-realization promoted in the 1960s and afterward as a significant factor in the spiking divorce rate. Others say liberal no-fault divorce policies made the divorce process easier. (No-fault is divorce granted without the need to establish wrongdoing by either party.) In turn, the feminist movement de-stigmatized divorce and created the "New Woman," who was encouraged to paddle her own canoe by becoming economically independent. It is also reported that newlyweds are older today as more and more young people decide to live together before tying the knot — often for the benefit of their children — and an increasing number of women compete in the workforce before settling into the domestic role. Finally, as attitudes change, the public is more accepting of same-sex parents fostering, adopting, and bearing children.

By far, the biggest impact on family patterns today has been the proliferation of the blended family. According to the U.S. Census, a blended family is made up of a husband, wife and two or more children, who are all step- or half-siblings brought into the marriage from previous unions by one or both parents. It should be noted that the term "blended" is largely a misnomer as it presumes that when two disparate families merge, their members will homogenize like a milkshake once they are put in the same container. This is far from the truth. As one woman who spent most of her life in a reconstituted family put it, "Mine was more like a soup, with each of my siblings and stepsiblings retaining our own texture and individuality."

The Trend

The latest statistics are still out, but in 1990, 5.3 million married-couple family households contained at least one stepchild under the age of eighteen. Two-and-a-half million children lived in blended families. According to the U.S. Bureau Census Report (1990):

Americans have seen the marriage and divorce norms and behaviors that are acceptable to our society evolve over the past 25 years — with a particular emphasis on the broadening of acceptable behaviors. Women feel freer to have and raise children without getting married. Couples are marrying later, and they are divorcing and remarrying in numbers that would have been beyond comprehension 25 years ago.... The data also show that divorce has peaked and will subside somewhat but will still remain high enough to continue to merit major attention as a social and economic issue. In addition, the data show that, although remarriage rates have fallen, the growth of consequent stepfamilies is significant, and that a large segment of the United States adult population flows into and out of several marital categories during their life course.

The Debate

Many believe the breakdown of the intact family is a sign of our nation's vitality, citing tolerance and diversity as indications of progress. For others, the breakdown is further proof we are neglecting our children. U.S. Senator Hillary Clinton of New York has written "...Children living with one parent or in stepfamilies are two to three times more likely to have emotional and behavioral problems as children living in two-parent families.... Every society requires a critical mass of families that fit the traditional idea, both to meet the needs of most children and to serve as a model for other adults who are raising children in difficult settings. We are at risk of losing that critical mass today" (Crouch, *The Marriage Movement*).

University of California family sociologist Judith Stacey, a senior scholar with the Council on Contemporary Families, who has studied the politics of family change and values in the postmodern age, is among those who argue that children do not need traditional family structures to thrive. Stacey says children's needs are best served by good parenting in any combination, restructured work schedules, adequate health benefits, and by correcting the economic inequities of divorce.

What about the Ex-in-Laws?

When your child remarries, he or she expects your primary allegiance to be with his or her new mate. Some parents have difficulty maintaining dual affiliation. If you have maintained a congenial relationship with the former daughter-in-law (and all the professionals say you should, for the sake of your grandchild), you will want to continue this relationship. How can you do this without offending the new daughter-in-law? Will you be showing disloyalty to the former spouse, who may not be thrilled with the remarriage? Maintaining relationships with the new and former spouse is going to test your diplomacy. You are on safe ground if you:

- Take your cues from your child about how close or distant you should be from the former spouse.
- Never compare in-laws, especially in front of your grandchild or stepgrandchild, who will bear tales.
- Look for ways to recognize and show respect for the new spouse. Go public with your praise, even if you have to dig deep.
- Do not play the present and former spouse against each other or share confidences with either one.
- Keep in mind that this new spouse is your child's heartthrob. This is the link to an ongoing relationship with your son or daughter.

It is not impossible to stay connected to the ex-son- or ex-daughter-in-law. I have spoken to more than one parent who keeps adding leaves to the Thanksgiving table each year as the family branches out. I know many siblings who have managed to remain close friends with former in-laws without offending the new relative or that person's sister or brother. It just takes tact.

The new family is a growing organism, vital and energetic. Intergenerational links should be maintained whenever possible, but you cannot afford to indulge in fantasies. Respect the feelings of ex-in-laws, who may have difficulty keeping these connections when they remarry.

> *Patty knew her son was uncomfortable having his ex-wife and her parents at his daughter's senior piano recital, so she decided not to invite the ex-in-laws back to her house for the dinner she had planned in celebration of Elizabeth's special occasion, even though her granddaughter would love to have everyone there. Patty hoped that the ex-in-laws would make their own plans with Elizabeth, considering the circumstances.*

Don't push family togetherness. Be thankful everyone is civil enough to one another not to cause a scene when they get together. Patty should breathe a sigh of relief that everyone was there to enjoy the event, and was wise to understand the boundaries of family togetherness.

•◀ *Pulling Away from the Family Moorings* ▶•

It would be to your benefit to anticipate some of the likely changes when your child remarries. It seems obvious, but many parents try to cling to "the way things always have been." In order to reach this final goal — family rebuilding — you will need to be realistic about the new life your child and your grandchildren have, and where this leaves you.

During the rescue and re-stabilization periods, your child may have reattached to your family. Appreciate the closeness you had when you were needed. It's logical that there is going to be a natural pulling away from the moorings you provided and seeking another shore in the new marriage relationship. Anticipate the following:

- Holidays will be divided among other sets of relatives. You will have to plan ahead to get everyone together. Put your bid in early.
- If the new spouse comes from a very different cultural or religious background, your child may embrace these new ways

and neglect your family heritage. You may be disappointed. Know this is your child's way of bonding and cementing the new relationship, not a rejection of your heritage.

- Remarriages are invariably kid-focused. Your child will be coping with increased demands on her time. When you visit, you may be struck by the "mayhem" — one parent's label for six kids coming and going, three cats and two dogs running around the house, and the telephone ringing every two minutes. Your son or daughter may not be able to have those late-night chats with you anymore.

- Economic pressures often surface when there are divorce payments in addition to the costs of raising a blended family. Your child may not be able to afford to visit you if you are a long-distance grandparent. You may be asked for financial help if the family is struggling to get on its feet. Refer back to chapter 3 for how to deal with the call "Mom, Dad . . . I Need Money."

•◄ Ties That Bind ►•

Today's families have many branches. According to 2002 U.S. population data, reported in July 2005 by Kreider and Fields, families with stepparents or adoptive parents are an increasingly large component of two-parent families. Diagramming your family tree may become more and more complicated as the years go by. The roots will spread out in all directions, but remember that the tree will be nourished by all the love and care you feed it.

Families need stability. You can only hope that your child will find permanent happiness in this next marriage. The best thing you as parents can do is validate the new family by conveying optimism, acceptance and respect.

That's what Nora is trying to do.

END NOTES

[1] Because of divorce and remarriage, many children have six to eight adults in the "grandparent" role in their lives. Between 20 percent and 25 percent of grandparents will be stepgrandparents either through their own or through their adult children's divorces and remarriages." http://www.legacyproject.org

Parental Guideposts: Chapter Ten

When Your Child Remarries

Continuity of family is important. Our parenting role is threefold. We want to:

Communicate our own history
Acknowledge the uniqueness of each new member
Create a new family identity.

Here are some suggestions.

- Mark family occasions such as special birthdays and anniversaries. Invite new members to join in the celebration.
- Learn about your new in-law's holidays and festivities, and make them a part of your family's repertoire.
- Create a unique family history by collecting photos, memorabilia, recipes, songs, etc. Create a new family photo album.
- Promote your blended family's identity by selecting holidays to celebrate, stories to tell.
- Share your family stories and encourage new members to share theirs.
- Include peculiarities with the positive traits. Example: Our family celebrates Thanksgiving on Fridays.
- Spend family time having fun. Organize vacations in new places.
- Acknowledge the individuality, the creativity, the special skills and abilities of each new member.
- Spend quality time with each person.

[2] 4.9 million children in the U.S. are living with a biological parent and a stepparent. Of these, 4.1 million were living with a biological mother and a stepfather. Fifteen percent of children (10.6 million) lived in blended families. One out of five children is not living in what Americans think is a traditional family with both birth parents.

[3] In the Ahrons study, five years post-divorce, 45 percent of mothers surveyed had remarried and 72 percent of fathers. By the end of year one, 4 percent of women and 22 percent of men; year two, 35 percent of women and 55 percent of men; by three years, another 23 percent of women and 21 percent of men had cohabitations.

✎ *Chapter Ten: Workbook Exercises*

1. Take a moment to ask yourself these questions:

   a. How do I feel about my child's remarriage?

   b. If I have reservations, what are they?

   c. How do I feel about my stepgrandparenting role?

   d. What can I do to support my stepgrandchildren?

2. Think about your role as your family's historian. What do you want to preserve and teach the new members about your family roots?

3. What are you interested in learning about the new member's history?

Nora's Epilogue

When I think back to what this divorce journey was like, I can't help sighing. Sometimes I wonder how I ever survived the ups and downs.

Ben, Ruth, Faith, and my grandchildren have busy lives these days. They are all juggling lots of balls in the air. Blended families are demanding! Two sets of grandparents and one set of stepgrandparents are always competing for their time.

The twins are old enough to take the train to visit their mother on alternate weekends. They have decided to continue to live with Ben and Ruth, but that may change at any time. We all understand that.

There is a lot less antagonism between Ben and Joan now that each has moved on and has his or her own life. Their ties will never be completely broken. How can they be? Their children will bind them forever.

I see far less of Joan since Ben's remarriage. Joan is working full-time in a New York law firm and seems happy in her career. The children have begun talking about someone named Jim, so I gather that Joan is in a serious relationship. Should she remarry, I doubt if I will be invited to her wedding, but I would certainly offer my congratulations and encourage my grandchildren to find a place for their stepfather in our ever-evolving family. Thankfully, Joan remains cancer-free after the five-year mark.

My new daughter-in-law, Ruth, and I have developed a warm relationship. Of course, it's different from the one I had with Joan. I guess I'm hesitant to get too close. I think that both Ruth and I have let our experiences with divorce make us just a bit tentative. That is sad.

Ruth is a wonderful mother and stepmother. I bless her for her patience with the twins and the happiness she has brought into Ben's life. They have a good marriage. I watch them work hard at getting over the rough patches.

As for Ben, I see many positive changes in my son that may or may not have to do with the experience of ending one marriage and beginning another. I believe these changes have more to do with his ability to look backward and finally get past his personal pain while fashioning a brighter future.

Recently Ben was offered a promotion that meant relocating the family to Texas. The track of ambition carries many cars, not just the engine. A move meant the twins would be separated from Joan, and Ruth would have the burden of resettling the children one more time. Ben declined the offer. Needless to say, Gary and I breathed a sigh of relief.

I know that many parents think of their child's divorce in terms of loss. Others who have watched their unhappy son or daughter from the sidelines call it a new beginning.

I see it as neither a beginning nor an end. It's a continuum, another one of life's challenges with new parental tasks, new obstacles, and new rewards. It's playing different roles at different stages in their child's divorce journey, knowing when to move to the foreground and when to step back.

It's not something we planned when our child got married. It's simply what we do to rebuild our family for the sake of future generations.

Guide

A Five-Stage Guide through Your Child's Divorce:

What You Can Expect...
What You Can Do to Help
the Family Rebuild

A Five-Stage Guide through Your Child's Divorce

What is the Stage?	What Can You Expect?	What Is Your Goal?
I. Accepting the News	Typically, after your child and his/her spouse have already made the decision, you will be told. Your child will measure your reaction, which can affect your future relationship and involvement in the next stages.	Maintaining objectivity and providing open-ended support during chaotic times.
II. Rescuing Your Child	In first weeks or months after the breakup, your child will feel emotionally and physically adrift. This dis-equilibrium may last three to six months.	Providing intensive emotional and/or emergency assistance to make sure your child and grandchildren have basic needs met and feel connected to the extended family.
III. Responding to Changes	After the initial crisis period has passed, your child will need to reorganize his/her life.	Helping your single-again child form a new identity, new relationships, roles, career. Providing family backup so your child will feel less isolated and more secure.
IV. Stabilizing the Family	After the divorce is final, your child will become more future-oriented and begin to set new goals for him- or herself.	Becoming your child's backup, not a lifeline. Allowing your child to re-assume responsibility for the changes in his/her life.
V. Refocusing and Rebuilding	When your family has branched out and reconfigured (especially if your child remarries), there will be some natural distancing between you/your spouse and your child again as you resume your life and your child forms new bonds.	Balancing your own and your family's needs. Accepting the new family constellation.

What Can You Do?	What Are the Obstacles?
Demonstrate loyalty to your child. Withhold blame. Focus on immediate needs. Keep lines of communication open. Go public with the news. Model loyalty for other family members. Reassure your grandchildren.	Lacking details behind the breakup. Having to choose sides. Dealing with gossip. Distancing from in-laws. Coping with your own emotions.
Offer financial assistance. Provide temporary housing. Help with childcare. Help with household management. Check in frequently. Research legal and financial information/help. Assist with pressing legal needs. Give emotional support to grandchildren.	Rushing in too soon. Exaggerating or underestimating the needs. Putting your own life on hold. Neglecting other family members. Sacrificing privacy. Having trouble maintaining loyalty after unpleasant revelations. Taking over. Prolonging this stage. Parent-child regression.
Encourage your child to set new goals (e.g., education, job, relocation). Provide in-kind assistance as appropriate to facilitate his/her new goal(s). Convey optimism about the future. Build bridges with ex-in-laws for sake of grandchildren. If loans were made, create a repayment schedule.	Reluctance to have child move away. Dwelling on inequities in the divorce settlement. Lacking confidence in your child's ability to move on. Blaming all problems on the divorce. Resistance to change.
Continue to support and encourage his/her work/education goals. Encourage problem solving. Continue to be involved with grandkids. Continue to build bridges with ex-in-laws. Return to your own "life" — invest in your own physical and emotional well-being.	Inability to establish appropriate boundaries. Allowing divorced child's problem to dominate your life. Resentment about changes in family. Hostility towards ex. Blaming all other family problems on the divorce.
Be open-minded and openhearted. Be inclusive. Carve out a unique place for new family members. Assume the role of stepgrandparent. Become your family's historian — a tradition maker. Take care of you!	Inability to break with the past. Clinging to hostility and resentment. Inability to accept your child's new spouse/kids. Creating guilt and indebtedness in your child for your past help. Unwillingness to negotiate holidays and making unrealistic demands on the new family that has many obligations.

Appendix A

Legal and Financial Issues
of Divorce

THIS APPENDIX IS OFFERED AS GENERAL INFORMATION on a few of the more common legal and financial concerns surrounding the divorce process. It is not a substitute for professional advice on legal or financial issues. Neither the author nor the publisher is engaged in rendering legal, financial, or other professional services. If expert assistance or counseling is needed, the services of a competent professional should be sought.

Although presented in the style and format of a chapter, this information is positioned as an appendix, because the information offered is rather complex and would have interrupted the flow of Nora's story through the book. *Don't ignore it* just because it appears here, however. The information you gain from these pages could be critical in your ability to help your child through the legal maze of divorce. It has been included to familiarize you with terms and legal issues related to your child's divorce.

> *In my practice, I am always delighted when a client brings along a family member or trusted friend. Since divorce and custody are extremely emotional issues, similar to visiting a doctor, you may recall little of the discussion at the meeting. Your trusted friend or relative will help you recall the meeting details, [as will] a memo of the meeting from your attorney.*
>
> — Wendy E. Prince, Attorney Mediator[1]

●◀ *Where Do the Parents of Divorcing Adults Fit In?* ▶●

There are many worthwhile pieces of advice, like the one above, for parents who are helping their child during his or her divorce. Divorces are often messy and complicated affairs. There are many legal and moral dilemmas when it comes to financial settlements, child custody issues, and grandparenting rights. Your job is to help and support your child, not to become embroiled in the couple's dispute. By being as objective and informed as possible, should you be asked, you will be equipped to offer intelligent advice. Even so armed, your best course of action is to refer your child to professionals trained in family law and divorce finances who can help families resolve disputes when there are knotty issues around property, business, and child custody.

◆ *Who Are the Experts?* ▶

Experts in divorce include a Certified Divorce Financial Planner (CDFP) or an accountant knowledgeable about business, real property (both commercial and residential), and retirement plans, and appraisers who can estimate the true value of employee option plans and personal property (e.g. art, wine, antique collections). These professionals can guide decisions during negotiations when good judgment is needed to assure your child's future well-being.

Many parents have strong convictions about how their child's divorce should be handled. It is likely that if you have "been there, done that" yourself, you would want your divorcing child to profit (literally and figuratively) from your mistake. Keep in mind that times are different. There are different options for *marital dissolution*. (Note even the word "divorce" has been replaced by a friendlier term.) Divorce laws are not the same in each state. The state where you sought your divorce, for example, may have different rulings and precedents about community property from the one where your child is seeking a settlement. Even within the same state in which you got divorced, state law may have changed since your proceeding.

A key consideration is that your child and the soon-to-be ex have their own views about how their divorce should be handled. You need to respect their decisions for the sake of your future relationship with both parties.

You may be asked to do some legwork to save time and money. Or, if your child is too overwhelmed by his or her circumstances to cope and you begin to play an active role, you will have to understand some divorce fundamentals. Keep in mind that the information in this chapter is general. Terminology, laws, and rulings keep changing.

This appendix is organized around several key topics: *Process, Pocketbook, Property, Parenting and Custody*, and *Grandparenting*.

Let's begin by reviewing the divorce itself — what we are calling *process*. We will consider four options, but before we consider the benefits and drawbacks of each one, let's define terms. The *action for dissolution of marriage* is a lawsuit that one partner brings against the other. The spouse who initiates the lawsuit is called the *plaintiff*, and the other spouse is called the *defendant*.

A key decision your child and his or her partner will have to make is how to untie the knot. There are many different options today, some of which may strike you as risky. In your day, you may have hired an expensive litigator, and now you want to provide your child with Mr. Nasty or Ms. Shark, who will also go for the jugular. Keep in mind that this is your child's divorce. The adversarial approach — *litigation* — is not always the best option for getting the best settlement. In fact, research has shown that couples who can agree amicably on the terms of their divorce outside the court are more likely to abide by those terms than those who must live with decisions handed down to them by a stranger.

Today, there are nicer ways people can get divorced. *Mediation* and *collaboration* methods are growing in popularity. They are fair, professional, less expensive, and just as binding as litigation. Mediation and collaborative divorce are non-adversarial options. Couples work together to prioritize the needs of their children. They try to be fair and objective and are able to maintain respect for one another as former partners in the marriage.

Some couples shun the expense of professional help and approach divorce as a *do-it-yourself* project. That method can work, if there are no children, little property, and the couple has maintained a *very* cooperative relationship.

Let's take a closer look at each of the four options.

Litigation: Each partner engages an attorney to hammer out the divorce settlement. The lawyers argue before a judge (there is no jury by peers in divorce cases), who hands down a decision that both parties must accept. Litigation inevitably results as a last resort in an adversarial situation. For example, when there is an imbalance of power on the emotional and/or economic levels between divorcing partners, and too many contested issues to negotiate a compromise, litigation is necessary.

Mediation: Involves a neutral 3rd party trained in conflict resolution and family law, who facilitates a dialogue between the parties to help them reach a consensus on all divorce-related issues including a parenting plan, alimony and child support, asset valuation and distribution, medical and life insurance benefits, taxes, college, allocation of property, grandparent visitation, etc. Clients may retain counsel to review the final contract, independent of the mediation process, before filing the papers before the court.

Collaborative Divorce: This is a middle ground — between litigation and mediation — for those spouses who are uncomfortable not having representation. Each client engages an attorney. The four parties sign a four-way agreement to resolve issues in an amicable way. If the negotiations break down, the lawyers agree to step down and the clients are free to hire new lawyers and move toward litigation.

Do-it-yourself: Some couples opt for a D.I.Y. variety or a "quickie" divorce. (By the way, there is no such thing really as a quickie in the U.S. Even Nevada requires a six-week residency requirement.) Don't despair if your child wants to avoid the hassle of a formal divorce. A lot depends on whether or not there are children or substantial property. According to a report in *USA Today*, as many as half of all divorcing couples decide to file without the assistance of lawyers or mediators (Moffett, 2003). Court clerks or paralegals may be available to assist people with court filings. Some states have D.I.Y. guides and forms that are available on their state websites. It is not necessary to purchase forms, because these forms are available at the courthouse or can be downloaded from the Internet. Instead, use the money to seek a lawyer's consulting time before completing or filing the forms.

Note: Since the mechanics of divorce differ from state to state, it is important for couples to know the laws of their state before deciding which option to choose. It is not difficult to check each state's divorce laws online or find guides in the library or bookstore. Court service centers are available for the asking and tend to be user-friendly.

Fault and No-Fault Divorces

In the cause of *fault divorce*, at least one spouse presents grounds or cause for filing for divorce. The traditional grounds are as follows:

Cruelty — inflicting unnecessary emotional or physical pain. This is the most frequently used ground for fault divorces.
Adultery — violating the marriage vows to be sexually faithful.
Abandonment — desertion for a specified length of time.
Confinement in prison for a set number of years.
Physical inability to engage in sexual intercourse, if it was not disclosed before marriage.

A *no-fault divorce* is a situation where the spouse suing for divorce is not obligated to prove that the other spouse did something wrong.

To file for a "no-fault divorce", one spouse must simply state a reason recognized by the state. In most states, it's as basic as stating the couple is incompatible, or there is an irretrievable breakdown of the marriage. However, when the parties cannot settle their case, fault can be taken into consideration by the judge when assessing distribution of property or the amount of alimony.

Note that with no-fault, neither spouse can prevent the divorce if the other thinks the marriage has broken down. In several states, the couple must live apart for a period of months or even years in order to obtain a no-fault divorce. The period of time differs with each state.

Fifteen states offer only no-fault divorces, and couples should consult a qualified attorney or mediator before petitioning for a divorce, whether it be fault or no-fault, to be sure they are complying with their state's laws.

Contested vs Noncontested Divorces. A contested divorce occurs when all major issues are in dispute. A noncontested divorce occurs when two people have agreed on the issues and the divorce terms can be negotiated to each partner's satisfaction.

●◀ *Pocketbook* ▶●

Money is always one of the stickiest wickets when a couple sits down to hammer out a divorce settlement. Right after the announcement, the divorcing couple will have to take stock of their financial situation. This will involve decisions around credit cards, bank accounts, health insurance, car loans, and any debt the couple has incurred during their marriage. Each should prepare a *budget* early in the divorce process.

A *budget* is a reasonably accurate forecast of needs that accounts for current living expenses. Projections take into advisement health, life, and disability insurance, repair and maintenance of property, and future expenses for children, such as schooling, clothing, and special needs.

Mediators and lawyers will request financial records to evaluate the couple's assets and liabilities in working up the final settlement. Typically, both parties will have to complete a standard financial affidavit, which is a sworn statement of financial status. Your child will have to produce these records:

Tax returns and recent pay stubs	Investments
Bank statements	Wills, trusts
Car loans	Pension, retirement
Mortgage and/or lease information	funds

Budget Worksheet

ANNUAL INCOME + + +	Month 1	Month 2	Month 3	(Etc.)	Annual
Salary/Wages/Bonuses					
Investment Income					
Rents/Royalties/Miscellany					
Grand Total Income					
EXPENSES	Month 1	Month 2	Month 3	(Etc.)	Annual
Home					
Mortgage/Rent					
Utilities (Gas, Electric, Water, Fuel)					
Phone(s)					
Mobile Phone					
Maintenance					
Improvements					
Landscape & Garden					
Property Taxes					
Homeowner's/Renter's Insurance					
Total Home					
Living Expenses					
Food — Groceries					
Food — Eating Out					
Laundry & Cleaning					
Housecleaning					
Pets					
Total Living Expenses					
Transportation					
Car Payment					
Fuel					
Insurance					
Maintenance/Repair					
Commutation to Work					
Parking					
Public Transportation					
Vehicle License Fees					
Total Transportation					

Budget Worksheet *(Continued)*

EXPENSES	Month 1	Month 2	Month 3	(Etc.)	Annual
Entertainment					
Books					
Music (CDs, etc.)					
Cable TV					
Video/DVD Rentals					
Movies/Plays					
Concerts/Clubs					
Home Entertainment					
Other					
Total Transportation					
Family					
Child Care					
Child Support					
Alimony					
Elder Care					
Other Dependents					
Children's Clothing					
Total Family					
Health					
Health Insurance/HMO					
Out-of-Pocket Medical					
Health Club					
Dental Expenses					
Vision Expenses (Eyeglasses, etc.)					
Total Health					
Education					
Tuition & Fees					
Books					
Supplies					
College Loans					
Miscellaneous Education (Music Lessons, Tutoring, etc.)					
Total Education					

Budget Worksheet *(Continued)*

EXPENSES	Month 1	Month 2	Month 3	(Etc.)	Annual
Vacations					
Plane/Train/Bus Fare					
Lodging					
Meals					
Souvenirs					
Pet Boarding					
Rental Car					
Other Vacation Expenses					
Total Vacations					
Recreation					
Sports Equipment					
Hobbies					
Team Dues					
Club Dues					
Toys/Child Gear					
Other Recreation Expenses					
Total Recreation					
Dues/Subscriptions					
Professional Association Dues					
Union Dues					
Magazines and Newspapers					
Internet Connection					
Subscription and/or Public Radio & TV					
Religious Organizations					
Charity					
Total Dues/Subscriptions					
Personal					
Clothing					
Gifts					
Grooming (Hair, Make-up, Other)					
Other Personal Expenses					
Total Personal					

Budget Worksheet *(Continued)*

EXPENSES	Month 1	Month 2	Month 3	(Etc.)	Annual
Financial					
Long-term Savings					
"Retirement (401k, Roth IRA)"					
Credit Card Payments					
Investment Expenses					
Bank Charges					
Accounting & Tax Preparation Fees					
Income Tax — Federal					
Income Tax — State					
Life Insurance					
Other Insurance					
Other Financial					
Total Financial					
Other Expenses					
Total Other Expenses					
GRAND TOTAL EXPENSES					
INCOME LESS EXPENSES					

Hiding income or providing misleading information is considered fraud and cause to reopen a case after settlement. It is a good idea for parents to be aware of some of the steps involved in negotiating the financial side of the divorce, but the real work should be left to the professionals, who can provide expert advice.

Where do I come in? Your child may ask for your help in drawing up a temporary budget, and you might glance at the numbers. If the figures don't balance, you may want to float a loan or make a gift to your adult child. If you do, this is a good time to negotiate a repayment schedule. Diplomatically set boundaries so your child knows how much money you can afford to commit and how long you are able to help. (See chapter 3 for a detailed discussion about parental financial support.) Attorney Wendy Prince suggests giving your child a loan with a promissory note. "This will become a marital debt, go down on your child's financial affidavit, and have a better chance of being paid from the marital assets. Be careful that any loan doesn't violate any court orders. (Some states have Automatic Orders.) A loan should be for usual household expenses. Be careful because regular contributory gifts may be considered as income."

Many couples work out an equitable settlement without hiring a financial consultant. In cases where there is a significant portfolio of investments or other assets, such as real estate, your child should seek the services of an expert who has experience in divorce cases. Attorneys specializing in family law or domestic relations have negotiating skills but may not have the kind of skills that will benefit your child tax-wise. In the long run, it is cheaper to pay an expert than to carry on an extended confrontational divorce over money.

●◀ *Some Things You Should Know about Financial Settlements* ▶●

- Each partner should agree to cancel joint credit cards and not run up any further joint charges.
- Each partner should establish his/her own independent credit.
- Each partner should agree to close joint banking and brokerage accounts.
- Outstanding debt must be divided and/or negotiated as part of the settlement.
- Once divorce papers are served, all assets are frozen.
- Property division must be in writing. Verbal agreements will not stand up in court.
- Each partner should seriously consider the long-term ramifications of any property negotiations. For example, women often negotiate to keep the house but find that they cannot afford the maintenance, upkeep, or taxes.
- Each partner should carefully consider income tax implications of decisions regarding property sales or division, child custody, alimony, etc. and be willing to look at arrangements that provide mutually beneficial tax reductions.

The terms *assets*, *community property*, and *separate property* pop up whenever we talk about divorce financial settlements so let's look at these, since they are related.

Assets refer to "Property," which includes real estate, jewelry, furniture, stocks, bank accounts, art or personal property collections, cars, business ventures, lottery winnings, club memberships, frequent flyer miles, season tickets, timeshares, etc. Some of the larger assets in a divorce case are the home, the retirement account, IRAs, and 401ks, employee stock options (vested and unvested). The Courts generally require an inventory of the property.

Community property is all property acquired during the marriage. Marital assets may be owned with a spouse, solely, or jointly with a family, friend, or business partner. Anything (truly anything) that an individual has an ownership interest in may be considered marital (community) property, including *separate property* in some states.

Separate or *personal property* is that which was owned before the marriage and that which is acquired by gift or inheritance at any time. In some states, separate or personal property owned before the marriage, including gifts and inheritances, is also valued as marital property.

State laws govern how community property is divided, since divorce is a state matter and not subject to federal law. Each state values the circumstances and conditions of the marriage differently and has a different approach to distribution of assets. Nine states — Arizona, California, Idaho, Louisiana, Nevada, New Mexico, Texas, Washington, and Wisconsin — are community property states and have the philosophy that marriage is a communal undertaking with each spouse contributing equally to its success. In community property states, the assets are divided equally between partners unless there was a prenuptial agreement.

In *non-community property states*, the assets are distributed "equitably," not equally. The only guidance here is the statute that the Court makes a "fair and just" division of the property based on certain factors. These can include: length of marriage; the causes for the breakdown; the age, health, station, occupation, amount, and source of income; vocational skills; potential for income; estate; liabilities and needs of each party; opportunities for future acquisition of capital, assets and income in addition to the contribution of each of the parties in the acquisition; preservation or appreciation value of the assets.

Note: Final division of assets is determined by an Order of the Court or is otherwise agreed to by the parties and entered as Order of the Court on the day of dissolution. The judge has the final word if an Agreement is fair and equitable.

Specifically, there are three kinds of assets: Family, Business, and All Others.

Family Assets refers to any property owned by one or both spouses and ordinarily used by a spouse or a minor child of either spouse for family purposes. A narrow interpretation of the phrase "family purpose" would be "a use connected with the family as a whole," and a broader interpretation would be assets owned and used by only one member of the family but intended for the family's future provision. This is a gray area. For example, your daughter might argue that the truck her spouse uses for business should be considered a family asset since she plans to use it to cart your grandson's soccer team to practice now that he made the team. It is best if the couple can work out these issues without bringing them into court, but negotiations often break down around matters such as these.

Business Assets refers to property not usually divided by the non-owning spouse. Business assets once valued can become part of the marital pot. If property is owned by one spouse to the exclusion of the other and is used primarily for business purposes, and if the spouse who does not own the property made no direct or indirect contribution to the acquisition of the property, the court may decide that the property is not a family asset. However, this is not always the case. Judgments about business assets vary by situation and state.

If you and your son- or daughter-in-law are in business together, any issues should be referred to a Civil Litigator to be argued in civil court. These cases are separate from divorce proceedings.

Other Assets generally include gifts, inheritances, jewelry, court awards for damages due to personal injury, and any property not intended for family purposes. Check the law in your state to determine if this kind of personal property is considered marital property.

Again:

It may not matter whether the asset was brought into the <u>marriage</u> by one spouse or obtained afterward, during the marriage.

The presumption that assets should be divided in half can be challenged or <u>rebutted</u> in court.

Division of assets is finally determined by an *Order* of the Court or is otherwise agreed to by the parties following an out-of-court *settlement*. The parties are free to work out their own division of the property, and the Court will encourage the couple to work out an agreement on the issue of property division.

Common Questions about Assets

• *My ex-daughter-in-law has Grandma's candlesticks. How can I get them back?*

Many parents lament the loss of treasured family heirlooms when their children split. According to the law, gifts received for the intent of the marriage become a piece of the marriage pie. Unless the ex-in-law is willing to return the candlesticks, it's your loss.

- *Am I entitled to get the money I gave my children toward a down payment on their house returned when they sell the house and settle the amount?*

Unless you have a mortgage agreement or a signed note in your possession, the court will very likely consider the down payment a gift; you would not be entitled to a return on "their" investment. "Parental gifts such as a house payment may be deemed marital property. Inquiries such as the length of the marriage and if the gift was part of an intended future inheritance should be discussed. For example, parental gifts towards the wedding and first home would be muddled in a marriage over ten years; however, in a marriage of less than one year, these fees should be reimbursed," advises Wendy Prince, LLC.

- *My daughter and son-in-law are filing for joint custody. They plan to take turns living in the same house after the divorce so the grandchildren have a stable situation. What happens to the property — the furniture, etc. — if the arrangement doesn't work out and they sell the house?*

Your children should have a schedule attached to their divorce and custody agreement, making clear who owns what contents of the house in the event of this situation. Even though the couple may say they have agreed to divide the contents if the arrangement fails, a signed court order is the best line of defense for those residing in the same residence. The court may not divide personal property after the marital dissolution.

●◀ Dealing with Your Child's Emotional Fallout over Possessions ▶●

I've heard many parents complain that, in the throes of their divorce, their children act irrationally when it comes to money. Talk straight to your enraged or depressed child about the danger of allowing emotionality to get in the way of good decision-making. Circumstances change. Tempers cool. Explain that your grandchildren may want to see their divorced parents' wedding album one day because it's their history, too, but most minor possessions aren't worth the time and energy they cost tying up the divorce. Things are only things. Help your child see the long view, and behave responsibly.

Here are some further guidelines that may assist you in coping with your child's property division issues:

- Suggest that each partner draw up a list of items he or she wants for any reason, then e-mail or snail mail the preferences to avoid a confrontation.

- Encourage your child to keep the lines of communication with the ex open.
- Don't dismiss items that have sentimental value to you, but do let go.
- If there are dual claims, let the lawyers handle it.
- Don't get in the way of "their" negotiations. You may place more value on an item than they do.
- Don't ask for or expect freebies from either child unless the couple is in complete agreement to give away possessions. Aunt Amelia's Crockpot will probably wind up at the thrift shop, and you can always buy it back.
- Offer to store special items your son or daughter might regret giving away.
- If your child gives you furniture that doesn't fit in his or her new place, shroud it in sheets unless your child is comfortable with you displaying it in your own home.
- Don't make an issue over why your child parted with this or that possession. Remember that everyone is hurting, and these are only things.

Since division of property surfaces significant economic, emotional and psychological undercurrents, it is a good idea to get a third party involved to help negotiate a settlement. Don't put yourself in the middle if you can help it.

●◀ When Parents Should Seek Legal Advice ▶●

Some parents have a financial stake in their child's marriage and suffer injustices or inequities due to the divorce. If you have questions about your personal legal rights or obligations, you would be wise to consult a lawyer. The following are some examples of legal entanglements that might need to be resolved during the divorce process:

- You are in business with your soon-to-be ex-son-(or daughter)-in law.
- You countersigned a loan before your child and his/her spouse broke up.
- You have a trust fund set up in your child's name and are worried about the ex gaining some control over it.
- Your grandchildren are named in your will, and you are concerned that the ex-spouse might have rights to the inheritance if your child predeceases you and the ex gains full custody.
- You gave your child a substantial sum as a down payment on his residence. Now his ex-wife wants half the proceeds for the sale of the house. Can she do that?

Alimony and *Child Support* are other important terms you should be familiar with. These can plague divorced couples long after the divorce because there are tax issues. (Again, it's best to seek a financial consultant before making any binding decisions about how to set these schedules to maximize the benefits.) Invariably the payor (usually the male who earns more than the stay-at-home-spouse) thinks the payments are too high and the recipient thinks she is getting too little.

Alimony, Maintenance, and *Spousal Support* are interchangeable terms. Alimony is the amount of money that the court orders one ex-spouse, who is considered the "bread-winner" or party with more financial resources, to pay to the ex-spouse of lesser means upon dissolution of the marriage. *Temporary alimony* may be allotted when the divorce is pending. Typically, alimony is the responsibility of the male, but in some cases, it is paid by the woman, or in same-sex legal partnerships, by the mate whose income is greater.

Common Questions about Alimony

• *How do the courts determine the amount of alimony?*

Many states have adopted formulas for alimony based on the income of each party. Payment is usually time-limited. In lengthy marriages, alimony may be lifelong. In some states, there is no formula for the amount of alimony awarded, and the court will consider additional factors such as cause of breakdown (e.g. one party's physical abuse of the other, alcoholism, drug addiction, etc.), in addition to other statutory factors to determine the amount. Furthermore, the court will take into consideration that the disadvantaged partner needs time to recoup economically from the marital dissolution.

• *Can the amount of alimony change?*

Any substantial change in circumstances such as illness, retirement, remarriage or improvement in financial circumstances can be grounds for the court to grant a modification or termination of the payment.

Note: Alimony is a tax-deductible expense for the payer but charged as income to the recipient. Couples should consider the tax effects of making payments as alimony as opposed to child support. In many states, child support is considered income and is taxable against the receiver. Alimony, however, normally terminates when the recipient remarries. Child support does not. But child support normally terminates when the child attains major age or graduates college. Alimony does not. Refer to local tax experts for current information.

Common Questions about Child Support

Child support is not the same as alimony. Child support is the obligatory set amount of periodic payment by the noncustodial parent owed to the custodial parent, caregiver, or guardian to attend to the care and support of children when a marriage or civil union has broken down by separation, annulment, or divorce.

Each state has different formulas for determining the amount of child support. In Texas, for example, children are subject to the jurisdiction of the Court until they become adults at age eighteen. Texas had a Family Code that regulates the amount of child support based upon the number of children and earnings of the payer. In this case, support is 20 percent of the net disposable income for one child; 25 percent for two children; 30 percent for three children; and 35 percent for four or more. In most jurisdictions, there is no need for the parents to be married, but there must be evidence of *paternity* and/or *maternity* to set a schedule.

- *What if my ex-son-in-law abandons my daughter and grandchildren and does not pay her child support?*

The law is quite clear that parents are responsible to pay for the support of their children whether on not they have legal or physical custody or visiting rights, and whether or not the child is living with one biological parent. Since visitation is viewed as a limited form of custody, the court may decide to suspend the privilege of visitation if the deadbeat parent stops support payments, although this may be seen as punishing the child, not the parent. Jurisdictions differ on this ruling, but generally, there is stiff enforcement for nonpayment of support, and penalties if a person refuses to pay such as suspension of a driver's license, garnishment of wages, or imprisonment. (Check Appendix B for Child Advocate Groups.)

- *Are there restrictions how child support payment should be used?*

There is typically no accountability on the part of the custodial parent as to how child support payments are used. The noncustodial payer may petition the court for a change of custody (not easy to achieve) if he or she considers the money is being used for purposes other than the child.

●◀ Property and Place ▶●

The arrangement for physical housing of the family members after the divorce is another issue that causes a great deal of turmoil. It's not always easy to decide which partner stays in the family domicile and which one moves out. There are legal considerations of ownership and economics that come into play. Some couples, of course, have already arranged a physical separation before the divorce. Still, negotiations as to who gets what piece of the family real estate are often labored. The basic options are (a) he moves out on his own, (b) he moves out with the children, (c) she moves out on her own, (d) she moves out with the children, (e) both move out into new residences, (f) everyone remains in the family residence until the court decrees the divorce settlement. Obviously, the unique circumstances of each family will determine which course they follow.

Some couples cannot afford to split up right away, and elect, usually with great reluctance, option (f) above — everybody stays. I've known couples who have drawn a line down the middle of their domicile and created inviolable boundaries — even designating "his" and "her" shelves in the refrigerator — until they reach a financial settlement!

Stanley Glasser, a New York City family law attorney, advises couples who must live together as a stopgap to make sure they have a signed Separation Agreement. He has had cases where couples do not want to distribute assets immediately and continue to contribute to their maintenance as in the past. Without a signed agreement, the partner who resides in a fault state (New York is one of the few) can be faulted with abandonment or adultery if he or she leaves the domicile or engages in extra-marital affairs.

•◀ *Parenting and Custody* ▶•

One of the most important topics that arise in divorce is *child custody and visitation*. We will examine these first as they relate to the parents; then we'll discuss rulings that affect grandparents' rights to access to their grandchildren.

Legal Custody in divorce settlements means a parent has the right and the obligation to make decisions about a child's upbringing such as schooling, religion, and medical care. In many states, courts regularly award *Joint (or Shared) Legal Custody*, and parents are expected to share the decision-making. If one partner is excluded from the decision-making process, he or she can go back to court and ask the judge to enforce the custody agreement or ask for a change in custody.

Sole Legal Custody means one parent is awarded full responsibility for the child, typically because the other parent is not living up to his or her responsibility in any way. In some cases, a parent will abdicate his or her rights to legal custody rather than spend the money to fight for it. The child will not necessarily be denied access to the noncustodial parent, and the noncustodial parent may still be a party to the decisions affecting the child.

Joint or Shared Legal Custody is the trend today. The court may award custody to both parents, which can be played out in different ways, depending upon the local jurisdiction and judge's discretion:

... One parent has Physical Custody, i.e. the child lives primarily with the mother or father and spends set time with the noncustodial parent according to a *visitation plan* that can be imposed by the court.

... The parents have *Joint Physical Custody*, and the child splits time, alternating weeks and weekends between both parents.

Joint physical custody works best if parents live near each other so a child has a somewhat normal routine. The obvious advantages are that the child has contact with both parents, and the burden of one parent having full responsibility for a child is alleviated. The obvious disadvantage is the child having to readjust to two households, two sets of friends, neighborhoods, etc. If the parents cannot cooperate, there is the added strain of the child bucking the conflicts and mixed messages of two parents, which will have a negative impact on the child's overall adjustment to the divorce.

Legal experts recommend that in situations of joint physical custody, parents keep careful financial records of the amount spent on groceries, school, medical care, and basic necessities caring for the child in the event one parent disputes what the other is spending.

Bird's Nest Custody is another joint custody arrangement, under which the children remain in the family home and the parents take turns moving in and out, spending their out time in separate housing.

If a parent is deemed unfit by the court, Sole Legal and/or Physical Custody may be in the best interests of a child. However, more and more states are awarding joint custody, even in this case, so both parents can have a significant presence in their child's life. Often, *supervised visitation* is stipulated so that the rights of the noncustodial parent are retained, and a show of good faith that the deficient parent can be rehabilitated with the goal of expanding his or her rights in the future is made.

Note that custody is modifiable. If one parent feels there is just cause to change the arrangement, he or she can appeal to the court to review the case.

The Language of Custody

Be wary of the terms, in this discussion. According to psychologist Philip Stahl, Ph.D., author of *Parenting After Divorce* (2000), "Lay people use the words 'joint custody' to mean equal time-sharing. This may not be the way that a mental health professional uses these words. To mental health professionals, joint custody may mean any plan where there is 'shared parenting' in the sense that both parents are responsible for the well-being of the children for a substantial period of time. To be shared, neither parent can have access only on alternate weekends and perhaps an overnight during the week that there is no access on the following weekend." With joint physical custody, children spend at least 33 percent of their time with each parent, alternating some weeks or negotiated schedule so children spend significant amounts of time with both parents.

The late California judge James Stewart, in *The Child Custody Book* (2000), applies a slightly different standard: "In some jurisdictions, the words 'joint custody' will be used to describe any plan where both parents have greater than 40 percent access to the children. With such a plan, it is likely that custody is truly shared in that both parents are involved in the children's health care, education, and transportation to various activities. These terms do not have any 'correct' meaning ... they mean different things to different people, and when someone uses the words 'joint custody', you [should] ask them to explain exactly what they mean unless it is obvious from the context in which the words were used."

There is one flagrant misuse of the words "joint custody." It is the effort by the evaluator or the judge to pacify the noncustodial parent by calling a plan "joint custody" when the noncustodial parent has such limited access to the child that custody is not "joint" or shared in any sense. In cases, for example, where a parent moves out-of-state, joint custody is not possible and clearly a misnomer. Also note that if one parent feels excluded from seeing his or her child, it is possible to go back to court and ask the judge to enforce the custody agreement or ask for a change in custody.

•◄ *Grandparenting* ►•

One of the legitimate fears grandparents have when they learn their children are getting divorced is a concern as to whether they will be denied access to their grandchildren, especially if the former in-law becomes the custodial parent, and the grandparents have a strained relationship prior to or after the couple divorces.

Current federal child welfare laws clearly favor parents over grandparents. Even in cases where there is evidence that a parent has been absent from a child's life, and the grandparent has been a primary caregiver, parental rights can take precedence. The pain of any grandparent who has been shut out of a grandchild's life cannot be minimized.

Chapter 9, "Grandparents as Stabilizers," sets out some practical advice about how to keep the lines of communication open with divorcing parents, but oftentimes the best efforts are rebuffed, and grandparents find themselves on the outs — victims in the power play of their embittered children. Should you find yourself shut out of your grandchild's life, the first step is to consult with a trained mediator. Such an individual can act as a third party and help you reconcile your difference with the recalcitrant parent. You can find experienced mediators online or through professional mediation associations. Also check with grandparenting groups, call the courthouse, or get referrals from a social service agency. Interview the mediator so you understand the process before you involve the other parties.

Many frustrated grandparents have no other recourse but to turn to a family law attorney, who will petition their case before the court. Know that the legal route is costly. States vary in their rulings, and more and more are upholding parental rights. Search online for the latest information about grandparents' rights by entering "grandparent rights" in Google or your favorite search engine. Check to be sure that the material you find applies in your state, however.

Historically, since the mid-1970s, grandparents' visitation rights have been debated in state legislatures across the country. There are a number of states that have upheld the rights of grandparents under two different statutes. All fifty states currently have some type of "grandparent visitation" statute, through which grandparents can ask a court to grant them the legal right to maintain their relationships with their grandchildren. Nevertheless, state laws vary greatly when it comes to the circumstances. Approximately twenty states have "restrictive" visitation statutes. Under the statute *parens patriae,* the state has the authority to act in the best interests of its children citizens and will consider the petition of the grandparent when there is some kind of disruption of the intact family, such as death of a parent, divorce, adoption, or termination of parental rights. Under the second statute, there does not need to be any kind of disruption of the intact family. More states have "permissive" visitation laws that say courts will consider a petition as long as the visitation serves the best interest of the child, although the grandparent may have to prove that there has been some prior relationship with the child. *In both cases, visitation remains a privilege, not a constitutional right.*

Both restrictive and permissive visitation statutes have been challenged in court by parents who argue that the laws are unconstitutional because they infringe on a parent's right to raise a child without interference.

The debate concerns the fundamental rights of parents to choose with whom their child should associate, versus the harm parent(s) do their child

Troxel v. Granville Supreme Court Decisions

The right of visitation by a non-parent was addressed by the United States Supreme Court on January 12, 2000, in the case of Troxel v. Granville. Justice O'Connor announced the judgment of the Court and delivered an opinion, in which the Chief Justice, Justice Ginsburg, and Justice Breyer joined.

Section 26.10.160(3) of the Revised Code of Washington permits "any person" to petition a superior court for visitation rights "at any time" and authorizes that court to grant such visitation rights whenever "visitation may serve the best interest of the child." Petitioners Jenifer and Gary Troxel petitioned a Washington Superior Court for the right to visit their grandchildren, Isabelle and Natalie Troxel. Respondent Tommie Granville, the mother of Isabelle and Natalie, opposed the petition. The case ultimately reached the Washington Supreme Court, which held that § 26.10.160(3) unconstitutionally interferes with the fundamental right of parents to rear their children.

In this case, the Court heard arguments on the rights of grandparents and other third parties to visit children over the objection of the children's parents. It was one of the rare times that the Court considered family law. It held that the grandparental visitation statute of that state was unconstitutional because it permitted the state courts to impose visitation without sufficiently considering the fit parents' objections.

State Court Decisions

The Supreme Court's decision in Troxel v. Granville is not the final word on grandparents' visitation rights. It's likely that grandparents will continue to challenge the decisions; however, the Court's decision has influenced rulings in other states that had permissive and restrictive visitation statutes. For example, the Court of Appeals in Wisconsin, which had a permissive statute, agreed with the Supreme Court decision and decided that their grandparent visitation statute was unconstitutional and limited the authority of parents. This was followed by Connecticut, Kentucky, North Dakota, Tennessee, and Washington, all of which held their statutes unconstitutional as applied. The first statute was revisited by Florida, Georgia, and Nevada which reversed their grandparent visitation statutes as violating the fundamental rights of parents. The court in Virginia also restricted the rights of grandparents under their statute. Grandparents in Virginia must prove that visitation would be in the best interests of the children and that grandchildren would suffer harm if visitation was denied.

by denying them the love and care of grandparents with whom they had an association.

Common Questions about Grandparents' Rights

• *What makes a grandparent's visit in the best interests of the child?*

The court would argue that the length and frequency of the relationship (actual contact) are factors. They would determine whether the parents and grandparents have an adversarial relationship that could possibly negatively affect the parent-child relationship. The "fuzzy factor" is whether the parent-grandparent hostility existed prior to or because of the lawsuit. The Court would also look at the family unit as a whole and consider the nature of the other relationships.

• *Should I pursue the legal course of action?*

There is no clear answer to this question. It's a matter of the heart and the ability to endure the pain of a legal course of action — one that would undoubtedly stir up old hurts. Much depends on the existing bond between grandchild and grandparent, and the degree to which it would put the child in the middle of yet another conflict. One must also take into account that even though a grandparent and grandchild may have had a positive past relationship, this does not guarantee that the grandparent will qualify for a court-ordered visitation.

• *If I decide to take court action, how do I proceed?*

Begin by researching the statutes of the state where your grandchildren reside and learn about any case precedents. Even if the parents are not married, you may still seek visitation. Should you decide to go the legal route, find a professional who specializes in non-parental third-party custody and visitation cases. Some state courts won't consider your petition for visitation until mediation has been attempted. Mediation means that you hire a neutral third party to help all of you create a legally binding agreement that everyone can respect and live with. If you are bent on going to court, you will save time and money by gathering evidence that supports your case in advance of seeing a lawyer. The documents should demonstrate that you and the children have had a loving and caring relationship, and that a continued relationship serves the best interests of your grandchild. You may need to call on witnesses.

• *What will happen after I engage a lawyer?*

The attorney will help you present your case. After you file papers to seek visitation, a judge will consider your request and make the final decision after evaluating the family situation. The judgment may be based on the legal standard in the state of your grandchild's residence. Some states are friendly to grandparents and acknowledge the importance of the grandchild-grandparent bond. Others will look more closely at whether or not your visits will be detrimental to the parent-child relationship and violate parental authority.

Some grandparents who think they are at risk of losing access to their grandchildren might ask their child to attach a paragraph to the divorce agreement giving them rights to see their grandchildren. Even if both parents sign the agreement giving the grandparents access, this paragraph may not be enforceable if tested in the future or even included in the original Family Court Order. The judge has the right to decide what is in the best interests of the nuclear family.

•◀ *Grandparent Guardianship and Custody* ▶•

There are more and more situations today in which grandparents need to step in to take care of a grandchild when their children cannot assume responsibility. Since guardianship and custody laws vary from state to state, you will need to familiarize yourself with the laws and consult a family law attorney if you are in this situation. There are many aspects to guardianship and custody of grandchildren, and a lot of bureaucratic tape.

• *What is the difference between custody and guardianship?*

Custody is temporary authority from the court to take care of your grandchild while the court decides who should be the guardian for the longer term. If you are appointed guardian through the court, you will make important decisions about your grandchild's education, medical treatment, and other daily care issues.

Informal Custody refers to grandchildren living with grandparents until the kids' home life is stabilized. The biological parents retain full legal rights and may regain custody of the child at any time.

Standby guardianship takes place when parents agree that their children should be placed in another relative's care that can last up to one year after the guardianship is activated. You will need a signed consent statement (in front of witnesses and a notary or attorney) that you have been authorized to take over until the parent(s) can resume responsibility. Standby guardianship may be necessary if you sense that your grandchild is in immediate danger due to a problem triggered by the divorce. It may be possible to transfer this authority to you without court involvement. As there are different guardianship arrangements, you will need to talk to a specialist in family law to understand the options and legalities in your grandchild's state.

This arrangement can be revoked at any time by the parent(s). You can challenge the revocation or request *temporary custody* if you think your removal will endanger the child, in which case you need to petition the probate court and file applications to get temporary custody. Court staff or an attorney can help you fill out the papers. Expect a hearing once the papers are submitted. A caseworker from child welfare will be appointed should you request removal or termination of the parents' rights to investigate the family situation in what is called a home study. The court may believe it appropriate to have your grandchild examined by a physician, psychologist, or psychiatrist. As you can see, this is an arduous process. Before you begin, know that most rulings respect the rights of parents as natural guardians and will work with the parents to help them resolve their problems. Situations where probate courts remove the parents and transfer legal authority to the grandparents (*full custody*) are usually:

The parent (parents) voluntarily gives up his/her (their) rights.

The child has been abandoned.

The child has been denied care, guidance, and control for his/her well-being.

The child has had injuries inflicted upon him/her by other than accidental means.

Grandparents who have a long-term relationship with their grandchildren may prefer *foster-care* status, which provides some measure of legal security to the child, although parents still have legal rights. Foster-care status entitles grandparents to apply for supplemental health and social service benefits, as well as tax benefits.

A couple of other helpful tips for grandparents who have a major role in parenting:

If you are thinking about taking a trip with your grandchild or know you will be the temporary caretaker, you may need to have a document called a "power of attorney" that requires the notarized signature of all custodial parents or guardians. Plan ahead and have your child check whether or not this is required in your case.

Advise your child to talk to your grandchildren's school to find out how they handle visitation. Schools are very careful about releasing children to individuals without formal authorization from the guardian.

• *What financial aid is available if I raise my grandchild?*

If you become your grandchild's legal guardian, you may be eligible for benefits from the company you work for, so check with the Human Resource or Benefits department. In addition, you may qualify for government assistance: Temporary Assistance for Needy Families known as TANF is available, depending on whether you need financial help for yourself or just to cover the needs of your grandchild. There are also subsidized guardianship programs and income tax benefits when you claim your grandchild as a dependent. Check your state's social welfare agency for more information about current state and federal programs. In some situations, housing may also be available.

Organizations such as AARP can guide you in matters regarding legal services, health insurance, tax benefits, and government subsidy benefits if your grandchild lives with you and you are the primary caregiver.

•◀ *In Conclusion . . .* ▶•

Keep in mind that litigation is a last resort. You'll want to avoid grandparent-parent conflict at all costs. Be proactive. Search for solutions that will prevent your going to battle. As a starter, make a list of people who might intercede in your behalf. Next, write some positive statements that will demonstrate to your ex-in-law your interest in maintaining a good relationship.

One piece of advice about legal issues affecting your child and your family bears repeating: Even though you have more life experience or knowledge about the law, the parties directly involved — the couple, their lawyers or mediators, psychologists, social workers, and the court — have the final say. Therefore, while your son or daughter is caught in the legal quagmire, debating claims to this or that, or even using your grandchild as a pawn in the highly emotional chess match, remind your child that nothing, nothing is more important than ties to extended family. With your love and fortitude, those ties will endure despite the difficult divorce journey.

THIS APPENDIX IS OFFERED AS GENERAL INFORMATION on a few of the more common legal and financial concerns surrounding the divorce process. It is not a substitute for professional advice on legal or financial issues. Neither the author nor the publisher is engaged in rendering legal, financial, or other professional services. If expert assistance or counseling is needed, the services of a competent professional should be sought.

ENDNOTE

[1] Wendy E. Prince of Greenberg & Prince, LLC. Attorneys & Counselors at Law, 350 Bedford Street, Stamford, Connecticut 06901. Attorney Prince is an attorney mediator, board member Connecticut Council for Divorce Mediation, committee chair Regional Bar Association, Connecticut Bar Association, Stamford Chamber of Commerce.

Appendix B

Divorce-Related Bibliography, Websites, and Resources

Recommended Readings on Selected Topics

Divorce Recovery for Adults

Ahrons, C. (1994) *The Good Divorce: Keeping Your Family Together When Your Marriage Comes Apart.* New York: Harper Collins.

Beattie, M. (1990) *The Language of Letting Go.* New York: Harper Collins.

Clapp, G. (2000) *Divorce & New Beginnings: A Complete Guide to Recovery, Solo Parenting, Co-Parenting and Stepfamilies.* New York: John Wiley & Sons, Inc.

Corman, A. (2004) *A Perfect Divorce.* New York: St. Martins Press.

Crouch, J. (1999) *The Marriage Movement: An Introduction to Divorce Reform and other Marriage Issues.* Retrieved from Internet on 11/30/05 from www.divorcerefor.org/mmo.html

Everett, C., & Everett, S.V. (1994) *Healthy Divorce.* San Francisco: Jossey-Bass.

Fisher, B., & Alberti, R. (2000) *Rebuilding When Your Relationship Ends.* (3rd ed) Atascadero, CA: Impact Publishers.

Fisher, B., & Bierhaus, J. (1994) *Workbook for Rebuilding When Your Relationship Ends.* Boulder, CO: Fisher Publishing Co.

Hetherington, E.M., & Kelly, J. (2002) *For Better or for Worse: Divorce Reconsidered.* New York: Norton & Co.

Holmes, T.H., & Rahe, R.H. (1967) The Social Readjustment Rating Scale. *Journal of Psychosomatic Research*, Vol II No. 2. August 1967 pp 213–218.

Kranitz, M. (2000) *Getting Apart Together.* Atascadero, CA: Impact Publishers.

Kreider, R.M. (2002) *Current Population Report.* U.S Dept of Commerce, Economics and Statistics Administration. Retrieved from internet from http://www.divorcemag.com/statistics/statsUS.shtml

Kübler-Ross, E. (1969) *On Death and Dying*. New York: Macmillan Publishing.

Marquardt, E. (2005) *Between Two Worlds*. New York: Crown Publishers.

Moffett, K., & Touborg, S. (2003) *Not Your Mother's Divorce: A Practical Girlfriend-to-Girlfriend Guide to Surviving the End of an Early Marriage*. New York: Broadway Books, Div. of Random House.

Rich, P., & Schwartz, L.L. (1999) *The Healing Journey of Divorce — Your Journal of Understanding and Renewal*. New York: Wiley & Sons.

Trafford, A. (1982) *Crazy Time*. New York: Harper and Rowe.

Vaughn, D. (1990) *Uncoupling: Turning Points in Intimate Relationships*. New York: Vintage Books/Division of Random House.

Wallerstein, J. & Blakeslee, S. (1995) *The Good Marriage: How and Why Love Lasts*. New York: Warner Book Edition.

Walton, B. (2000) *101 Little Instructions for Surviving Your Divorce: A No-Nonsense Guide to the Challenges at Hand*. Atascadero, CA: Impact Publishers.

Webb, D., Ph.D. (2000) *50 Ways to Love Your Leaver: Getting on With Your Life After the Breakup*. Atascadero, CA: Impact Publishers.

Wegscheider-Cruse, S. (1994) *Life After Divorce: Create a New Beginning*. Deerfield Beach, FL: Health Communications, Inc.

Finances, Child Support, Custody and Basic Legal Issues

Belle, M., & Krantzler, M., Ph.D. (1988) *The Complete Guide for Men and Women: Divorcing*. New York: St. Martin's Griffin.

Berry, D.B. (1995) *The Divorce Sourcebook*. Los Angeles, CA: Lowell House.

Cassidy, R. (1977) *What Every Man Should Know About Divorce*. New York: Simon & Schuster.

Gold, L. (1996) *Between Love and Hate: A Guide to a Civilized Divorce*. New York: Penguin.

Smith, G. R., & Abrahms, S. (1998) *What Every Woman Should Know About Divorce and Custody*. New York: Perigee.

Stewart, J. (2000) *The Child Custody Book*. Atascadero, CA: Impact Publishers.

Warshak, R. A. (1992) *The Custody Revolution: The Father Fiction and the Motherhood Mystique*. New York: Poseidon Press, Simon and Schuster, Inc.

Wild, R. & Elllis, S. (2005) *The Unofficial Guide to Getting a Divorce*, (2nd ed). Hoboken, NJ: Wiley Publishing, Inc.

Wittmann, J. P. (2001) *Custody Chaos, Personal Peace: Sharing Custody with an Ex Who Drives You Crazy*. New York: Perigee Book.

Parenting During and After Divorce

American Academy of Matrimonial Lawyers. Stepping Back from Anger: Protecting Your Child During Divorce. *Academy Materials*. Chicago, IL. http://www.aami.org.

Brodr, A. (1999) *The Single Father: A Dad's Guide to Parenting Without a Partner*. New York: Abbeville Press.

Corman, A. (2004) *A Perfect Divorce*. New York: St. Martin's Press.

Fetterman, C., (ed). (1999) *Participant's Guide Putting Children 1st — Skills for Parents in Transition*. Connecticut: Council of Family Service Agencies.

Glenn, N.D. & Marquardt, E. "Poll Says Even Quiet Divorces Affect Children's Paths." *New York Times*, November 5, 2005.

Goldstein, S. (1987) *Divorce — Your Child*. New Haven, CT: Yale University Press.

Grollman, E. (1989) *Explaining Divorce to Children*. Boston: Beacon Press.

Haley, C. (2005) The Weekend Daddy. *Dads Today Divorce Series, Part One*. Retrieved from internet from http://dadstoday.com/resources/articles/ divorceept1.htm

Lansky, V. (1996) *Divorce Book for Parents: Helping Your Children Cope With Divorce and its Aftermath*. (3rd ed). New York: America Library.

Long, N. & Forehand, R. L. (2002) *Making Divorce Easier on Your Child: 50 Effective Ways to Help Children Adjust*. New York: McGraw Hill.

Newman, G. (1999) *101 Ways to Be a Long-Distance Super Dad — or Mom, Too*. (rev). Mountain View, CA: Blossom Valley Press.

Ricci, I. (1997) *Mom's House, Dad's House: Making Two Homes for Your Children*. New York: Simon and Schuster.

Schneider, M. F., & Zuckerberg, J. (1996) *Difficult Questions Kids Ask (and are afraid to ask) About Divorce*. New York: Fireside.

Stahl, P. M., Ph.D. (2000) *Parenting After Divorce: A Guide to Resolving Conflicts and Meeting Your Child's Needs*. Atascadero, CA: Impact Publishers.

Thayer, E., & Zimmerman, J. (2001) *The Co-Parenting Survival Guide: Letting Go of Conflict after a Difficult Divorce*. Oakland, CA: New Harbinger Publications, Inc.

Wallerstein, J. S., & Blakeslee, S. (2003) *What About the Kids? Raising Your Children Before, During and After Divorce*. New York: Hyperion.

Guidance for Stepfamilies and Stepparents

Berry, J. (1990) *Good Answers to Tough Questions About Stepfamilies*. Chicago: Children's Press.

Burt, M. (Ed.) (1991) *Stepfamilies Stepping Ahead: Eight-Step Program for Successful Family Living*. Lincoln, NE: Stepfamily Assoc. of America.

Einstein, E., & Albert, L. (2005) *Strengthening Your Stepfamily*. Atascadero, CA: Impact Publishers, Inc.

LeBey, B. (2004) *Remarried with Children: Ten Secrets for Successfully Blending and Extending Your Family*. New York: Bantam Books.

Grandparenting and Raising Grandchildren

Callander, J. (1999) *Second Time Around: Help for Grandparents Who Raise Their Children's Kids*. Morton Grove, IL: Albert Whitman & Company.

Cherlin, A.J. & Furstenberg, F.F., Jr. (1986) *The New American Grandparent: A Place in the Family, A Life Apart*. New York: Basic Books, Inc.

Cohen, J. S. (1994) *Helping Your Grandchildren Through Their Parents' Divorce*. New York: Walker and Company.

Gottlieb, D. W., Gottlieb, I. B., & Slavin, M.A. (1988) *What to Do When Your Son or Daughter Divorces*. Toronto: Bantam Books.

Jendrek, M. P. (1993) *Grandparents Who Parent Their Grandchildren*. Available through AARP/Andrus Foundation.

Kaplan, W. (1988) *Grandparenthood*. New York: Routledge.

Kornhaber, A. & Woodward, K. L. (1985) *Grandparents/Grandchildren: The Vital Connection*. New Brunswick, NJ: Transaction.

Kornhaber, A. (2002) *The Grandparent Guide: The Definitive Guide to Coping with the Challenges of Modern Grandparenting*. Chicago: Contemporary Books.

Le Shan, E. (1993) *Grandparenting in a Changing World*. New York: Newmarket Press.

Lewin, T., Financially Set, Grandparents Help Keep Families Afloat, Too. *New York Times, National*. July 14, 2005.

Ruiz, D. S. (2004) *Amazing Grace: African-American Grandmothers as Caregivers and Conveyors of Traditional Values*. Westport, CT: Greenwood Publishing.

Turtletaub, S. (2001) *The Grandfather Thing*. Los Angeles, CA: Tallfellow Press.

Wasserman, S. (1990) *The Long-Distance Grandmother: How to Stay Close to Distant Children*. Port Roberts, WA: Hartley and Marks.

Family Renewal

Guerin, P.J. Jr., Fogarty, T.F., Fay, L.F., Kautto, J.G. (1996) *Working with Relationship Triangles: The One, Two, Three of Psychotherapy*. New York: Guilford Press.

Paul, P. (2003) *The Starter Marriage and the Future of Matrimony*. New York: Random House.

Pipher, M. (1996) *The Shelter of Each Other: Rebuilding Our Families*. New York:Ballantine Books.

Wallerstein, J. (1989) *Second Chances*. New York: Ticknor & Fields.

Wallerstein, J., Lewis, J., & Blakeslee, S. (2001) *The Unexpected Legacy of Divorce: The 25 Year Landmark Study*. New York: Hyperion.

Readings for Children of Divorce

Young Children

Banks, A. (1990) *When Your Parents Get Divorced: A Kid's Journal*. New York: Puffin Books. (ages 7–10)

Brown, L. K., & Brown, M. (1986) *Dinosaurs Divorce: A Guide for Changing Families*. New York: Little Brown & Co. (ages 4-6)

Heegoard, M. (1991) *When Mom & Dad Separate: Children Can Learn to Live With Grief from Divorce*. MN: Woodland Press. (grades 1 and up)

Lansky, V. (1998) *It's Not Your Fault: Koko Bear*. Minnetonka, MN: Book Peddlers. (ages 3–8)

Le Shan, E. (1978) *What's Going to Happen to Me?* New York: MacMillan.*

Mayle, P. (1988) *Why Are We Getting a Divorce?* New York: Harmony Books. (ages 4–8)

Rogers, F. (1996) *Let's Talk About It: Divorce*. New York: Penguin Putnam. (ages 3–6)

Schuchman, J. (1979) *Two Places to Sleep*. Minneapolis: Carolrhoda Books.*

Thomas, P. (1999) *My Family's Changing — A First Look at Family Break-up*. NY: Barron's Educational Series.

Teens and Older Children

Ahrons, C. (2004) *We're Still Family: What Grown Children Have to Say About Their Parents' Divorce*. New York: Harper Collins.

Boekman, C. (1980) *Surviving Your Parents' Divorce*. New York: Franklin Watts.

Getzoff, A., & and McClenahan, C. (1984) *StepKids: A Survival Book for Teenagers in Stepfamilies*. New York: Walker.

Gurganus, A. (1989) *Oldest Living Confederate Widow Tells All: A Novel*. New York: Knopf distributed by Random House.

Krantzler, M., & Krantzler, P. B. (2003) *Moving Beyond Your Parents' Divorce*. New York: McGraw Hill.

Rofes, E.E. (Ed) (1981) *The Kids' Book of Divorce By, For and About Kids*. Lexington, MA: Random House.

Staal, S. (2001) *The Love They Lost: Living With The Legacy of Our Parents' Divorce*. New York: Delta Publishing. (memoirs)

Divorce — Related Websites

Key words to help you find information on your browser:
  Child custody
  Child support
  Divorce + name of your state to get state-specific information
  Divorce mediation
  Divorce support groups (parents, grandparents, children)
  Grandparents raising grandchildren
  Grandparenting rights
  Stepfamilies

Some helpful Websites by topic:

Legal Information

  http://www.findlaw.com Comprehensive online library of legal resources, but a bit technical.

  http://www.law.cornell.edu Sponsored by Cornell University's Legal Information Institute. Extensive information about divorce law, custody, support and division of assets.

  http://www.lawyers.com Nation's leading directory of lawyers by geographic area. Paid subscription service. Smaller firms are not listed.

  http://www.aaml.org Official Web site of the American Academy of Matrimonial Lawyers with clear, state-by-state information in their divorce manual, available by requesting: "A Client Handbook"

  www.divorcenet.com This site has a number of chat support groups, an attorney center, and a listing of state-by-state legal provisions.

  http://www.divorceline.com Online database for lawyers, accountants, therapists, with advice and Q&A.

  http://www.divorcesource.com General state-by-state links to find information about divorce law in specific jurisdictions.

  http://www.acf.dhhs.gov/programs/cse Links to the Federal Office of Child Support Enforcement and provides useful information about each state's child support laws. There are links to each state's child support enforcement agency.

Financial Resources

  http://www.FamilyLawSoftware.com This company offers online bundled and unbundled divorce-planning software components to calculate financial costs.

http://www.cfainstitute.org Lists chartered financial analysts (CFA), which are similar to certified financial planners (CFP).

www.institutedfa.com Helps locate financial analysts who specialize in divorce, who must also be licensed CPAs or CFPs.

Stepfamilies

http://www.saafamilies.org Stepfamily Association of America, Inc. A non-profit organization of people concerned with helping stepfamilies live successfully.

Support Groups and Information for Divorced Parents

http://www.parentswithoutpartners.org For information about support groups with a directory of local chapters.

http://www.divorcecare.com Features a searchable database of divorce support groups.

Support Groups and Information for Grandparents

http://www.aarp.org American Association of Retired Persons is a good source for the latest information about grandparent rights. Their publication has articles about roles, things to do with grandchildren, and travel ideas.

http://www.aarp.org/grandparents has fact sheets, a newsletter, and directory of local support groups for grandparent caregivers.

http://www.grandsplace.com Grands Place is a Web site offering grandparents information on local resources and online discussion of issues relating to raising their grandchildren.

http://www.grandparenting.org Dr. Kornbacher's Foundation for Grandparenting is dedicated to raising grandparent consciousness and grandparent identity. Also includes information about camping with your grandchild.

http://www.caregiving.org http://www.caregiving.org is the National Alliance for Caregiving Web site. The Alliance connects families with information on caregiver resources and local services.

http://sierraclub.org/outings The Sierra Club offers trips specially designed for grandparents and grandchildren to enjoy.

http://grandtrvl.com Grandtravel.com offers stateside and international tours for the express purpose of providing a learning and bonding experience for grandparents and grandchildren.

General Information

http://www.aboutourkids.org is an educational Web site sponsored by New York University Cornell Medical Center. You will find professionally authored articles about child rearing, divorce, grandparenting and stepfamilies.

Divorce-Related Advocacy Organizations

AAML (American Academy of Matrimonial Lawyers) was founded in 1962 "to encourage the study, improve the practice, elevate the standards and advance the cause of matrimonial law, to the end that the welfare of the family and society be protected." There are currently more than 1500 members in all 50 states. Members are experts in divorce, prenuptial agreements, postnuptial agreements, annulment, child custody, visitation, property valuation and division, alimony, and child support. (800) 422-6595.

Children's Rights Council is an international, nonprofit children's advocacy organization based in the Washington D.C. area, with 51 chapters in 39 states as well as Canada, the United Kingdom, and Japan. Formed in 1985, the Children's Rights Council (CRC) works to assure children meaningful and continuing contact with both their parents and extended family regardless of the parents' marital status. (301) 559-3120.

National Organization for Children's Rights is an advocacy group for child support, joint custody, and visitation and custody reform. (202) 547-6227.

U.S. Department of Health and Human Services in Washington, D.C. helps locate parents who are not paying child support or who have kidnapped their children. It operates, develops, and improves child support enforcement programs according to federal regulations. (202) 401-9373.

National Council on Family Relations maintains an online database with a bibliography of marriage and family literature and publications. (612) 781-9331.

National Organization of Single Mothers is a networking resource for women raising children on their own. (704) 888-5437.

United Fathers of America provides counseling assistance and referrals and seeks equal rights for fathers in child custody cases. (714) 385-1002.

National Domestic Violence Hotline is staffed 24 hours by trained counselors and can direct the caller to help in their local area. (800) 799-7233.

For information about divorce workshops or family counselors in your area, check with your local mental health association, university, community social service agency, pastor or company's employee assistance department for referrals. You can also check the listing in the telephone book under "Divorce" or call Infoline.

Index

Please see the following page for more books.